AGAINST HAPPINESS

AGAINST HAPPINESS

OWEN FLANAGAN, JOSEPH E. LEDOUX,
BOBBY BINGLE, DANIEL M. HAYBRON,
BATJA MESQUITA, MICHELE MOODY-ADAMS,
SONGYAO REN, ANNA SUN,
YOLONDA Y. WILSON

WITH RESPONSES FROM CRITICS
JENNIFER A. FREY, HAZEL ROSE MARKUS,
JEFFREY D. SACHS, AND JEANNE L. TSAI

Columbia University Press *New York*

Columbia University Press
Publishers Since 1893
New York   Chichester, West Sussex
cup.columbia.edu
Copyright © 2023 Columbia University Press
All rights reserved

Library of Congress Cataloging-in-Publication Data
Names: Flanagan, Owen, Jr., 1949– author.
Title: Against happiness : subjective well-being and public policy /
Owen Flanagan, Joseph E. LeDoux, Bobby Bingle, Daniel M. Haybron,
Batja Mesquita, Michele Moody-Adams, Songyao Ren, Anna Sun,
and Yolonda Y. Wilson.
Description: New York : Columbia University Press, [2023] |
Includes bibliographical references and index.
Identifiers: LCCN 2022048474 (print) | LCCN 2022048475 (ebook) |
ISBN 9780231209489 (hardback) | ISBN 9780231209496 (trade paperback) |
ISBN 9780231557962 (ebook)
Subjects: LCSH: Well-being. | Happiness—Philosophy. | Economics—
Psychological aspects. | Social policy—Psychological aspects.
Classification: LCC HN25 .F58 2023 (print) | LCC HN25 (ebook) |
DDC 301—dc23/eng/20230120
LC record available at https://lccn.loc.gov/2022048474
LC ebook record available at https://lccn.loc.gov/2022048475

Cover design: Milenda Nan Ok Lee
Cover image: Victor Chaika © Shutterstock

AUTHORS

Bobby Bingle, philosophy, Duke University

Owen Flanagan, philosophy, psychology and neuroscience, neurobiology, Duke University

Daniel M. Haybron, philosophy, St. Louis University

Joseph E. LeDoux, psychiatry, neural science, and psychology, New York University

Batja Mesquita, Center for Social and Cultural Psychology, University of Leuven

Michele Moody-Adams, philosophy, Columbia University

Songyao Ren, philosophy, University of Texas at Dallas

Anna Sun, sociology and religious studies, Duke University

Yolonda Y. Wilson, health care ethics, African American studies, philosophy, St. Louis University

CRITICS

Jennifer A. Frey, Philosophy, University of South Carolina

Hazel Rose Marcus, Psychology, Stanford University

Jeffrey D. Sachs, Center for Sustainable Development, Economics, Columbia University

Jeanne L. Tsai, Psychology, Stanford University

To the memory of Paul Farmer, M.D.
All royalties to Partners for Health

CONTENTS

Preface xi

Introduction 1

I HAPPINESS PHILOSOPHY AND HAPPINESS SCIENCE

1 The Happiness Agenda 29

2 Varieties of Theories and Measures of Well-Being and Happiness 43

3 How Should We Think About the Emotion of Happiness Scientifically? Lessons from the Science of Fear 75

4 Why Averaging Happiness Scores and Comparing Them Is a Terrible Idea 97

II CULTURE AND HAPPINESS

5 Positive and Negative Emotions: Culture, Content, and Context 107

6 Happiness and Well-Being as Cultural Projects: Immigration, Biculturalism, Cultural Belonging   117

7 Happiness and Well-Being in Contemporary China   127

III RACE, RACISM, RESIGNATION

8 Happiness, Race, and Hermeneutical Justice: The Case of African American Mental Health   149

9 Interpreting Self-Reports of Well-Being   163

IV CONCLUSIONS

10 Recommendations for Policy Use of Happiness Metrics   185

11 Universal Rights, Sustainable Development, and Happiness: Two out of Three Ain't Bad   191

V RESPONSES BY FOUR CRITICS

12 On Ersatz Happiness, by Jennifer A. Frey   205

13 Why the Analysis and Assessment of Happiness Matters, by Hazel Rose Markus   213

14 Three out of Three Is Better, by Jeffrey D. Sachs   227

15 What the Gallup World Poll Could Do to Deepen Our Understanding of Happiness in Different Cultures, by Jeanne L. Tsai   235

Notes 249
References 295
Index 333

PREFACE

We are a diverse group representing philosophy of mind, ethics, political philosophy, race theory, bioethics, the philosophy and science of happiness, cross-cultural philosophy, cultural psychology, sociology, religious studies, and the neuroscience of emotions. Our team began its life in June 2020 as a task force on "Ethics, Psychology & Neuroscience" representing the Science and Ethics of Happiness and Well-Being Initiative (SEH) of the Center for Sustainable Development at Columbia University and the Vatican's Pontifical Academy of Social Sciences. We tasked ourselves with thinking hard about the nature of happiness alongside other more practically focused task forces working to make policy recommendations for promoting happiness during the COVID pandemic for the Global Happiness Council (https://www.happinesscouncil.org/council.html).

We evolved into a monthly seminar over the course of 2021 and into 2022, thinking and writing together about the nature of happiness, its status in the order of goods, and the ethics of promoting happiness and well-being as a worthy personal, social, and political goal. Our eyes were especially set on whether and how concepts, measures, and uses of happiness metrics capture what matters, and especially whether and how they were sensitive to the well-being of the worst off, to cultural and intracultural variation on what matters, on how happiness is conceived, and how valuable happiness is in the order of goods.

This book is our opinionated assessment of "the happiness agenda," a specific version of happiness philosophy and science, which conceives the ultimate aim of policy as maximizing the number of people who are subjectively happy with their lives or, what is different, maximizing the total amount of happiness for humans. Our hope is that this book can serve as a reliable introduction to recent thinking about happiness and that it will engage both advocates and critics of the happiness agenda to think more carefully about happiness as a policy goal. The happiness agenda is conceptually disunified and overreaches rhetorically. One goal is to rein in the happiness agenda and return happiness to its proper place as one good in a panoply of goods. Another goal is to make the case for happiness policies that are constrained by culture and tradition specific conceptions of happiness, which are themselves constrained by commitments to human dignity, equal worth, universal rights, sustainability, and the demands of justice.

The views expressed in these pages are the authors' alone. They do not represent the Science and Ethics of Happiness and Well-being Initiative (SEH), Columbia's Center for Sustainable Development, the Global Council for Happiness, or the Vatican's Pontifical Academy of the Social Sciences. We have been the beneficiaries of working closely with colleagues from all these initiatives and institutions.

AGAINST HAPPINESS

INTRODUCTION

Happiness is the ultimate good because, unlike all other goods, it is self-evidently good. I believe that Bentham's idea—that all laws and actions should aim at producing the greatest possible happiness—was right and that we should fearlessly adopt it.
—Richard Layard, *Happiness: Lessons from a New Science,*
second edition

Well-being is about how people feel.
—U.K. *Well-Being Guidance for Appraisal: Supplementary Green Book Guidance to HM Treasury Green Book*

The purpose of life is not to be happy. It is to be useful, to be honorable, to be compassionate, to have it make some difference that you have lived and lived well.
—Ralph Waldo Emerson

Happiness, as currently understood, is not necessarily a desirable state, and the maximization of happiness is a political ideal of which we should be suspicious. What matter are the expectations and desires of both the happy and the unhappy and to identify and interpret these is a work of some complexity.
—Alasdair MacIntyre, *Ethics in the Conflicts of Modernity*

In some ways it seems like a no-brainer: Who could object to happiness as the goal of a human life or of public policy? Didn't Aristotle teach that happiness is the *summum bonum*? Actually, Aristotle didn't teach that, and we don't think that happiness is the highest good, either. Whether happiness, conceived of as a hedonically positive subjective mental state or as life satisfaction, is good depends on the contours of happiness, what the happiness is about, what causes it, what good if any it produces, and so on. It is almost certainly false that happiness is the *summum bonum*, the ultimate good, the final end, the one thing in the universe that has noninstrumental value, and at which all other things of value—rights, love, friendship, meaningful work—are means. There is no sense of "happiness" advanced and measured by social scientists or public policy wonks that is anything like the happiness advocated by philosophers and theologians as true happiness.

Happiness exists. It comes in varieties. It is a *prima facie* good, nice to have if you can get it, and its study and measurement are worthwhile activities. The scientific study of happiness is a good thing like the study of anything else. There is a fantastically rich and valuable literature that studies what people think will make them happy and what in fact does, and there is a vast literature on techniques to be happier. And there are no doubt some legitimate uses of happiness metrics for policymakers.

But the worth of happiness and the importance of promoting it in public policy are overstated by fans of "the happiness agenda." The happiness agenda also known as the "Happiness Movement," or even "The World Happiness Movement," is an *episteme* in Michel Foucault's sense, a currently prominent way of thinking and speaking about what allegedly matters most, that endorses itself to guide government policy, and that has elevated happiness to supreme importance, the end that can unify us despite our diversity.[1] The happiness agenda tends to elide the clear distinctions between happiness, well-being, the quality of life, and what is good, right, and just. It overstates what is known about happiness (many generalizations are local), and collapses or ignores the happiness/well-being distinction, as well as the distinction between 1. experiential utility, the quality of experience one desires or prefers; 2. preference utility, the goods one wants; and 3. the goods that are good for you, but that you (or your community) haven't yet discovered or don't see are so.[2]

United Nations Resolution 65/309 of July 2011 observes that "happiness is *a* fundamental goal."[3] It does not say that happiness is *the* fundamental goal. The indefinite article matters. The UN's Resolution goes on to invite member states to develop new indicators of happiness, to share them, and to consider ways to use such information "to guide their public policies." That is, the UN calls for nation-states to consider using information about the happiness and well-being of their people for their people. It did not call on anyone to develop metrics to use to compare happiness across all nation-states and to recommend international policy or international comparisons on such bases.

We represent no member state, but we offer our wisdom on how and how not to think about the nature of happiness, how and how not to measure it, and how and when to use such knowledge for public policy. Here we share our findings.

HUMILITY ABOUT HAPPINESS

There are two reasons for humility about happiness as an individual, social, and political goal. One reason is that it is philosophically parochial. The other is that the human sciences suffer a general methodological deficiency: surmises about human nature are based typically on unrepresentative samples of WEIRD people: Western, educated, industrialized, rich, and democratic. The fact that such people prize happiness especially is a datum about the psychology of some people not a finding about universal psychology.

Alfred North Whitehead remarked that the safest generalization to make about Western philosophy is that it is a "series of footnotes to Plato." His idea was that the lineage that runs from Socrates to Plato to Aristotle to Augustine, Aquinas, Averroes, and Maimonides plays a foundational role in philosophical and theological education in the North Atlantic and its imperial outposts. One might observe, as Whitehead did not, that this lineage contains lots of discussion of happiness, true happiness, earthly happiness, and eternal happiness. People in the "footnotes to Plato" lineage comprise about a billion people of the earth's population. There are eight billion people on earth, which means that the ratio of people not thinking in the "series of footnotes to Plato" mode to those who are is 7:1.

Even if one thinks that the Abrahamic religions also channel the "footnotes to Plato" tradition in virtue of these two traditions having mutually accommodated each other, and that in that blended form (Augustine is a Platonist; Aquinas, Averroes, and Maimonides are neo-Aristotelians) they have infiltrated the thinking of 3.5 billion people, this still does not represent most people on earth. Furthermore, insofar as there is a consensus in the "footnotes to Plato" lineage about happiness, it is that happiness is a conditional good. Whether any variety of happiness is an all-things-considered good depends on its causes, contents, constituents, and composition. The dominant, but not uncontested view, in ethics and political philosophy in the platonic lineage is that rights and justice are prior to and constrain the pursuit of happiness, and thus that happiness is neither the first nor the ultimate good. Plato himself conceived of the good life as one directed at what is Good, True, and Beautiful. Being happy or blessed (μακάριος, makários) might be an accompaniment of this quest. But it is not the aim of the exercise.

Second, one aspect of the self-image of Western psychology (like Western philosophy), the science that established itself as separate from philosophy in 1879, when Wilhelm Wundt began "brass instrument psychology" in Leipzig, is that it discovers universal truths, psychological kin of $f = ma$, the inverse square law of universal gravitation, or $E=mc^2$. This universalist pretense was exposed as such in an important 2010 paper by Joe Henrich, Steve Heine, and Ara Norenzayan.[4] They confirmed that most psychology, like most social science, is based on research with one of the most unrepresentative groups in the history of humanity, North American college students. Findings about universal human nature or intuitions about what everyone wants based on data and conversations internal to one tradition have no empirical warrant. This finding cannot be highlighted enough. It means that, at least for the time being, social scientists should not claim that their generalizations apply beyond the larger population that their sample represents. This entails that we should assume that most findings that pertain to complex goods and ends are local. And indeed the evidence in cultural psychology and anthropology reveals that different peoples, cultures, and subcultures conceive of happiness in different ways and value it differently.

There is an additional reason for humility about the happiness agenda. The happiness agenda is entirely human-focused. Many traditions think that insofar as ethics attends to happiness, it ought to attend to the happiness of all sentient beings, which includes all nonhuman animals. Policy that weights the happiness and well-being of nonhumans highly will result in radically different policies from one that does not do so. Unless we get things right at the get-go, we could go seriously wrong ethically in promoting human happiness.

IS HAPPINESS NECESSARY FOR WELL-BEING?

Suffering and ill-being are bad. Ancient Indic philosophies are excellent sources that direct attention to the sources of suffering, which include objective conditions such as disease, poverty, and famine, and subjective conditions, especially our rapacious egos, which want more than they need. Good people and good politics work to overcome ill-being and suffering. These traditions are also excellent in explaining that eliminating suffering and ill-being is not equivalent to aiming for happiness. One eliminates ill-being and suffering out of love and compassion, not because eliminating ill-being and unhappiness will make people happy. Typically it will not make them happy. It will make them not-suffering, and it will allow them to get on with living a meaningful human life. As Amartya Sen pointed out,

> Happiness has two basic problems in its claim to stand for well-being. First, as it is interpreted in the utilitarian tradition, happiness is basically a mental state, and it ignores other aspects of a person's well-being. If a starving wreck, ravished by famine, buffeted by disease, is made happy through some mental conditioning (say, via the "opium" of religion), the person will be seen as doing quite well on this mental state perspective, but that would be quite scandalous. Second, as a mental-state concept, the happiness perspective may give a very limited view of other mental activities. There are mental states other than just being happy,

such as stimulation, excitement, etc. which are of direct relevance to a person's well-being. Furthermore, mental activities involve *valuation* of one's life—a reflective exercise—and the role of valuation in the identification of the person's well-being cannot be seen in terms merely of the happiness that such reflection itself creates. It is hard to avoid the conclusion that although happiness is of obvious and direct relevance to well-being, it is inadequate as a representation of well-being.[5]

Advocates of the happiness agenda support the use of indicators across cultures that measure happiness by asking directly about happiness (how happy/unhappy are you?), about life satisfaction (how satisfied/dissatisfied are you with your life overall?), or about pleasant/unpleasant experiences, positive emotions/negative emotions, or balance, harmony, peace, and cheerfulness. None of these concepts is the same as each other, and every one of them can be contested as an indicator of happiness. See table I.1. 'Happiness' in the wild is not a simple univocal descriptive concept; it an essentially contested polysemous normative concept. "True happiness," as it has been conceived of over world historical time and across traditions, rarely stipulates subjective satisfaction, feeling happy, or feeling cheerful as necessary conditions.

There are many reasons not to embrace the claim that happiness is the *summum bonum*, that it can be measured adequately in any of these ways, and, what is different and additional, that it is the proper ultimate aim of public policy.

- There are many different concepts of happiness, so what happiness even is, is contested. There is happiness conceived of as a cognitive judgment about life satisfaction, either overall or domain by domain; there are numerous hedonic or emotional

Table I.1 WIDELY USED HAPPINESS QUESTIONS

Survey	Variable	Question
World Happiness Report	Life Satisfaction	Please imagine a ladder, with steps numbered from 0 at the bottom to 10 at the top. The top of the ladder represents the best possible life for you and the bottom of the ladder represents the worst possible life for you. On which step of the ladder do you feel you personally stand at the present time?
General Social Survey	Happiness	Taken all together, how would you say things are these days? Would you say that you are very happy, pretty happy, or not too happy?
World Values Survey	Life Satisfaction	All things considered, how satisfied are you with your life as a whole these days? Please use this card to help with your answer [range of 1–10 with 1 labeled "Very Dissatisfied" and 10 labeled "Very Satisfied"].
European Social Survey	Happiness	Taking all things together, how happy would you say you are? Please use this card [range of 0–10 with 0 labeled "Extremely unhappy" and 10 labeled "Extremely happy"].
European Social Survey	Life Satisfaction	All things considered, how satisfied are you with your life as a whole nowadays? Please answer using this card, where 0 means extremely dissatisfied and 10 means extremely satisfied [range of 0–10 with 0 labeled "Extremely dissatisfied" and 10 labeled "Extremely satisfied"].
European Quality of Life Survey	Happiness	Taking all things together on a scale of 1 to 10, how happy would you say you are? Here 1 means you are very unhappy and 10 means you are very happy.

Survey	Variable	Question
European Quality of Life Survey	Life Satisfaction	All things considered, how satisfied would you say you are with your life these days? Please tell me on a scale of 1 to 10, where 1 means very dissatisfied and 10 means very satisfied.
German Social Economic Panel	Life Satisfaction	In conclusion, we would like to ask you about your satisfaction with your life in general. Please answer according to the following scale: 0 means "completely dissatisfied," 10 means "completely satisfied." How satisfied are you with your life, all things considered?
British Household Panel Survey	Life Satisfaction	How dissatisfied or satisfied are you with your life overall [range of 1–7 with 1 labeled "Not satisfied at all" and 7 labeled "Completely satisfied"]?

state senses of happiness. One theory conceives of happiness as the state of experiencing a surplus of pleasant over unpleasant experiences, feelings, or sensations over a time interval. Another conceives of it as a mental state involving cheerfulness, serenity, and vitality.[6] Still another conceives of it simply as the state constituted or produced by a surplus of positive to negative emotions or a favorable ratio of positive to negative emotions.[7] And yet another operationalizes happiness as the state reported by people when asked about how happy they are and how happy they think they are compared to their peers.[8]

• We know from social and cultural psychology, anthropology, and religious studies that there is variation in how people conceive of both happiness and its value. Although happiness conceived of as life satisfaction dominates measures favored by proponents of the happiness agenda, it is not the dominant view of what happiness is among laypersons across cultures.[9]

- Psychiatrists, clinical psychologists, and social workers regularly counsel people who judge their lives satisfactory, even objectively amazing, but who are miserable.
- The worth of happiness (every kind) is contested. Some people think it matters a lot; some think it matters little. Most survey measures get at happiness in a thin sense, a least common denominator sense.[10] Thick senses are left to philosophy, religion, cultural psychology, sociology, anthropology, and political theory.
- Philosophy and psychology teach that humans are imperfect judges of their own mental states, as well as what is good for them.[11] Aristotle was one of the first to argue that a person is a good judge of whether her own life is eudaimonic (one in which she flourishes) only if she has been taught (by an excellent value education) the correct standards for judging a life, has internalized these standards, and assesses her own life truthfully without self-serving spin. If any of these conditions are not met, the judgment is not accurate; it is mistaken, confused.
- There is no evidence of a reliable connection between a meaningful life and a happy life in either direction. Many meaningful lives are wrenched with angst, and many perfectly happy lives involve little in the way of challenges, growth, or meaningful projects. This matters because many people on earth think living a meaningful life is more important that living a happy life if one cannot have both.
- No conception of happiness currently on offer in the social sciences claims any reliable connection between happiness and goodness. This matters because many people on earth think living an ethically good life is more important that living a happy life if one cannot have both.

- No conception of happiness on offer in the social sciences claims that happy individuals live in a just society or are actually endowed with human rights. This matters because many people on earth think living in a just society is more important that living a happy life if one cannot have both.
- Cognates of "happiness" in Greek philosophy and the Abrahamic religions are not life satisfaction or emotional state happiness. Aquinas, for example, identifies such analyses of happiness as the folk concept (*ratio communis*) of it. But this is not the kind of happiness, *beatitudo* that we should care much about. The right kind of happiness is one that aims, in accordance with Aristotle's definition of *eudaimonia*, at moral and intellectual excellence, exemplified for Aquinas by "living in Christ." Furthermore, perfect happiness comes for Aquinas, if it does come, only in the hereafter.
- This point generalizes outside of Greek philosophy and the Abrahamic religions. For example, in Confucius the word for happiness or joy is *le* (樂). It does not refer to ordinary happiness, except insofar as such happiness consists in a measured Confucian appreciation of the best things in life, such as friendship, and warm family relations (see *Mencius* 11.26), but rather to a very specific positive state of mind that follows from, or supervenes on, or is constituted by living in accordance with the Confucian Way, *dao* 道.[12] In Buddhism, the kind of happiness that is desirable involves distinctively ethical attitudes of compassion (*karuna*) and lovingkindness (*metta*) for all sentient beings.[13] Lacking the virtues of compassions and lovingkindness a seemingly (even to themselves) happy Buddhist person isn't happy.
- The concept of well-being also comes in varieties and except among hedonists, it does not mean the same thing as happiness.[14] Well-being can mean that certain objective conditions are met (food, shelter, education, medical care); it can mean that

a person judges that such conditions are met; it can mean a life that is happy and meaningful and ethical. The list of objective goods and subjective goods that make up well-being is vast. Almost no one who has ever studied the matter has thought that possession of even the total set of good things (excellent relationships, meaning, rights, etc.) is good because they yield a single psychological state such as happiness, conceived of either as a judgment of overall life satisfaction or an emotional state of feeling happy. Indeed, such things as rights are good independently of whether they produce any distinctive cognitive or psycho-emotional state whatsoever. Rights would be good even if they reliably made people feel unhappy, which they might since many rights are constraints that tell people what they are not allowed to do even if they really want to.

- The study of happiness, like any kind of study, entails nothing about what to do with knowledge about the causes, constituents, and effects of happiness so conceived of, and certainly nothing about using this information to guide public or government policy.
- It is a peculiar and rare idea in the history of political philosophy that government should aim to produce happiness or that "Happiness is the only ultimate objective of public policy."[15] But it is very popular among proponents of the happiness agenda, such as Paul Frijters and his colleagues:

> We can begin with the problem of how to spend a given sum of money so as to deliver the best value, where value is measured in units of happiness. Thus, in the case of government expenditure, we take the size of the state as given, and we assume initially that the problem is how to maximize the aggregate happiness of the relevant population, subject to that constraint. The correct approach is then to rank all possible policies in terms of the extra happiness which they

generate per pound of expenditure, starting with the most effective and working down. We then undertake as many policies as it is possible to do before the total money available is exhausted.[16]

- In fact, there is only one political philosophy in the history of political philosophy that has promoted happiness in any subjective sense(s) as the goal of politics. This is Bentham's political philosophy. There are some arguments that can be made in its favor if one thinks politics cannot legitimately take any positions on what is good or right or best, so that making the greatest number of people happy independently of the whys, wherefores, and contents of their happiness is good. But such arguments are rarely offered by proponents of the political happiness agenda. (And no, Bhutan is not an exception. The happiness endorsed in the Bhutanese constitution and tracked inside Bhutan is Buddhist through and through. Vajrayana Buddhism is the state religion of Bhutan.)
- The happiness agenda has this general problem conceived of as a cross-cultural imperative: liberal countries will need to promote happiness with indifference to its nature since liberalism is (or is required to be) neutral or indifferent about different ways of pursuing happiness. That is, a liberal state promoting happiness should be indifferent to whether the happiness produced produces happy (satisfied) hedonists, libertarians, communitarians, and so forth. But a country committed to a particular theory of the good such as Bhutan will require policy that produces good Vajrayana Buddhists, not good Chan Buddhists or good Theravada Buddhists and certainly not just any old kind of happy or satisfied people.
- One can circle back at this point and think it is actually too bad that liberal societies might be required to promote the good while being entirely indifferent to its form. One thought

would be that liberal societies should promote character development in such a way that commitment to rights, justice, sustainability, and obligations of mutual benevolence and for the common good constrain the pursuit of happiness and thus its healthy forms. But this move (a good one) denies that happiness conceived of as a subjective emotional state or life satisfaction is the *summum bonum*. And if it is not that, then its promotion as a good is conditional on its form, and its promotion requires considerable delicacy.

- One job for all human beings, not just for social scientists and politicians, is to end suffering, unhappiness, and ill-being. But ending suffering, unhappiness, and ill-being is not the same as aiming to make people happy. A person is depressed or anxious. We prescribe an antidepressant or an anti-anxiety drug. It works. Is the person happy? That's not the aim; they are less depressed, less anxious, possibly okay, back to baseline to get on with their life. Happiness is not the aim or the point. The COVID pandemic caused sickness, death, economic problems, and serious problems for children and their parents, especially mothers. All these things are bad, worthy of remedy. But they are not bad because these bad things made people unhappy, although they did, but because they are bad. Schoolchildren were not educated; mothers were stressed out trying to balance things; the economy suffered; anxious and depressed people became more so, and so on.
- The usual situation is that government is charged with a disjunctive set of jobs, which include promoting order, harmony, and public safety; providing defense; promoting a stable economic system; developing systems to prevent poverty, famine, and poor health; offering public education; distributing resources fairly; protecting human rights such as those in the UN Declaration of 1948 and promoting sustainable development.[17] Doing

all this well might have a reliable effect of whether people are happy in the life satisfaction sense or various emotional state senses. If so, this is a welcome effect of government's doing well what it is supposed to do. But producing happiness is not the main or best reason that government should do all the things on its mission list. It should do all those things because they are important in their own right. And they would be right, even if they don't also make people happy.

- The promotion of rights, the aims of equitable distribution, and the requirements of sustainable development often have happiness costs because they involve sacrifices. These costs are worth it because rights and sustainability and justice are more important than happiness.
- Finally, public policy focus on happiness as the *summum bonum* is legitimately perceived as shallow, frivolous, avoidant, even gaslighting with respect to the subjects of racism, sexism, colonialism, economic exploitation, ethnic hatred, and those who suffer from depression, anxiety, PTSD, mood disorders, schizophrenia, and addiction. Love, compassion, and justice are virtues. The promotion of feeling good or feeling satisfied, though doubtless well-intentioned, isn't even a political virtue. No liberation movement anywhere in the world asks for happiness from its oppressors. The happiness agenda can seem patronizing, condescending, the next nice thing on the list of achievements for antecedently well-off people to get more of for themselves and to bless others with.

HAPPINESS POLITICS

Our aim in this book is to explore these and several other pressing foundational issues in the study of happiness and well-being and unhappiness and ill-being. The simplest way to put our central message is that the promotion of happiness and, what is different, well-being is not a culturally or politically neutral exercise. What happiness is, what exactly the words in its semantic family mean across languages, whether it is valuable, and if so how valuable it is, are all contested. Furthermore, happiness and subjective well-being can compete with goods such as social and economic equality, as well as racial, gender, and intergenerational justice. We press this point by discussing many findings that highlight intra-cultural and cross-cultural disagreements about what happiness is, and where it is situated among plural goods. Our view is that happiness and subjective well-being are important public goods only if they are circumscribed by and produced by circumstances of equality and justice.

One caveat is this: We keep our critical focus on the nature and worth of happiness rather than on the nature and worth of well-being. Proponents of the happiness agenda often speak of happiness or well-being, and even flourishing, interchangeably and as synonyms, as when the intended sense of well-being is subjective well-being.[18] They are not. Well-being as subjective satisfaction is a narrow category, which is then glossed as happiness. And sometimes happiness is used as a synonym for subjective well-being, which includes many states that are not happiness or components of happiness, such as absorption or calm. The concept of well-being as used in philosophy, psychology, and economics is a much more capacious category than happiness and allows inclusion of any and all states of mind and heart, as well as all the other goods—air quality, public education, health insurance, national defense, economic equality, rights, and so on—that are not states of mind and are not good because they make people happy. That said, sometimes we let the concept of subjective well-being, as used by others, stand for happiness, but only when we judge that they intend something in the vicinity of happiness.

We are mostly worried about the conceptual and rhetorical creep of "happiness" to name or include all good things. Some well-being researchers worry about a related problem: the conceptual creep of the concept of well-being to include everything good, and thus as unhelpful analytically and politically:

> We question whether science is usefully advanced by calling a host of distinct phenomena, such as objective indicators of socioeconomic status (educational attainment, income, standard of living), diverse indicators of health (health conditions, functional capacities, life expectancy), and multiple subjective indicators (happiness, life satisfaction, purpose, self-realization) *all* "well-being." Such inclusiveness, in our view, muddles important scientific agendas regarding what it means to be well, for whom opportunities of wellness are or are not available, and what health consequences well-being may have.[19]

With this caution about the conceptual creep of both happiness and well-being in mind, we proceed often to use evidence about well-being in the wider sense to show how narrow and parochial is the focus on happiness or narrow subjective well-being as a guide to policy. Remember: we are focused on the agenda that insists that there is a well-defined, measurable, and comparable (across individuals and collectives, including nations) state of mind called "happiness," which is both what everyone wants and the *summum bonum*, and that should be the aim of public and government policy. There is no kind of happiness that everyone wants. The type of happiness put forward as the kind everyone wants and that should guide policy is typically so thin as to be uninformative, and it suffers from being culturally parochial in virtue of conceiving happiness as a state of individuals rather than social wholes.[20] Furthermore, insofar as happiness matters to public policy, it is not average happiness but the distribution of happiness. However, because of many problems with self-reports (adaptation, opacity, low expectations, variation in norms of expression) distributions can be completely uninformative. For example, in both Atlanta, Georgia, and St. Louis, Missouri, Blacks who live in objectively terrible conditions report high life satisfaction. Comparing and ranking nation-states by average happiness scores inherit all these problems.

The upshot is that there is almost no sensible public or government policy question to which happiness is the answer.

OVERVIEW

Part I, "Happiness Philosophy and Happiness Science," contains four chapters.

In chapter 1, "The Happiness Agenda," we introduce readers to a movement that promotes the use of happiness and well-being metrics, often conflating them, as an important and possibly the best guide to policy. Its alleged merits are that everyone knows what happiness is and agree that they want happiness, and thus that promoting it is warranted and politically neutral. All three claims are false.

In chapter 2, "Varieties of Theories and Measures of Well-Being and Happiness," we provide an overview of the main theories of what happiness and well-being are and measures used to assess them. We discuss the relations among such concepts as *a good life*, *well-being*, and *happiness*. We defend the claims that all these concepts—a good life, well-being, and happiness—are normative, by which we mean that they embed norms and ideals and express values. A person lives a good life, lives well, is happy relative to some standard. The standard can be one the person herself endorses, or one endorsed by others—her community, culture, nation-state, or certain experts, theologians, philosophers, psychologists, or policy wonks.

In chapter 3, "How Should We Think About the Emotion of Happiness Scientifically? Lessons from the Science of Fear," we mark the distinction among happiness as a universal psychobiological state, happiness as a culturally constructed emotional state, and happiness as a cognitive judgment about, for example, life satisfaction. We explore some foundational controversies about what emotions are generally and what the emotion of happiness is specifically. To illustrate, we use the most well-studied and understood emotion, fear, which serves well to reveal the evolutionary-cultural-psychological-neurobiological features of emotion. The emotion of happiness is less well-understood than the emotion of fear, but we can expect it to have similar features, especially its social construction and cultural variation. The emotion of happiness is important to some theories of well-being, but not all. Some indexes of well-being track happiness as a simple well-understood emotion; others track happiness conceived of as life satisfaction; still others as a medley of positive features of one's psycho-emotional or psychosocial ecology. We provide conceptual clarity on these matters, and on the question of whether, and in what sense, various happiness measures measure happiness.

In chapter 4, "Why Averaging Happiness Scores and Comparing Them Is a Terrible Idea," we take up two common practices of proponents of the happiness agenda. First is representing the happiness of countries based on average subjective satisfaction scores. Second is ranking countries in terms of averages. Both are terrible practices. Insofar as happiness is an important political goal, what matters is its distribution, not its averages. Averages (mean), as well as median and mode, are uninformative about distributions. A country might have a high average happiness, while certain groups, ethnic minorities, immigrants, or women are very unhappy. Graphs are informative about distributions; single numerical values for mean, median, or mode are not. Ranking countries requires averaging and inherits all the problems of averaging. If graphs were used to represent distributions of happiness, rather than averages, it would not be possible to rank countries by happiness scores. But then again—a constant refrain in our analysis—even graphs can be uninformative because we find often that oppressed, discriminated-against people who live objectively unsatisfactory lives express higher life satisfaction scores that people whose lives are objectively much better.

Part II, "Culture and Happiness," consists of three chapters.

In chapter 5, "Positive and Negative Emotions: Culture, Content, and Context," we focus on one view of happiness that conceives of it as an emotional state that arises from, or is identical to, a state where there are more hedonically positive emotional episodes than negative ones (day-by-day, week-by-week, etc.), or where there exists a favorable ratio of positive emotions to negative ones. We provide lots of evidence that cultures differ in terms of which emotions they think are positive and negative, including the kinds of happiness—for example, low arousal or high arousal—that are desirable. We give many examples and discuss implications for the study of happiness and well-being. There are cultural norms, scripts, and permissions for when emotions are apt or fitting and when their expression is at the mean between too much and too little. Emotions can be positive hedonically but negative evaluatively depending on their content, depending on what they are about; for example, happiness over a rival's woes might feel good but would be cruel, callous, and unworthy. Or emotions can be negative hedonically, but just right and perfectly fitting, for example, sadness at a personal loss or another's suffering. We also show that different indexes of happiness such as subjective life satisfaction, positive/negative emotions, and balance/harmony measures, yield very different results. This matters because the happiness agenda says that happiness is the *summum bonum* and that public policy ought to promote it. But there is no single measure, nor is there a set of measures that reliably measure what it is that is to be promoted. Different metrics yield different countries as exemplars of happy ones.

In chapter 6, "Happiness and Well-Being as Cultural Projects: Immigration, Biculturalism, Cultural Belonging," we develop the thesis that a component of subjective well-being is *cultural belonging* and that this requires some sort of cultural fit. We provide additional examples of the ways cultures and traditions differ in their norms and ideals for emotional expression, including their ideals for happiness and subjective well-being. We discuss research on the special challenges faced by immigrants who are called upon to fit into their new environment. Immigrants are burdened with learning a new language, but also with learning new habits of the heart and mind. There are subjective well-being benefits to learning to belong, fitting in, assimilation. But there are also costs: alienation from the prior normative ecology, generational conflict, loss of a homeland. There are additional problems when immigrants are called upon to fit in and belong to multicultures. Which culture ought one to assimilate in order to maximize happiness and subjective well-being? The dominant culture that holds power and resources? The normatively nearest subculture from among the options? The subculture that will have you? The other new kids on the block, which is often another socioeconomically bad-off group? There are studies that claim that the average happiness of immigrants, measured by subjective satisfaction, quickly moves towards the average of the home population.[21] We think this shows that subjective well-being is a weak and uninformative measure. The reason is that all the other findings about the immigrant experience (unless they are rich, mobile, immigrants of choice) show that there are significant costs to immigrants, often lasting generations, on both emotional state happiness and every variety of well-being.

In chapter 7, "Happiness and Well-Being in Contemporary China," we offer an exportable model for deep understanding of another culture that turns on isolating significant "habits of the heart" that a people or various subcultures use to orient themselves toward the good. It is intended as one model that might provide thick, ecologically valid assessments of happiness and well-being as conceived of in particular nation-states and at a time, where the assessment aims, among other things, to track contestations about whose happiness and well-being is at stake, and which kinds of happiness and well-being are desirable. The conception of flourishing we uncover in China is ethicized, and it is ethicized in a manner that reveals the powerful effects of Confucian philosophy, as well as both traditional Chinese religions and imported Abrahamic ones. Next, we provide a case study of the feminist movement in contemporary China and focus specifically on current contestations between liberatory languages (with sources in communism and the Western enlightenment), which conceive of well-being and flourishing as requiring gender equality and justice, and traditional Confucian discourse, which prizes filial piety and a certain conception of a well-functioning family as the basis for the good life. These contestations are primarily about the importance of equality and rights in a good life, hardly at all about happiness.

Part III, "Race, Racism, Resignation," contains two chapters.

In chapter 8, "Happiness, Race, and Hermeneutical Injustice: The Case of African American Mental Health," we argue that even if subjective well-being measures can provide useful information for certain purposes, getting reliable data about subjective well-being is not as easy as some researchers have thought, especially in societies shaped by persistent patterns of marginalization and discrimination against some social groups. *Hermeneutical injustice* exists when there are differential permissions among groups to speak truthfully about how they are faring, and more specifically when histories of discrimination and oppression create deficiencies in interpretive resources that "external" inquirers use to understand certain groups and sometimes that members of these groups use to describe their own situation. *Affective injustice* exists when there are "feeling rules" that apply to emotional expression of different groups, for example, that women and Blacks should not be shrill, whiney, scary, or "uppity." We argue specifically that the resources available for describing and understanding subjective experience are likely tainted by their origins in belief systems that embody discriminatory or stigmatizing stereotypes and prejudices. The finding that older African Americans are an unusually happy population is one example of a finding that deserves suspicion that it is due to the dynamics of hermeneutical injustice and affective injustice (encouragement to speak in certain positive ways, adaptation, resignation, lowered expectations) rather than to the fact that older African Americans are in fact an unusually happy population. We examine the workings of hermeneutical injustice in the domain of mental health, ill-being, and psychosocial suffering (something which is not entirely in the head on any plausible account), especially the effects that hermeneutical injustice and affective injustice has had on the diagnosis and treatment of depression and the prevention of suicide among African American males.

In chapter 9, "Interpreting Self-Reports of Well-Being," we further reflect on the informativeness of self-report measures, specifically measures in the broad area of subjective well-being, which encompasses people's judgments about their lives as well as their emotional responses to their lives. Much more work needs to be done to understand whether and how subjective well-being measures warrant comparing and ranking dissimilar social and cultural groups inside communities, states, and nation-states on the same scale of life satisfaction. Otherwise, we risk failing to grasp what the data are really telling us and thus, ironically, basing policy on a distorted understanding of a population's experience of their lives—perhaps even worsening the situation of the most vulnerable groups. In the St. Louis, Missouri, metro region, we found self-reported stress in Gallup daily surveys to be lowest not in affluent white municipalities but in several predominantly Black neighborhoods that would appear to be among the most severely distressed parts of the region from metrics of health problems, violent crime, life expectancy, poverty, and so forth. We recommend extreme caution about computing average happiness scores in populations that we antecedently know are faring differentially well. And we recommend adding a complement of qualitative ethnographic interviews to interpret life satisfaction data, again with the caveat that even if the nature, causes, constituents, and effects of life satisfaction are better analyzed, it is not a remotely adequate tool to measure whether a person or a people live good lives or have objective well-being.

Part IV, "Conclusions," contains two chapters.

In chapter 10, "Recommendations for Policy Use of Happiness Metrics," we collect some lessons for the philosophy and science of happiness, and we discuss implications for policy.

In chapter 11, "Universal Rights, Sustainable Development, and Happiness," we sum up and conclude our analysis by explaining the modest role that happiness should play in public policy and insisting that equality and justice are significantly more important than happiness.

Part V, "Four Responses by Critics," includes comments and insights from Jennifer A. Frey, Hazel Rose Marcus, Jeffrey D. Sachs, and Jeanne L. Tsai.

I

HAPPINESS PHILOSOPHY AND HAPPINESS SCIENCE

1

THE HAPPINESS AGENDA

There are two trends in policy circles that deserve close attention. First, there is increased advocacy for "the happiness agenda" as a guide to public and government policy. Second, there is a disconnect between alleged empirical findings about happiness (it is high and trending higher with some bumps) and objective reality (there is the COVID pandemic, climate disaster, multiple epistemic crises, epidemics of anxiety and depression, deaths of despair, increased authoritarianism, political hatred, racism, xenophobia, war, terrible refugee crises, and rising economic inequality). We take these in reverse order.

THE DISCONNECT: "1,000,000 OF US DIED AND WE ARE THRIVING!"

The long years of COVID-19 began in early 2020. We do not know when the global epidemic will end. As we write these words in the spring of 2022, almost one million Americans and six million people worldwide have died due to COVID. Many indexes show alarming rises in economic insecurity, stress, loneliness, and mental illness. In July 2021, the CDC reported that American life expectancy fell 1.5 years: three years for Blacks and Hispanics and 1.2 years for whites.[1] In April 2022, the CDC reported a slight uptick in a disturbing long-term trend: four in ten teens felt "persistently sad and hopeless," and one in five said they had contemplated suicide.[2]

But in that very same month that the CDC reported the extraordinary drop in American life span, a drop presumably being matched or exceeded across numerous nations, regions, and continents and alongside consistent findings that American teens are suffering a terrible scourge of anxiety, depression, and hopelessness, Gallup reported that Americans had reached the highest level ever of the percentage of the population who consider themselves "thriving"—plotting themselves at 7 on an 11-point scale (0–10) of the best possible life for them, and predicting themselves at 8 on that scale in five years.[3]

Relatedly, the *World Happiness Report* editions of 2021 and 2022, also based largely on Gallup data, found little change in average life evaluation scores across the world during the first two year of the global pandemic.[4] Furthermore, in data gathered over several years in Atlanta, Georgia, Blacks had only slightly lower current life satisfaction (they were "thriving" as well or are pretty close to "thriving") than whites, but 50 percent of Blacks thought they would be at 10 in five years (compared to 7.6 for Americans overall). We found the same pattern in poor Black neighborhoods in St. Louis, Missouri, where reported stress was low while objective conditions are maximally stressful.

Various hypotheses have been offered for the stark conflicts among indicators and disconnects between positive life assessments and the negative situation on the ground: resilience, optimism, adaptive preferences, self-deception, COVID-19-induced discoveries about what really matters in life, poor measurement tools, and human inability to accurately answer abstract questions, among others.

THE HAPPINESS AND WELL-BEING AGENDA(S)

In the 1970s, economists discovered that personal happiness did not always rise with income, nor at a national level did it always rise with GDP per capita. More precisely, the Easterlin Paradox, also called the happiness-income paradox, says that: (1) in the short term, happiness and income tend to move together; (2) there are income levels below which people are generally unhappy; but (3) over the course of a decade or so, average happiness does not rise reliably with income. That is, once income reaches a certain level, more of it doesn't reliably increase happiness.[5]

Betsey Stevenson and Justin Wolfers claim that Easterlin is wrong and that there is no satiation point at which average ordinary happiness ceases to rise with income, but because the effect is logarithmic it takes a lot more money once one is pretty happy to become more so.[6] One credible interpretation is that money doesn't quite so much make people happier and happier as they get more, albeit at a slower rate once one already has a lot of it, but that money decreases one's precarity, fragility, and vulnerability to terrible misfortune. In countries with strong social safety nets people feel less threatened by thoughts of getting ill or losing work not because they individually are rich but because their country is rich enough and compassionate enough to protect them from such misfortune. Is feeling safe the same as feeling happy? Not in ordinary speech.

In any case, such results mean that money doesn't bring happiness, or isn't the main thing that brings happiness, or doesn't bring true happiness, something that countless religious and philosophical traditions have insisted on for millennia.

One of the aims of the happiness research in economics is to figure out what brings happiness, given that money, or money alone, or at least money once one hits a decent middle-class standard doesn't.

It is important to emphasize that the happiness agenda began in economics as an internal disciplinary correction due to Easterlin-like findings. GDP doesn't track everything that matters.[7] Economists need to measure what else matters. At the time, no other discipline—not philosophy, psychology, sociology, theology, political science, or public policy—had the problem economics did because they all had plural conceptions of what matters. Happiness was on all their lists, but it was not the main thing.

Then something happened, a perfect storm in which the burgeoning field of positive psychology met the economics of happiness, and some economists but almost no psychologists proposed the idea that all the things that matter collect themselves in the *summum bonum* as happiness or subjective well-being. For example, Martin Seligman, the founder of the positive psychology movement, like most psychologists, thinks subjective happiness is only one aspect of a good human life. To it are added purpose and meaning, high-quality relations, various often difficult achievements, expressions of talents, and so on. Seligman calls this the theory of "authentic happiness."[8] Happiness conceived as a single emotional state or as a summary cognitive judgement about life satisfaction is not considered an essential element of authentic happiness so conceived. This view of happiness is best characterized as *eudaimonistic* or *eudaimonistic* and *existentialist*, since it blends features of Aristotle with an existentialist focus on meaning, difficult projects, and achievement. It is one among many theories of true happiness, not a theory of ordinary happiness.

The happiness agenda goes one step further than simply investigating all the other things that matter besides GDP and that are good to promote. It is the movement that in addition to claiming to study the nature of happiness, its causes and effects, endorses the use of happiness and subjective well-being metrics to guide public policy. It comes in strong and weak forms. The strongest form says that we have known since the time of Aristotle that happiness is the highest or ultimate good, the good at which all other goods aim (setting aside that it is entirely false that Aristotle thought this or that it is true). Politics should promote the ultimate good, which is happiness. The weak version says that happiness is one of the good things in a plural package of good things that should be considered in creating public policy, and furthermore any practically wise public policy (keeping power might depend on it) should be interested in the happiness effects of those policies. But even in arguments for the weak view, wise thinkers sometimes can't resist stating the strong and implausible view: "The ultimate goal of public policy should be to enhance citizens' subjective well-being."[9]

The happiness or well-being agenda is not, in fact, conceptually unified. To put it more favorably, it is a very wide umbrella that includes traditional concerns with rights and justice that can compete with happiness. David Cameron and Nicholas Sarkozy were both caught up in the memetic atmospherics and the emerging rhetorical posture of celebrating happiness as the *summum bonum*, and thus they expressed support for the happiness agenda. But Cameron was sensibly capacious when he proclaimed himself an advocate of the happiness agenda, and thus he was inaccurate about what happiness is or what the word "happiness" means. For Cameron, happiness includes meaning, what matters, and rights, none of which in fact is happiness or reliably causes happiness: "You cannot capture happiness on a spreadsheet any more than you can bottle it—and if anyone was trying to reduce the whole spectrum of human happiness into one snapshot statistic I would be the first to roll my eyes, [but such measures] could give us a general picture of whether life is improving and lead to government policy that is more focused not just on the bottom line, but on all those things that make life worthwhile."[10]

Sarkozy's happiness agenda wasn't particularly concerned with happiness. He was advised by the economists Joseph Stiglitz, Amartya Sen, and Jean-Paul Fitoussi—none of whom are fans of the view that happiness or subjective satisfaction is the *summum bonum*—and was focused on the distribution of income, quality of the environment, and what Sen calls "capabilities," roughly, the genuine opportunities to do and to be who and what we want to be. In the capabilities approach, well-being is conceived in terms of whether a person has genuine chances to be well-educated, to get good work, to save money, to travel, to learn to play a musical instrument or a sport, to be treated with respect, and so on. Do capabilities lead to happiness? Sometimes, maybe. But that's not why capabilities are good or why they should be promoted by sound public policy.

Conceptual confusions such as these suggest that the happiness agenda is coming unglued internally and becoming a plural well-being agenda. We predict that the idea that government should promote happiness will be shortly seen for what it is: a fad, a passing fancy, a branding overreach. Excellent work in economics such as Anthony Annett's *Cathonomics* and Jeffrey Sachs's forthcoming work on Aristotelean economics are entirely concerned with happiness in thick senses that embed Catholic social gospel values in Annett's case and Aristotelean *eudaimonistic* ones in Sachs's case.[11] In Sachs's work especially, human rights and sustainable development are offered as consensus conditions that set a baseline for global human flourishing. Neither Annett's nor Sachs's views depend at all on what brings subjective satisfaction; or better, neither Annett nor Sachs thinks subjective satisfaction matters unless it comes with living in accordance with virtue and good values, and in states that respect universal human rights and aim at sustainable development.

In American English, the semantics of the main terms of art "happiness" and "well-being" skew respectively personal (happiness is a psychobiological state of an individual person) and impersonal (well-being is a state of individuals when one is faring well and collectives, as in "the common good"). Among philosophers, well-being consists in how well your life goes for you. But even this is ambiguous between how well your life goes for you subjectively (which also divides between how you feel about it and how you judge it) and how well it goes for you objectively (your income, savings, heath care, etc.). A life can be going well for you even if you feel or think it isn't and are not, as we say, happy. Often happiness and subjective well-being are treated as synonyms, which again can be very confusing, since (1) subjective well-being is often measured by judgements about life satisfaction, which can easily come apart from feeling happy or being happy. There is nothing peculiar about saying that one's life is going very well but that one is unhappy; (2) there are many states, such as calm, engagement, attachment, that are not happiness or varieties of happiness but that can indicate subjective well-being; and (3) there are numerous measures of both happiness and subjective well-being, and they yield different results as to who is happy or has subjective well-being.

Some theorists claim that well-being is distinct not only from happiness but also from goodness. The inspiration here is Callicles, Socrates's interlocutor in Plato's *Gorgias*, who celebrates the life of the immoralist who is quite pleased with his life and lives well by doing exactly what he wants. Others follow Aristotle by claiming that moral goodness is one of the things that is good for a person herself, not just for those with whom she interacts, and that true happiness (*eudaimonia*) consists in or requires intellectual and moral excellence. On views that make goodness a necessary condition for happiness, Callicles—as pleased, healthy, and self-satisfied as he is—just isn't happy and doesn't have well-being, period. He is not *eudaimon*, as the Aristotelians would say.

Discussion of happiness is all around us on TV, in journalism, in self-help sections of bookstores. William Davies calls it "the happiness industry" and subtitles his book of that name "How the Government and Big Business Sold Us Well-Being."[12] The happiness industry of which the happiness agenda is one component is highly visible in new journals dedicated to happiness, well-being, and positive psychology. And it has a world-famous annual vehicle in the form of the *World Happiness Report*, which has been published since 2012, and that ranks countries on the basis of average happiness, conceived as subjective life evaluation. Christopher Barrington-Leigh, in *World Happiness Report 2022*, devotes a chapter to tracking the dramatic rise of the word "happiness" in economics journals and policy circles: "It appears that the flexibly-defined language around 'well-being' and 'quality of life' serves as a rhetorical and conceptual gateway to recognizing happiness as an important or even central policy outcome, and incorporating happiness data and insights into policy formation."¹³ He judges this "rhetorical and conceptual gateway" a good thing. We judge it a fad, an unfortunate overreach.

Bhutan was the first country to adopt happiness as an explicit policy aim. If people were paying attention starting in the 1970s when the king of Bhutan first announced that "gross national happiness" was more important than gross domestic product, they could have seen right away that what Bhutanese Buddhists mean by happiness is not American-style happiness. Bhutan's *Gross National Happiness Index* explicitly endorses in the Constitution of 2008 an ideal of happiness that cannot be achieved by being a happy individual, whereas American-style happiness is paradigmatically achieved by individuals. The government of Bhutan says that no one is happy unless everyone is, which although possibly empirically false even in Bhutan is ethically true for Bhutanese Buddhists.¹⁴

The romanticism and mythmaking about Bhutan's role in (re)awakening the world to the importance of happiness and the government's role in advancing happiness looks suspiciously "orientalist" in Edward Said's pejorative sense.¹⁵ Happiness is predominantly an Anglo-American obsession or a North Atlantic obsession, not a worldwide one, and casting a small landlocked Buddhist country—a constitutional monarchy with a very mixed human rights record toward ethnic Nepalis— as the exotic locale in whose company we can regain our bearings is magical thinking.

At least four additional countries—New Zealand, Iceland, Scotland, and the United Arab Emirates—have also adopted well-being agendas as public policy frameworks, where well-being is glossed as happiness or is connected by advocates to the use of happiness metrics. Jacinda Arden, the prime minister of New Zealand, says that her ministers need to be prepared "to prove that you are going to improve inter-generational well-being."[16] The government of New Zealand favors measuring "gross national well-being." Examined closely favoring "gross national well-being" is not the same as favoring "gross national happiness." One but not the only criterion of well-being in New Zealand is how happy (that is, satisfied with their lives) people say they are. But any scheme to promote intergenerational well-being will need to acknowledge that there may need to be sacrifices of happiness now for the happiness and well-being of future generations. Guiding reasons to make such sacrifices will not be hedonic, emotional, or psychological, or straightforwardly happiness promoting reasons, but reasons of ethics, specifically reasons of intergenerational justice.

Nicola Sturgeon, the first minister of Scotland, calls for promoting "a vision of society that has well-being not just wealth at its very heart."[17] And Katrin Jakobsdottir, the prime minister of Iceland, is leading an effort to guide and measure whether public policy works to advance goals that actually matter the most to people.[18] These include advancing the role of women in work and men in child care, and reducing depression (Iceland leads the world in antidepressant prescriptions).

It is not always entirely obvious whether and how well-being and doing what matters to the most people or, what is entirely different, what is judged to matter the most by experts is related to overall happiness. One set of complexities come from the fact that New Zealand's well-being metrics start with goods that appear on the Organisation for Economic Co-operation and Development (OECD) *Better Life Index*, only one of which (out of eleven) is happiness in the subjective sense.[19] The others are such things as income, safety, quality of health care, and housing. These things are as they are independently of how people subjectively feel about them or how people judge them to be.

In Iceland, gender equality is a major focus. One can imagine that achieving gender equality might involve tough sledding and thus costs in terms of how people—and not only sexists—feel, while nonetheless being for the best ethically. To put it another way: even if gender equality does not matter to most people, it might be what matters the most to those, possibly a numerical minority, who see sexism as an obstacle to general social health and well-being. Gender equality is a perfectly legitimate aim of public policy, but not because it will make most people happier. In the short term it might do the opposite.

Scotland's *National Performance Framework* is based in large measure on achieving the United Nations' 2015 seventeen Sustainable Development Goals (SDGs).[20] But none of the SDGs mentions happiness or subjective well-being explicitly. In virtue of aiming at peace, security, good education for all the boys and girls on Earth, environmental quality, and less economic inequality inside and among nations, the SDGs will almost certainly enhance well-being. And there are correlations between where nation states are in achieving the SDGs (at present no country is meeting benchmarks for success by 2030) and the average subjective well-being (glossed as happiness) in the nation-states that are doing the best. But achieving the SDGs also involve sacrifices for the sake of future generations and economic redistribution that might need to make some, possibly many or most, less happy, but again for the greater good.[21]

This indicates the two main problems with a single-minded policy focus on happiness. First, it is impossible to sustain this focus because there are many things that matter (wealth redistribution, environmental justice, equal rights, capabilities) that are not aspects, features, or types of happiness nor reliable causes or effects of happiness. Second, the solution to the greatest existential crisis of our time, the climate crisis, requires policy that will almost certainly reduce happiness, although perhaps not the greatest happiness overall and eventually. The wider class of things that matter might credibly fall under a theory of subjective and objective well-being, but then we are back to the situation where what matters is a plural set of goods, not one ultimate good, and within that set happiness has no special status.

The United Arab Emirates explicitly calls its initiative "The Happiness Agenda." The government aims to develop a sound happiness experience (HX) strategy that will make its largest city, Dubai, "the happiest city on earth" and that can serve as a model for the rest of the world. Although the UAE holds the highest position (20) of any Arab state in the *World Happiness Report* 2012–2014, this ranking is the result of the weighted average of two very different groups, citizens and resident aliens (it is ranked 21st in the WHR 2021 and 25th in the WHR 2022).[22] The overall population of the UAE consists of approximately 1.5 million citizen nationals versus 9.2 million resident aliens, a ratio of one citizen to every six resident aliens. Some resident aliens are wealthy international businesspeople, but most are people from poor countries in South Asia, Southeast Asia, and Africa who often work in miserable conditions with very limited freedom. If human rights and subjective well-being were both measured and weighted (as they might be in a measure of overall well-being), it is inconceivable that the UAE and Saudi Arabia would rank higher than Spain, Italy, and Japan.

There is another problem: 2012 Gallup subjective well-being polling in the UAE was only in Arabic, whereas between 2013 and 2019 it was in Arabic and English. Nonresident aliens who speak Hindi, Persian, Urdu, or any of the dozen other languages spoken by immigrant workers were not represented in polling until 2020. This means the data on subjective well-being in the UAE were unrepresentative until 2020. Averages are uninformative when there is a bimodal economic distribution plus two different sets of rights. How subjectively happy are the denizens of the UAE? No one knows. It is easy to judge, however, that the migrant workers in the UAE do not have high objective well-being (even if, as some say, they are better off working in the UAE than being unemployed in their home country). Thus if we discover that they are on average subjectively happy, this would show only that happiness measures don't measure what really matters.

Finally, there is this really interesting fact. The OECD *Better Life Index* asks people to say what matters to them and how much it matters to them from a list of eleven goods, only one of which is subjective life satisfaction.[23] The others are such things as housing, education, environment, safety, community, civic engagement, income, jobs, health, and work/life balance. In many countries, according to the OECD, subjective life satisfaction is not what matters most.

Happiness conceived as subjective life satisfaction matters most to Americans, the British, the Irish, those in the UAE, and among Indians, but not to Canadians or Mexicans or Chinese. It matters the most in Nigeria, Zimbabwe, and Libya, but not the most in Ethiopia, Somalia, or South Africa. And it does not matter the most to the residents of any country in South America.

THE META-HAPPINESS PARADOX

So there is a paradox beyond the Easterlin paradox. Call it the meta-happiness paradox: the happiness agenda is premised on the idea that government policy should aim at what matters the most to people. What matters the most? What do people value the most? Happiness. Therefore, governments should aim to promote happiness.

But here's the rub: in measures that let people choose what matters most, most people in most nations do not universally or reliably rank happiness, conceived as subjective well-being or, it seems, conceived in the emotional state sense, as what matters most. In many places they are more interested in health, housing, income, and rights.

One move is to point out that across the earth happiness matters a lot to people, and that it is one of the good things that contributes to well-being. Fair enough, but there are other things that matter to people, including things like justice, freedom, equality, and human rights. Rights and such are valued and valuable independently of any happiness they might produce. That is not their point.

2

VARIETIES OF THEORIES AND MEASURES OF WELL-BEING AND HAPPINESS

Philosophy, psychology, and economics have active research areas devoted to the study of happiness and well-being. There are abundant fruitful intra- and interdisciplinary debates about the nature of the phenomena, about vocabulary (well-being, welfare, utility, happiness, *eudaimonia*, and flourishing, about measurement, about whether happiness is unidimensional or multidimensional, and about the sensitivity of various indicators.

There are also complex normative debates in, between, and across these disciplines: Are there universal generalizations about what *comprises* happiness and well-being? Are there universal generalizations about what *produces* happiness and well-being? Are standards of happiness and well-being so culture- and tradition-specific that only local, nation-specific, or subculture-specific generalizations are possible? Are comparative assessments of happiness and well-being theoretically and empirically sound? Should criteria of happiness and well-being be ethically and politically neutral? Can criteria of happiness and well-being be ethically and politically neutral? Should governments be in the business of aiming to produce the greatest amount of happiness or well-being, or should they be in the business of aiming to produce justice and equality (or order and public health), assuming these aims can conflict as they sometimes do?

It is easy to see how the ends of justice and happiness can conflict. Imagine a tax policy that is good for social justice but makes those who are taxed at the higher rate less happy. If there are enough people negatively affected, this could result in lower average happiness, while still being for the best. De Neve and Sachs provide empirical evidence that at least two of the seventeen Sustainable Development Goals, 12 (responsible consumption of resources) and 13 (climate justice), require actions that have costs to subjective well-being.[1]

Finally, are indicators and assessments of happiness and well-being attuned enough to hear the voices of those who are downtrodden, oppressed, and shortchanged, who are encouraged by histories of mistreatment to have very low expectations, and who are often also socialized not to complain about their situation, to show a stiff upper lip or to praise God almighty for the most meager bounty?

WHAT IS CONTESTED

The concepts of a good life, well-being, and happiness—are normative. They are like such concepts as physical health and mental well-being. They embed norms and ideals and express values. A person lives a good life, lives well, is happy relative to some standard. The standard can be one the person herself endorses, or one endorsed by others—her community, culture, nation-state—or by certain experts, theologians, philosopher, psychologists, or policy wonks.

Most everyone thinks that living a good life, well-being, and happiness matter. *Living a good life* and *well-being* are more abstract and general concepts than *happiness*. A common view is that well-being consists in, is produced by, and/or involves achieving some set of goods that includes, depending on the theory, desire satisfaction, good interpersonal relations, meaningful work, a decent income, a low Gini coefficient, a strong social safety net, clean air, potable water, a reasonably long life, good health, educational advancement, moral decency, human rights, and so on. Some of the goods on the list are objective. They are as they are independently of anyone's feelings or opinions about them. The feelings and opinions are subjective.

It is an odd failing of most happiness research that it largely ignores the history of reflection on the nature, status, and varieties of happiness across the world's great philosophical and theological traditions. Ignorance is the only explanation for the widespread claim that rigorous thinking about happiness and well-being are new things. It is rare in the history of reflective thinking about happiness to say that a good human life or well-being consist in happiness alone or that happiness is sufficient for well-being. Most theories of well-being say that happiness is one desirable component of a life well-lived. Some theories say something stronger: that happiness is all there is to well-being or, at least, that happiness is a necessary component of well-being. If true, this entails that unless one is happy one cannot, despite possessing all the other goods in the requisite set be judged to be living well or to have lived a good life. Socrates is thought to have lived well, but no one who has read the Platonic dialogues closely would say that Socrates was reliably and regularly subjectively happy in the ordinary emotional state sense.

It is true that Socrates was almost certainly satisfied with his life, even if not happy. This is good for theorists who propose that life satisfaction is what matters and needs to be tracked. The trouble is that across Plato's *Dialogues*, it is typically Socrates's sophist interlocutors, like Thrasymachus in book 1 of *The Republic* and Callicles in *Gorgias*, who think that "it is better to seem good than to be good" and that it is every ego for itself, who are perfect 10s on life satisfaction. A very similar set of observations about very self-satisfied souls is discussed throughout Confucius's *Analects*. Confucius calls such people "glib tongues" and "village worthies," noting their extraordinary life satisfaction alongside their social indifference and moral vacuity.

There is disagreement about what happiness is, even among those who agree that it is a desirable component of a good life. Some theories stipulate that it is only "true happiness" that is desirable or necessary, where "true happiness," is used to mark off happiness that passes some kind of qualitative inspection, and which is not achieved on the cheap by the satisfaction of superficial or immoral desires. A narcissist with entirely frivolous desires could, after all, be happy in one familiar sense; although perhaps not "truly happy." And Socrates, who taught that the unexamined life is not worth living, might, according to such a conception, be judged happy in the "true happiness" sense, given that he reflectively endorsed how he lived his life. He is happy in one sense, the life satisfaction sense, but not happy in another sense, the emotional state sense.

Some say happiness is pleasure, that pleasure is produced by desire satisfaction, and that happiness can be measured moment by moment.[2] Others say that happiness (of the right sort) comes from the satisfaction of reflectively endorsed desires and values.[3] Others say that happiness is an emotional state that consists in feeling happy or in experiencing a favorable ratio of feelings of cheerfulness, engagement, and energy to feelings of sadness, stress, and lethargy.[4] Still others say that happiness is the cognitive-evaluative state of being satisfied with how one's life is going or how one is living one's life.⁵ Happiness in this cognitive-evaluative sense need not involve what we colloquially think of as feeling happy or being happy, although it might. Finally, but still not exhausting the theoretical space, there are those who claim that a life that is judged to be satisfactory as a whole or domain by domain—work, family, health, physical environment, and so forth—will reliably yield a subjective state of overall satisfaction that is what happiness is, or at any rate, is the kind of happiness we ought to be interested in tracking and making use of in public policy.

NORMATIVE

All theories of happiness and well-being are normative. They describe a state or condition that is judged to be good or healthy or desirable, and they involve value judgments. The World Health Organization (WHO) defines health as the "state of complete physical, mental and social well-being and not merely the absence of disease or infirmity."⁶ Once a norm or set of norms for physical, mental, and social health, happiness, or well-being is in place, we can construct instruments to measure whether and to what degree the norms are met or satisfied by and for some population. The quality and ease of a measurement tool is an empirically and conceptually separate matter from the quality of the theory it serves.

Consider: physical health is an emergent system level property of an organism-in-the-world. A complete blood and metabolic panel at an annual physical for someone with good insurance in America involves more than twenty different blood tests, each of which is designed to detect subsystem irregularities. The measures taken together are good indexes of overall health. No measure taken alone reliably marks good or ill health. And all the measures taken together are not perfect indicators of health. When an irregularity shows up in a particular subsystem, one is sent for further, more sensitive tests. One suspects the same sort of situation applies to mental health and psychosocial well-being. In the case of physical health, psychological heath, and well-being, some people who feel good or pass inspection according to a battery of tests are not in fact well. And some people who feel or judge that something is off are just fine physically.

It is common that when theorists discuss how to measure happiness or well-being for the sake of public policy, they debate what is the shortest and easiest way to do so.[7] This puts the cart before the horse, allowing the ease of a measure to dictate the conceptualization of the target phenomenon. If happiness matters, and in addition is the goal of public policy, one better have it theorized correctly. Life satisfaction is typically offered as an atheoretical or theoretically light measure since it is content-free; it doesn't concern itself with or measure what a person's or community's or nation-state's normative conception is; it is indifferent to the whys, wherefores, components, and contents of happiness so conceived. This indifference, some say, is desirable in liberal cultures that are neutral across conceptions of the good. What matters is that you are happy, not what you are happy about.

LOGICAL AND EMPIRICAL DISTINCTNESS

Thanks to the important study of Margolis and colleagues, we know that when one studies subjective well-being (three of the five measures are standard happiness ones) via the instruments designed to measure what different theories of happiness and/or well-being claim needs measuring, one sees positive correlations, ranging from .5 to .79 across the different measures.[8] But the correlations do not remotely approach unity. This strongly suggests that the theories of happiness and subjective well-being glossed earlier (moment by moment pleasant feelings, more positive than negative emotions, desire satisfaction, life satisfaction, etc.), which are logically and conceptually distinct from each other, are also empirically distinct. The conflicting indicators during COVID 19, where stress, economic precarity, depression, unemployment, and death rates were all dramatically up at the same time as indicators of life satisfaction held stable, even that the percentage of Americans who are thriving reached all-time highs, are almost certainly due to multiple measurement weaknesses.

As a general policy, it is always best to say exactly what theory of happiness or well-being is in play, what was measured and how, life satisfaction, ratio of positive to negative emotions (and which ones), objective lists, emotional state happiness, and so on, and not to elide the concepts of happiness, subjective well-being, and objective well-being or to simply assert that one has discovered such and so about happiness and well-being. Indicators are indicators. What they indicate requires interpretation. A thermometer can tell whether a child has a fever or not. It provides no information about what the underlying problem is if the child has a fever. And, of course, a child can be sick even if it doesn't have a fever.

CAUSES, CONSTITUENTS, CONTENTS

Well-being theories or models inquire into at least six different aspects of happiness and/or well-being: preconditions, causes, correlates, components/constituents, contents, and effects of happiness and/or well-being. They yield generalizations at a time and in a location. It is too early to know whether and if so how much universality any observed patterns have. Even when generalizations find, for example, that subjectively happy people are also generous (or selfish), they are at best representative of a certain population in a place and at a time, but never so far representative of humankind.

Theorists aren't always careful about which features of well-being they are discussing or where those features sit—as preconditions (being alive) or causes (good government, social trust), as constituents or components (feeling happy), or as effects (generosity)—in the general framework of well-being being advocated. Finally, of course, there are separate questions about what people are happy about, what philosophers call "content." The evidence might indicate that happiness is caused by high income, good education, and good government, but a person might judge that what she is happy about is almost exclusively the quality of her personal relationships.

Theories and measures line up along a spectrum where some focus on objective aspects, such as income per capita, whereas others assess subjective aspects or indicators, such as life satisfaction. Many theories are hybrids, tracking correlations among objective and subjective factors.

Theories toward the subjective side of the spectrum say that affective states, such as feeling happy or being happy, or cognitive states, such as being satisfied or judging one's life to be going well, are necessary components or constituents of well-being. Normally theories that claim subjective states as the key components or essential constituents of well-being also cite certain objective conditions as typical causes of the subjective states, that is, being happy or satisfied, which constitute or make up well-being. One reason to track both the subjective and objective is due to the familiarity of cases such as these. Suppose both A and B say their life satisfaction is 8. Average life satisfaction for this dyad is 8. Analysis reveals that A is highly motivated to speak well of her life, having been raised by people who teach that one ought to "accentuate the positive, eliminate the negative." B was raised by pessimists who always see what is bad. A has goods 1, 2, 3 in her life. B has 1, 2, 3 + 4 and 5. B's life is, in fact, objectively better than A's, but B is less happy than A.

Theories toward the objective end of the spectrum, on the other hand, will say that the objective conditions of, for example, income above a certain level, a strong social safety net, clean air and water, a certain level of education, a low Gini coefficient, and so on, are what well-being consists in. People can be faring well even if they are not reliably feeling happy or recognizing their bounty. But theories toward the objective side will agree that happiness in the emotional state or cognitive state senses is a common accompaniment or effect of these objective conditions obtaining, and the reason is that basic and universal subjective desires are guaranteed to be satisfied whenever such objective conditions obtain.

Sometimes an objective theory will stipulate that for purposes of theoretical precision measures of objective well-being should be kept separate from measures of subjective well-being. One principled philosophical reason to do this is emphasized by Kant: it is one thing to be happy, it is another to be good. Another reason is that people can become accepting of, or okay with, or adapted to objectively bad conditions.[9] A third principled reason to prise apart the objective and subjective is in order to determine the causal direction between the subjective and objective dimensions of well-being, or to determine bidirectionality if it obtains. And a fourth reason is to track all the most significant correlates, causes, and effects of well-being.

Some prominent reports, such as the *World Happiness Report* series, focus on six useful predictors and correlates—GDP per capita, social support, healthy life expectancy, freedom, generosity, and absence of corruption, which are then also used "to explain the variation in happiness across countries."[10] One could in principle track these six variables objectively or subjectively. The WHR tracks GDP per capita and life span objectively, but freedom, generosity, and corruption subjectively. It asks people how free their life choices seem, how much they believe business and politics are corrupt, and how generous they have been to strangers. There are extraordinary obstacles to getting objective information about degree of freedom or corruption and the like, in part because effectiveness at restricting freedom or being corrupt involves concealing how and that one is doing so. Nonetheless, it matters that the subjective measure of how satisfied with life people are is assessed in relation to several other subjective judgments rather than to a set of six objective states of affairs. Without independent evidence that actual freedom or actual lack of corrupt politics and business exists, the inferences are about the relations of some subjective judgments to other subjective judgments, not from objective states of affairs to the subjective life satisfaction judgment. Consider, for example, that most Americans will say that America is a democracy. But when one factors in and pays attention to the role of big money, and thus of American oligarchs, complete control of most elections by two political parties, voter suppression, low voter turnout, and so on, one sees that quick subjective impressions are belied by the objective situation. Can ordinary people see this easily? No. Keeping us in the dark is the idea.

Furthermore, we know antecedently that these six causes (preconditions or predictors) are not all the important causes and preconditions of either happiness or subjective well-being. Others include neurochemistry, temperament, years and quality of education, natural and human made beauty, reliability of news/journalism, food choices, religion, defense spending/security, shared values, and political polarization.

In fact, the authors of the *World Happiness Report* state that employment rate and equality (likely both political and economic equality) are antecedently known to effect subjective well-being, but they are not assessed as structural causes of happiness in the cross-country regressions, because there is lack of data on them.[11] This matters because one natural response to the happiness agenda is to say: show me how economically and politically equal a society is, and then, and only then, will I be interested in how happy the people are. But there is insufficient data on things that we antecedently know are important factors (preconditions, correlates, causes, and constituents) of happiness and well-being. So these factors are not included in developing the theory of subjective well-being.

The six-causal-variable model has two further weaknesses. First, these variables are not fine grained enough to track significant local causes; for example, the people are predominantly stoics or hedonists or egalitarians, or they are responding to a unique environmental crisis or advantage that is not one of the six tracked features of common life. Second, in many places on Earth, the quality of close personal relationships—romantic, familial, and communal—is the best predictor of happiness, and it, like employment rate and equality, is not tracked by the world's most visible happiness instrument (the wallet return question is not itself a measure of the quality of personal relations).[12]

One difference at the two ends of the theoretical spectrum that appears to be substantive is this: subjective theories will insist that some psychological states (surplus of pleasant sensations or experiences or an emotional state, such as being happy, or a cognitive state, such as judging one's life as satisfying) are necessary conditions of well-being. A subjective theory might even say that these subjective states are sufficient, that is, enough, to declare that a person or a people satisfies the conditions of well-being. Objective theories will deny this, and they will do so for familiar reasons that have to do with mistaken judgments and mistaken preferences. That said, almost all objective theories claim that there is a reliable empirical connection between objective well-being and subjective well-being. Thus, most theories are hybrid theories recognizing both objective and subjective components of well-being and happiness.

There is one kind of theory that denies that there is a necessary or even a reliable connection between objective measures of well-being and subjective feelings or judgments of well-being. Philosophical *eudaimonistic* theories are sometimes put forward in the spirit of thinking that the standards for living a good life are, or ought to be, a form of excellence.[13] Compare this to the standards for being a good runner. If you ask people if they are good runners, most might say good or good enough. But the perfectionist claims that who is and isn't a good runner ought to be determined not by average jogging standards but by track and field standards. A good 1,500-meter runner in the 18–30 age group can run it in under five minutes. This is about 25 percent slower than the women's world record and is probably not something 99 percent of people in the 18–30 age group can do. This means that most people in that age group are not good runners, and their opinion about the matter is irrelevant. It does not mean that the standards for being a good runner are off, but rather than people's subjective opinion of the matter is off. Some ethicists who work on well-being claim that high scores on well-being or happiness measures (for example, the recent findings that Americans are thriving at all-time highs) simply serve to show that, in this case, Americans have low standards of—take your pick—what *eudaimonia*, a good life, well-being, or happiness really consist in.

John Rawls, who is not a political Aristotelian (he insists that a theory of rights and justice is prior to and independent of the quest for any kind of good or happy life), nonetheless defends the view that human flourishing involves what he calls "the Aristotelian principle": "This principle of deep motivation affirms that other things equal, human beings enjoy the exercise of their realized capacities (their innate or trained abilities), and [that] this enjoyment increases the more the capacity is realized, or the greater its complexity."[14] Flourishing, on Rawls's view, involves the exercise of realized capacities and the enjoyment that accompanies this exercise. The excellences one can develop depend on talent, discoveries that take world historical time (the invention of football, paint and painting, basketball, jazz), and the actual availability of these practices and excellences to individuals and societies.

The common way of understanding Aristotle's idea of *eudaimonia* in contemporary worlds is to think of it as requiring or presupposing the social and political conditions that make possible a person's development of her potential excellences, moral, intellectual, athletic, musical, and so on. Sen and Nussbaum's capabilities approach to well-being develops these insights. The key idea is that a good society will provide the conditions (income, education, health care) that allow people to pursue their potential excellences, develop them, and possibly achieve or actualize them. A person who develops excellences will experience pride, self-respect, and self-esteem. Will they be happy? Maybe, maybe not.

HAPPINESS AND MEANING

So far we have said that happiness is normative because it is considered good—but not the highest good—across almost every conception. We say "almost" because there are a few religious conceptions that judge all kinds of earthly happiness worthless or evil, the guise of the devil. And, as we will discuss shortly, there are many cultures and traditions that think of happiness as a childish state, not one available to or desirable for adults. Some conceptions of happiness—*eudaimonia, beatitudo, le* 樂— are normative in a stronger sense; they incorporate ethical requirements. One is happy in these senses only if one is in the happy state at least in part because one is good in the Aristotelian, Christian, or Confucian way. Being this way (Christian, Confucian, and so on) partly makes up or constitutes one's "happy" state. It does not cause it, nor does it result from it, although once in the state the cycle is self-sustaining.

Some traditions emphasize another normative dimension of happiness or true happiness. This is meaning, as in the meaningfulness of a life. Great thinkers like Marx and Nietzsche were attuned to the human importance of living authentically, engaging in activities especially in the domains of work, friendship, love, and communal life that are genuinely meaningful. And they were well aware of a host of techniques oppressors use to make people think they are happy, even to make them feel happy while they are living unfree and alienated lives. Just as the concepts *eudaimonia, beatitudo,* and *le* refer to happiness that is not a simple matter of feeling happy, but rather require feeling happy (if one does) in part because one is ethical according to the relevant conception, there are views that add to the required content and causes of happiness that one be happy in part because one lives in a meaningful way. True happiness involves living authentically, which once again might not involve feeling happy at all.

The conditions of meaningfulness are contested, but freedom to choose among worthwhile projects is thought to be essential. America guarantees political freedom in its Constitution. In early 2022, two-thirds of Americans were living paycheck to paycheck.[15] Are they free to pursue what gives meaning or not? One answer is that they are politically free to pursue any and all meaningful activities, but they are not practically free to do so. Most people across the earth are less well-off than Americans, so the point generalizes. But recall that according to life satisfaction measures the average American is thriving, and this despite the fact that 40 percent of American teens suffer "persistent sadness and hopelessness."[16] Hopelessness, anomie, ennui are not friends of either happiness or meaningfulness.

If we think meaningfulness is another reasonable feature of a good human life in addition to being morally decent according to one conception or another, we will want to know whether happiness guarantees meaningfulness, or if it doesn't guarantee it, whether it at least has a reliable connection to it. The reason this matters is that the only good reason to want policy to focus univocally on happiness as its goal is if feeling or being happy is a reliable cause or indicator of such things as moral decency and meaningfulness.

What do contemporary data show? Is there a reliable connection between happiness in the subjective state sense ("feeling happy," which is the ordinary folk understanding) and meaning? Even judging only by U.S. data, the answer seems to be no.

Here are ways they differ and come apart in American populations:[17]

- Happiness is fleeting. Happiness is an emotional state one is either in or not, and thus is a present-tense state, a *now* state.
- Meaning is not fleeting. Meaning involves a sense of engaging in worthy projects that are existentially satisfying over time.
- Money, achievements, and desire satisfaction matter a lot to happiness; they don't matter much to meaning. Meaning often comes from commitment to projects that are difficult individually or collectively to achieve. Nietzsche writes: "If you have your '*why?*' in life, you can get along with almost any '*how?*' People *don't* strive for happiness, only the English do."[18]
- Health, physical and mental, is linked to happiness but not to meaning. Disabilities are often cited as sources of difficulties and unhappiness but are not similarly considered obstacles to meaning. Abraham Lincoln had bipolar disorder, but he lived an extraordinarily meaningful life (hopefully even by his own lights).
- Meaning often comes from giving, from doing things for others. But there is some evidence that "takers" are happier than givers.
- Parenting reduces happiness but increases meaningfulness. One expects that this point generalizes to lots of meaningful work.
- Experiencing bad events reduces happiness, but bad events are correlated with greater meaning.
- Wisdom, reflectiveness, and existential anxiety (but not, of course, hopelessness) are associated with greater meaning, but not with happiness.

These results are significant because the question of which matters most, a happy life or a meaningful life, is nontrivial. It would be trivial if happiness entailed meaningfulness or if happiness were sufficient for meaningfulness. But happiness isn't sufficient for meaningfulness conceptually or empirically. Is happiness necessary for meaningfulness? Certainly not.

WELL-BEING SUPERORDINATE, HAPPINESS SUBORDINATE

Well-being, welfare, a good life, *eudaimonia*, human flourishing are theoretical concepts, terms of art. *Happy* and *happiness* are ordinary folk concepts that can also be used once regimented as terms of art and science.[19] The usual semantic situation is that "well-being" is considered a superordinate category relative to "happiness." That is, according to most theories of well-being, happiness is a component of well-being or a typical and highly desirable effect of well-being. To make things more complex: it is common to think that a good life is superordinate to well-being. Aristotle, who is almost always claimed as a fan of well-being and happiness theorizing and measurement, is explicit that he is interested in the quality of a complete human life, in something like the form of an overall life assessment that could be made by an objective eulogist. A person is *eudaimon* if she has lived a full human life in which she has attained intellectual and moral excellence as far as her nature permits, and—crucially for Aristotle—as judged by experts. If an individual knows herself and has the proper normative standards, she might be a reliable judge of the quality of her own life. If she doesn't, she isn't.

There are some promising theories of what emotional happiness is and how to measure it.[20] Advocates of such theories are explicit that their theories of happiness are not intended to provide a theory of everything that falls under a general theory of well-being. Similarly, theories that favor life satisfaction measures also often employ other measures. For example, in the *World Happiness Report* for 2021 and 2022 there was the surprising finding that average life evaluation scores were relatively stable during the first two years of the Covid-19 pandemic. This requires interpretation, and various ones were offered: people are resilient; Covid-19 focused people's minds on what matters most in life; life satisfaction is not a sensitive instrument; there are performance demands to show a stiff upper lip; and so on. But even as life satisfaction held stable, measures of positive (amusement, enjoyment) and negative emotions (sadness, anger, fear) did show an uptick in negative emotions. In addition, the WHR uses a measure of trust in the form of predictions about whether a lost wallet would be returned (as a proxy for social trust), as well as a recommendation to include measures of how many years of high-quality nondisabled life one can expect, called WELLBYs. The point is that the WHR, despite historically favoring life evaluation measures for well-being, in fact reveals its commitment to a hybrid model by its use of hybrid methods. It is called the *World Happiness Report*, but none of its instruments that are used to rank countries by happiness measure happiness in the feeling or emotional state senses, which are the only consensus senses of the words "happy" or "happiness." The cognitive judgment senses of happiness, where one says how satisfied one is with one's life or how good one thinks one's life is going on a scale of 1–10, are judgments about life satisfaction or how one thinks one's life is going relative to one's aspirations. The semantics of "satisfying" and "satisfaction" vary considerably across languages from the semantics of "happy" and its cognates. In American English there is no oddity, let alone inconsistency, in saying "I am very happy/satisfied with my life, but I am unhappy/dissatisfied about my anxiety disorder, my weight, the political climate, economic inequality, sexism, and racism." And there is no oddity in judging in the first or third person a life that achieves what one wants or hopes for as not very good all things considered.

WHICH SIDE IS ARISTOTLE ON?

There is a final undisputable fact about happiness and well-being studies, which is that many theorists say that their theory captures what Aristotle thought about human flourishing, what he called *eudaimonia*. It is amusing that so many think that one needs the imprimatur of a Greek philosopher from two millennia ago.[21]

Aristotle held a *eudaimonistic*/perfectionist theory that says that flourishing consists in achieving and enacting excellence, specifically some set of demanding intellectual and/or character traits over the course of a life. *Eudaimonia* is an active life of reason and virtue, of developing one's intellectual and moral potential (possibly one's physical, musical, artistic gifts as well). It is a reliable effect of living such a life that one experiences real, true, or genuine happiness. But it is not at all clear from anything Aristotle says that the experience of being *eudaimon*, of achieving *eudaimonia*, is anything like what we call "happiness." A *eudaimon* experiences her life as good. She experiences—although even this is to speak anachronistically—self-esteem and self-respect. She is good; she knows it. But, of course, she doesn't brag about it or experience herself as a character in

"La-La Land." She is living as a well-developed human ought to live. Aristotle compares the feeling associated with living a life of *eudaimonia* with "the bloom [on the cheeks] of youth" that comes with and indicates robust physical health.[22] The bloom is not the main event, and it is certainly not the *summum bonum*. In the case of "the bloom of youth," it is the underlying state of physical well-being that is the ultimate good which the glow indicates; and in the case of *eudaimonia*, it is the psychosocial/moral/intellectual excellence that is the *summum bonum*. If we are lucky, a pleasant feeling accompanies such excellences. The feeling is a side effect of or supervenes on the flourishing, but it isn't the aim (*telos*) of someone who seeks to flourish.

There is a scholarly consensus among experts as to what Aristotle thought. Aristotle reports on a survey in the *Nicomachean Ethics*, where he explains that all his informants use the same word, *eudaimonia*—roughly, to be "good spirited"—for the highest goal in life.[23] But most of his contemporaries are confused about what *eudaimonia* consists in, thinking it involves pleasure or money or fame. Furthermore, most of his compatriots felt or judged, according to criteria they used—pleasure, public acclaim, wealth—that they were *eudaimon*. But they were wrong. They were not living an active life of high intellectual achievement and high moral character. They were chasing fleeting goods on the hedonic treadmill. And the happiness they experienced was not true happiness, not the real deal.

The proper theory of well-being, Aristotle thought, was a matter for moral and political experts to determine and was not to be left to the feeling or judgment of *hoi polloi*. Some people are shocked and say, "But that would make Aristotle an elitist!" He was.

To put it in modern terms: a survey that shows that everyone is satisfied or happy with their lives would carry weight for Aristotle only if the judgment or feeling results from holding the right standards, which for him were that such a life is lived according to the highest intellectual and moral standards. Being subjectively happy or satisfied is a good only if the individual is happy about a life that is objectively excellent. The quality of art or philosophy or music or science is a matter of expert judgment for Aristotle, not common taste or opinion. The same holds for well-being.

The subjective well-being methodology in the *World Happiness Report* is defended this way: "The central role [for using happiness measures in public policy] is and should be played, as argued by Aristotle, by people's own evaluation of their lives."[24] But Aristotle thought the exact opposite. The *hoi polloi* are terrible judges of how their lives are going, about whether they are *eudaimon*. Only experts with the right normative standards can judge such matters.

One needs generally to be very careful about importing ancient wisdom to modern circumstances. Aristotle shares with Plato the view that physical, moral, and intellectual education are required to acquire the correct standards for judging a life as a good one. It is interesting that both Plato and Confucius thought that philosopher queens and kings in training or sages on the path were not in a position to make reliable judgments about virtue, well-being, harmony, and so on, until they are at least forty years old and have received the highest quality education available.

Most modern people are elitist, or better "principled," in similar ways insofar as we would judge a slave society or a colonialist society with high average life satisfaction because of the slaves or the riches from the colonies, to be happy for the wrong reasons, not "truly happy," as we might say. Or we would judge such people as happy, but not living well. In either case, no social policy ought to support slave or colonialist policies even if it reliably produces a happy majority or a satisfied majority or high average life satisfaction (one can imagine that the oppressed group is small and/or suffers from Stockholm syndrome). This ethical point generalizes to all well-being and happiness policy-making. That said, one could stipulate and thus restrict the meaning of the concept of happiness, as some do, to a purely subjective qualitative state of how people feel or whether they judge themselves happy. If one is up front that this is how the concept is being regimented and used, this is not a problem. But it isn't how Aristotle conceived happiness or flourishing. And it is not clear how much happiness so conceived is worth. One might claim that surely everyone values that kind of happiness as the goal of life. But this too is entirely false.

POLITICAL NEUTRALITY?

Happiness is a normative concept, or a hybrid descriptive-normative concept. Happiness, across its various meanings, describes a psychobiological state that is *prima facie* good or conditionally good. Things that are *prima facie* goods are sometimes good all things considered, and in more or less every context. But not always. Physical health is an all things considered good. Ice cream and wine, despite being good, are not good for everyone at all times and so on. Happiness is a *prima facie* good, but whether it is an all things considered good, or among the greatest goods, depends on what kind of happiness we are talking about.

The normativity of every notion of happiness obtains whether anyone tries to measure or promote it. If a state of affairs is judged good or bad, favorable or unfavorable, the judgment is normative. If any group or especially if any governmental agency endorses a conception of happiness and tries to promote that conception, which is already normative, it is rendered political.

There is an interesting connection between standard public opinion polling and happiness polling. When some large percentage of a people (a plurality at least) says they favor Donald Trump (or Adolf Hitler, Vladimir Putin, or Viktor Orbán) for their leader, one can, according to folk psychology, infer that this will make that plurality happy or satisfied, possibly very satisfied, if that individual is elected, and conversely their election will make the minority unhappy (or unhappier). There are two things of note: elections have the result of making a plurality—often not the majority—happy or satisfied, and others less satisfied. Do democratic elections (non–ranked choice ones) contribute to greater happiness overall? Not necessarily. But second, and more important, we assign no special normative status to the opinions of ordinary people. If people judge these leaders as good, better than the alternative, satisfactory, and/or satisfying, they are just confused and have bad standards. There is no *a priori* reason to think that the standards by which people judge their own emotional well-being and life satisfaction are of higher quality. To be sure, they have their opinions. But opinions (*doxa*), Plato taught us, usually originate in the shadows and images of the cave.

One thought is that happiness standards should not be neutral and left to the vagaries of shifting fads and socialization but should incorporate principled and demanding standards of say, true happiness. But another is that at least in liberal precincts the state just better be neutral across conceptions of happiness.

Are current conceptions and/or measures of happiness and well-being politically neutral? Should they be neutral? One might put the two questions this way: Do the surveys that measure happiness favor any substantive political values? If they do, is that a problem? Why?

In order to answer these questions it helps to take the conceptions and measures one by one. Consider measures that ask how satisfied one is with one's life on a 0–10 scale. Life satisfaction measures are in fact entirely neutral about what makes one happy or satisfied and what one is happy about. For any individual or collective it might be that they are satisfied because their life is filled with pleasure, or because they possess lots of stuff, or because of the economy, their work, the moral quality of life, the quality of their personal relations, the political form of life, or all of these. The measure doesn't inquire into the causes or contents of the happiness, and thus it neither favors nor disfavors any set of causes and contents. If Pope Francis and Hugh Hefner, the hedonist founder of the *Playboy* empire, are a 9, they are the same, "thriving" as far as life satisfaction goes and equally happy in that sense.

Neutrality on the causes and contents of happiness conceived as subjective well-being goes well with a certain kind of liberal neutrality about one's comprehensive conception of the good. Libertarians, hedonists, sadomasochists, narcissists, Buddhist nuns, and Irish Christian Brothers can all be equally happy, each in their own way and for their own reasons. The conception, the measurement tool(s), and policies to advance this kind of happiness are neutral on that. Again it is worth noting that the happiness agenda as conceived and tracked in Bhutan is not neutral across forms of life. It explicitly favors happiness that incorporates Buddhist values such as compassion for all sentient beings, and it makes it a condition of individual happiness that all be happy. If life satisfaction was equivalent to happiness, then no Bhutanese informant ought to say they are satisfied with their life.

However, when one applies the life satisfaction instrument and isolates what appear to be structural causes of higher and lower life satisfaction scores, one sees that overall rich, democratic countries with strong social welfare policies score highest.

So the measure is neutral, but it yields evidence that favors some forms of political economy over others, assuming that one prizes higher (average) subjective well-being as measured with indifference to its causes, character, and content. That is, if happiness conceived as average life satisfaction is a goal, then living in a rich, democratic country with strong social welfare policies is wise or provides the right structural conditions. Finland is no doubt a good country because there is little precarity—there are long maternity and paternity leaves, free childcare from eight months until formal schooling begins, health care for all, protection from unemployment, and so on. This makes people feel secure, and they correctly judge their lives as satisfactory. Life satisfaction is the result of good policies, not the reason for the good policies.

That said, theorists like Nietzsche, Durkheim, Weber, Anscombe, and MacIntyre think that the focus on happiness (conceived hedonistically or as personal satisfaction) as a goal of life or as an aim of social policy is itself a product of a certain kind of consequentialist thinking, common especially in Anglophone precincts, which antecedently favors "happy" souls, as conceived in the value neutral way that such instruments as life satisfaction instruments measure. Thus, prizing measures of happiness over measures of rights or political or economic equality or social harmony or sustainability is itself a political exercise with a certain historical lineage and imprimatur.

The situation repeats if one uses the conception of happiness as involving a surplus of positive to negative emotions or a certain favorable ratio of positive to negative emotions. At first glance, such measures are also neutral about causes and contents of the positivity, measuring only whether there is a surplus of positive to negative emotions or whether the ratio is above a certain threshold, say 2:1 or 3:1 positive to negative (according to most findings, the world average is approximately 2:1). But analysis reveals that Latin American countries with strong familial and communal cohesion do best; better, at any rate, than the rich, democratic Nordic nations that do best on life satisfaction measures. Thus, if policymakers favor high positive/negative emotion ratios as a more desirable kind of happiness than life satisfaction, then being rich and democratic with a strong social safety net will recede as policy aims, and growing familial affection and community solidarity will become focal. And moving from Finland to Paraguay might be smart.

Things get messier if one adds a new study that appears in the WHR 2022, which is neither a life satisfaction nor a positive/negative emotions study. This study examines whether people find their lives to be in balance and harmony.[25] But here's the rub, which reveals the disunity of metrics for happiness.

We've already said that if you want to live where you have the best chances of being happy, life satisfaction and positive/negative emotions measures will give conflicting guidance. On the first metric you should move to the Nordic countries. On positive and negative emotions measures, try Central and South America.

What about if you aim for balance and harmony? Now Malta, Portugal, Slovenia, Romania, and Lithuania appear in the top 10. Things get worse: if happiness is identified specifically with "feeling at peace," then Taiwan and Saudi Arabia are good places to be, whereas if one wishes to "feel calm," Vietnam, Jamaica, the Philippines, and Kyrgyzstan receive 5 star ratings.

What to do? You think you have a problem, well, what about nation states that avow the happiness agenda for public and government policy? Which measure should they use? If they use life satisfaction, they will try to be like Finland. If they value positive emotions, they will try to be like Costa Rica or Paraguay. And if they use balance and harmony, they will try to model whatever it is about Romania or Lithuania or Portugal that makes Romanians, Lithuanians, or Portuguese balanced (see table 2.1).

One might reply, "let's use all these measures"—promote wealth, democracy, human rights, justice, strong social safety nets and communal trust and cohesion, life satisfaction, positive emotions, and balance and harmony. That's fine. In many places on Earth there is agreement that these things are valuable. But they are not valuable because these things are happiness or make people happy. They are valued because they are good for multifarious reasons. Finally, implementing these three (or any other) metrics into coherent public policy is not neutral, and it is conceptually and logistically challenging. Each metric offers up a different list of policy models. The burden is on advocates of the happiness agenda to work all this out, not their critics. We will return to this topic in the conclusion.

Suppose, finally, that one endorses a conception of happiness that is ethicized, that is, one that requires happiness to have certain content, so that, for example, even if Pope Francis and Hugh Hefner, Donald Trump, and Vladimir Putin (Putin is religiously very devout) are equally happy as far as subjective life satisfaction goes, only Francis is truly happy because some set of virtues and excellences partly constitute or cause his happiness. Any such conception is straightforwardly political insofar

Table 2.1

Metric	Questions Asked	Top Five "Happiest" Countries
Life Evaluation	Please imagine a ladder, with steps numbered from 0 at the bottom to 10 at the top. The top of the ladder represents the best possible life for you and the bottom of the ladder represents the worst possible life for you. On which step of the ladder do you feel you personally stand at the present time?	(2019–2021) Finland Denmark Iceland Switzerland The Netherlands
Positive Emotions	Did you experience the following feelings during a lot of the day yesterday? 1. Laughter 2. Enjoyment Did you learn or do something interesting yesterday?	(2021) Panama Indonesia Paraguay El Salvador Honduras
Negative Emotions	Did you experience the following feelings during a lot of the day yesterday? 1. Worry, 2. Sadness 3. Anger	(2021) Estonia Kyrgyzstan Latvia Russian Federation South Africa (These countries experienced the least negative emotions)
Balance	In general, do you feel the various aspects of your life are in balance, or not?	(2020) Finland Malta Switzerland Romania Portugal

Metric	Questions Asked	Top Five "Happiest" Countries
Peace	In general, do you feel at peace with your life, or not?	(2020) The Netherlands Iceland Taiwan Finland Norway
Calmness	Did you experience the following feelings during a lot of the day yesterday? [Followed by a series of feelings, including . . .] How about Calmness?	(2020) Vietnam Jamaica Philippines Kyrgyzstan Finland

as it endorses a certain sociopolitical (although possibly not a governmental) conception of happiness as the right kind.

This highlights an odd situation: Any conception of true happiness such that the quality of happiness is assessed in terms of its causes and contents (Is it caused by healthy social circumstances? Is it partly constituted by a certain set of virtues that make up a person's character? Is it partly constituted by commitment to good values?) will be associated with a particular ethical tradition and conception. These conceptions will be parochial, they will be hedonistic or Confucian or Stoic or Christian or communist or liberal conceptions of a *truly* happy person. One could try to find an overlapping consensus of virtues and values that partly make the happy people across distinctive forms of life truly so. This can succeed to a point.[26] But again one will meet, especially in liberal precincts, the view that even if happiness is the business of the political order, no conception of true happiness is!

A common response to this situation is to accept that different groups will have different parochial conceptions of true happiness and to require political neutrality among them. Perhaps one conceives the situation as allowing these different conceptions of true happiness duking it out in the marketplace of ideas. Is this politically neutral? No. It favors relativism about the good or state neutrality about the good, or both over any particular comprehensive conception of the good or true happiness.

One upshot is that even if measures of happiness such as subjective life satisfaction measures or ones that measure ratios of positive to negative emotions or multidimensional emotional state ones that measure six factors—cheerful, energetic, tranquil vs. sad, lethargic, and stressed—or ones that track feelings of balance and harmony (and peace and calm) are neutral as to causes and contents of the judgment or the positive to negative surplus or ratio, or of the multidimensional emotional state, or a state of balance and harmony, using any of them as a guide to government policy is not neutral. It advances a specific view of what happiness is and fixes the aim of public policy on achieving that state.

This is easy to see. Accept that happiness in any of these four senses is a *prima facie* good. First pass, it is better than the alternative if people judge their lives as satisfactory, or if they experience more positive than negative emotions, or if they are generally cheerful, energetic, and tranquil rather than sad, lethargic, and stressed, or if they feel balanced and in harmony. Ideally but not necessarily (they might be opiated in various ways), this means that the social and political conditions are in place that help make it so. But it doesn't follow that it is wise government policy to promote whatever social and political conditions make it so. In America, we conceive of ourselves as having certain inalienable rights: "to life, liberty, and the pursuit of happiness."

Government must protect these rights. There is nothing about government's promoting happiness (Which kind? Which version?), only the right to pursue it. One can imagine all sorts of reasons on the left and right to resist governments from using happiness as a policy goal. These include: there is no consensus on what kind or kinds of happiness are best; there is no agreement about where happiness, however conceived, sits in the order of goods that include rights, liberty, pluralism, cultural autonomy, sustainability; and, finally, the idea of government bureaucracies planning outcomes for deeply private aspects of life is dystopian—what could go wrong? Wole Soyinka's *Chronicles from the Land of the Happiest People on Earth* (2020) is a chilling satire about a troubled African nation that creates a "Ministry of Happiness," which then brands its people "the Happiest People in the World."[27] It is, of course all, smoke and mirrors, tricks and gimmicks. But it works—until it doesn't.

That said, it is hard to see what there is to complain about as we get more and varied information about types of happiness and all their significant social causes and conditions. Knowledge is power, and transparency is good. But it is not obvious that governments claiming responsibility for producing happiness and wielding power over the production of any kind of happiness is something anyone should want.

3

HOW SHOULD WE THINK ABOUT THE EMOTION OF HAPPINESS SCIENTIFICALLY?

Lessons from the Science of Fear

Suppose we wish to measure happiness itself as an emotional state (and not, say, as a judgment about life satisfaction) because we think it a good state, a state at which we ought individually and collectively to aim. Put aside for now questions of whether happiness is associated with goodness, moral decency, and justice and even with whether (and how) it is associated with certain objective states of affairs, life expectancy, income, relative wealth, tax rates, clean air, and potable water.

What is happiness? For that matter, what is an emotion, and what exactly are we referring to when we use emotion words like happiness, sadness, anger, and fear? Unless we can answer this question, we cannot use such words to help us know what a good life is, assuming—what not every theory assumes—that happiness is a necessary or sufficient condition of a good life. We have already said that the happiness agenda pays remarkably little attention to the rich and long-lived conversations about happiness and its place in the order of goods across the world's wisdom traditions in theology and philosophy. It may surprise the reader to learn that "the happiness agenda" also contains remarkably little theorizing about happiness as conceived in the sciences of the mind.

Fear is the most extensively studied emotion in evolutionary psychology and neuroscience (anger and shame are more extensively studied in cultural psychology). By contrast, happiness is far less studied and is not well understood in terms of brain mechanisms. Part of the reason for this discrepancy is that fear has characteristic bodily expressions in behavior and physiology that can be studied with scientific precision in the brains of animals, but happiness cannot.

EMOTION COMMOTION

The topic of emotion is, and has long been, highly contentious. There are many theories (models) of emotion. We focus on two theories: basic emotions theory and cognitive theory.

Basic emotions theory built on Darwin's notion that an emotion is a state of mind inherited from mammalian ancestors by way of natural selection affecting the nervous system.[1] Contemporary representatives assume that an innate neural structure called an 'affect program' underlies emotions such as fear, happiness, sadness, surprise and disgust, but the list varies to some extent for different theorists.[2] Basic emotions are contrasted with higher-order emotions (e.g. envy, jealousy, or pride) that are said to be learned and influenced by one's culture.[3]

The study of the role of cognition in emotion was largely started by Stanley Schachter and Jerome Singer in the 1960s.[4] They proposed that emotions are cognitive interpretations of the external situation one is in at the time and signals from physiological arousal in the body. Contemporary representatives of the cognitive approach call upon various sorts of attributions, cultural specifications, appraisals, schemata, norms, and other factors to account for the emotion that one has in the moment.[5]

According to the cognitive view, what fear, sadness, and happiness, and all the other emotions feel like, what causes them, what expressions of them are judged to be warranted or apt, and how they fit with a good life is more due to individual experience and to cultural norms than to innate biology. But individual and cultural factors are not completely independent since one's personal experiences are shaped in part by their culture. These facts have two consequences. Emotion terms are less well regimented and precise than terms for physical objects. Emotion terms are more individually and culturally idiosyncratic than physical object terms.

FEAR FOLLIES

The starting point in discussions about the neurobiology of fear is typically the brain area called the amygdala, which has been implicated in the expression of behavioral and physiological responses elicited by threatening stimuli.[6] Such findings are consistent with basic emotions theories that emphasize that the affect program of the amygdala is responsible for both the bodily responses and conscious experience of fear.[7] While the role of the amygdala in the control of behavioral and physiological responses is firmly established, its role in conscious feelings of fear has been challenged by cognitive theories that emphasize that the conscious experience of emotions, including fear, depends on higher-cognitive processes involving the prefrontal cortex.[8]

Studies of fear thus suggest that external dangers are detected by the sensory systems and then take two paths through the brain.[9] One goes to the amygdala to control the objective sequalae; that is, the readily measurable behavioral and physiological changes. The other path goes to cognitive circuits in cortex, where the conscious feeling of fear is constructed. The latter depends on schemata, organized bundles of information that people use to conceptualize the situations in which they find themselves. The difference between emotional and nonemotional experiences, and between different kinds of emotions, is not due primarily to different brain circuits but to the processing of different information by the cognitive circuits.

In such a model, it is danger, not fear, that is universal.[10] People in all cultures encounter danger and have subjective experiences in dangerous situations. But just because we can translate the words used by different cultures in dangerous situations into the English word "fear" does not mean that the experience itself is the same across cultures. This point is strongly supported by recent research on the lexicon of emotion in different cultures.[11]

Emotion words are conceptual anchors through which people understand and remember their experiences.[12] While specific words are not required to feel emotionally aroused, they are necessary in order to feel the emotion named by the word. Lacking specific emotion words, a young child cannot experience a state of the same conceptual complexity that an older child experiences as fear because the child has not accumulated the memories required to conceptualize experience that way. At the same time, even in adults, the nonconscious underpinnings of emotions are not always sufficiently elaborate to produce an experience that is clearly identified with a common emotion word. As a situation unfolds, vague feelings of being uncomfortable, concerned, or distressed may progress to one labeled and experienced as fear, which might, with additional information, morph into anger or jealously or to relief.

HAPPINESS HEADWAY

Let's apply the lessons from fear to happiness. Consider these six questions and their answers:

1. Is happiness a well-defined emotion? *Answer*: It is not well defined in folk psychology or ordinary speech. And it is not well defined in scientific psychology. Although given what we have said one sees how one might study happiness by tracking its semantics and natural history in different socio-moral ecologies.
2. What and where is the underlying dedicated neural circuitry or neurochemistry for the emotion of happiness? *Answer*: There isn't one postulated or predicted by any model. Bartels and colleagues argue that there is biological basis for happiness.[13] In fact, little is known about brain mechanisms or neurochemistry that subserve various kinds of positive emotions; and nothing is known about brain or bodily states that subserve life satisfaction judgments.
3. What causes happiness? What activates the emotional happiness system? *Answer*: Naturally pleasant experiences and activities, personally interesting activities, and culturally endorsed activities.
4. What behavior typically results from happiness? *Answer*: Many different kinds. Smiling, restful sleep, generosity, selfishness, and often nothing at all.
5. How does happiness seem phenomenologically? *Answer*: Happy people have whatever feeling or range of feelings that their verbal community tried to corral and teach individuals to identify when it taught the language of "happy" and "happiness." *A second answer*: Happy people are cheerful (they endorse how they are living, how their life is going) and

energetic (they are engaged with making things happen in their lives); and, in some cultures, they are not stressed or frazzled (they are attuned to the flow of their lives, secure, largely in equanimity). *A third answer*: Happiness feels many different ways, and whether the kind of happiness that is desired is high-arousal or low-arousal is culturally variable. Some cultures and some personality types prefer a somewhat frazzled, intense type of happiness over the serene, contented type.[14] In some cultures norms and scripts are such that a happy person ought to be kind and generous; in other cultures self-satisfaction and self-absorption are perfectly acceptable for achieving such a delicious state. (Lomas and colleagues think most people, in most countries—Vietnam and Georgia are exceptions—like excitement less and balance and harmony more than Tsai predicts.)[15]

HAPPINESS MEASURES

Advocates of the happiness agenda who study subjective well-being announce with great rhetorical flair, and with policymakers' rapt attention, that they study happiness and that average happiness is a reliable measure of the relative quality of nation-states. Some studies of subjective well-being do in fact ask directly about happiness.[16] A job site, Indeed.com, tracks answers to this question: "*To what extent* [on a scale of 1–5] *do you agree or disagree with this following statement: I feel happy at work most of the time?*" This survey instrument doesn't ask about satisfaction but about feeling happy most of the time at work.

But many measures that are advertised as measuring happiness do not even try to measure the emotion of happiness or the feeling of happiness in any direct or scientific way, although they sometimes create an instrument that can serve as an indicator for some feature that ordinary speech and science judge as relevant to inferring (some aspect of) happiness. This is paradoxical but true.

Consider the 2021 and 2022 *World Happiness Report*, which like their predecessors uses several different instruments. Not one of the measures used involves asking people if they are happy, if they remember being happy yesterday, whether they expect to be happy tomorrow, or at the end of their life, how they conceive their own happiness or the emotion of happiness, why they consider happiness of value, and what kind of value it is.

The two main instruments used are life satisfaction and positive/negative affect measures. They involve:

- Asking people how they evaluate their lives on a scale of 0–10 (and sometimes how good they expect their lives to be in, say, five years). Only this measure—not the next one on positive/negative affect—is used in the national rankings.
- Asking people if they smiled and laughed a lot and experienced enjoyment a lot the previous day; and if they experienced any of the three emotions of worry, sadness, and anger a lot the previous day.

In both years there was also a new measure:

- Asking people whether they expect a lost wallet to be returned by police and/or other residents of their community.

The first, the life evaluation measure, asks nothing about any emotion, including happiness. It asks for a judgment about overall life satisfaction relative to how one imagines the best life for oneself. The second measure asks nothing about the emotion of happiness, but only about enjoyment, laughter, and smiling (in 2022 a new question was asked about whether one had learned something new and interesting, which is not an emotion or a feeling or an affect), and worry, sadness, and anger.

Any claims to measure happiness of individuals or countries by these three instruments must be because there are background assumptions in play about the links of life satisfaction to happiness, so that, people who are satisfied with their lives would also judge themselves happy (or what is different, would also *be* happy, experience themselves as happy), and possibly in the other direction that happy people are satisfied with their lives; that some reliable relations exist of ratios of positive vs. negative emotions (Fredrickson says 3:1 is very favorable)[17] to feelings of happiness or the condition of being happy; and there exists a connection between trust and happiness, where happiness is conceived as life satisfaction.

WHOSE HAPPINESS? WHICH HAPPINESS?

One should mark three different senses of happiness used in well-being philosophy and science. First, there is happiness as a short-lived emotional state, the state of feeling happy at a moment or time. Second, there is happiness as a state or condition of being happy.[18] Third, there is happiness in a sense that, weirdly enough, does not require feeling happy or even satisfying the conditions of being happy in the stable emotional condition sense. This last sense is used when theorists elide the happiness vs. well-being distinction and say that a society or person that satisfies some set of conditions of well-being is happy. The *World Happiness Report* tends to encourage this mistake systematically by claiming that high scores on measures of life evaluation are or are also high happiness scores. This is misleading because, according to most theories of well-being, subjective happiness as a feeling state or as a stable condition is only one component of well-being, not identical to or a logical consequence of judging one's life as satisfactory or living meaningfully, thinking one is thriving, or trusting one's compatriots.

Other measures have related weaknesses. For example, the Gallup *Global Emotions Report* claims to assess emotions and to rate and rank countries on average daily quantity of positive emotions.[19] The questions it asks are about positive experiences. There is no assessment of the quality of emotions outside of positive or negative valence. This is a problem because I might be equally happy that my enemy died as that my grandchild was born; a population might be happy in part because it is militarily and economically most powerful, "masters of the universe." The instrument by itself is crude.

The distinction between quantity and quality of happiness is the distinction John Stuart Mill marks in his question about whether it is better to be a satisfied pig or a dissatisfied Socrates.[20] Many people who lived great and noble lives, possibly in their own eyes, such as Jesus, Dorothy Day, or Martin Luther King Jr., were not in any obvious way blessed with either a surplus of happy moments or the emotional condition of sustained happiness. Perhaps they experienced self-esteem and self-respect (as they well deserved) and were satisfied with their lives. But from what we know, neither they nor close friends and loved ones would rate them as emotionally happy, or often happy, or dispositionally happy, or generally in a stably happy state. The former president of Finland, Tarja Halonen, captures the basic insight well when in response to Finland's status as the happiest country on various *World Happiness Reports* she remarks that (we paraphrase) 'We Finns are on the dour side as a people; we are happy in the sense that we are secure because we have a good social safety net.'

Most philosophers and scientists who are not involved in producing the *World Happiness Report* think the report measures some aspects of well-being, not happiness in the emotion condition sense. This might be considered a good thing or a bad thing. If the emotional state senses of happiness—either short term or as a stable condition—is not being studied, despite the constant rhetorical suggestions that it is, this would be good if it turns out that the emotion of happiness is not at all well understood in emotions science, and if in addition, emotional happiness in several common ordinary senses is not normatively all that important; or at least it is differentially important depending on culture.[21] What matters is well-being, which if it includes feeling happy is fine, perhaps even better than if a life is good but not happy; but that such a life is also happy is not the most important thing. Furthermore, many think that what matters to well-being is not mainly, or only, that you are satisfied with your life but whether it is satisfactory.

Some cultures think happiness in the emotional state or condition sense matters a great deal to well-being; others do not.[22] For example, Jeanne Tsai and colleagues have shown that different cultures model different emotions for children.[23] Bestselling children's books in the United States model high arousal positive happy faces, whereas East Asian books model low arousal positive faces. And Mesquita distinguishes between a "my" sense of happiness that emphasizes the inner feel to the individual of happiness and that is common in North Atlantic precincts from an "our" sense of happiness that emphasizes that our relationships are going well, which dominates in other parts of the globe.[24] These different ways of conceiving and parsing emotions are conceptually anchored to particular forms of life and ways of speaking and thinking about emotions and value. There is no reason to think that the carving, parsing, and value assignments across cultures and subcultures are the same.

There is one further complication. Normative disciplines, ethics and psychiatry for example, insofar as they are concerned with happiness, typically focus on the content of happiness, what an individual is happy about, and the ideals that an individual aspires to and thinks would make for a good and happy life. The reason is that the content of what one is happy about and one's ideals for a good life reveal value. A life built around a vision of a happy life that involves selfish or unworthy values is not, according to such criteria, a good or happy one, even if it is judged as satisfying or happy making by its owner. Some psychologists think that the ideals and values, the satisfaction of which make certain contemporary people happy, possibly "super happy," as they say, are highly narcissistic and hyper-egoic.[25]

SEMANTICS IS NOT (ALWAYS) PEDANTIC

Science and philosophy typically call for precision that ordinary language and common sense do not possess and were not designed to possess. The demand to distinguish the (at least) two senses of happiness, one the emotional state sense, the other the well-being sense are also required by findings from psycholinguistics and sociolinguistics. Researchers find that in American English, there are two common uses of the words *happy* and *happiness*.[26] There is happy in the emotional state/psychological sense, and there is happy in the evaluative sense. The second sense involves what philosophers, from Aristotle on, call *eudaimonia*.

In ordinary speech, and across religious and philosophical traditions, it is glossed as "true happiness," or flourishing, living well, living meaningfully, or having a good life. Used in this way, even among ordinary people, there is no requirement that people *feel* happy in any inner phenomenological sense. People who are happy in this second sense—the well-being sense—might well judge their lives as good, meaningful, well-lived, but might not claim to be happy.

Anna Wierzbicka offers a related set of linguistic reasons to be wary about the validity of comparing self-reports that ask people to rate how happy they are across linguistic communities.[27] Her reason is that the word *happy* means different things in different languages. For example, English differs from German, French, Italian, Russian in that the adjective *happy* is much weaker—often meaning something akin to feeling "okay"—than the noun *happiness*, which names a more positive state that is nonetheless still ambiguous between naming a good emotional state or something more like "living satisfactorily."[28] Second, self-reports about happiness are colored by cultural norms, which involve different conceptual structures (schemata) about what happiness is (same for well-being), whether it is a very important value or not, as well as norms for expressing happiness. Americans, Chinese, and Poles have different standards for what sensibly produces happiness (money or friendship or family), what counts as funny or fantastic, how often one should smile, when laughter is appropriate, and so on.

On the social-cognitive view of emotions, when a person reports that she is scared or lonely or angry or happy or satisfied, she is not reporting a certain narrow qualitative feeling or phenomenal state. She is actually invoking a culturally understood schema that relates an emotion to its causes, contents, and effects. When one says one is happy or satisfied, one is not naming a cross-culturally identical phenomenal state, instead one invokes a form of life, a way of world-making, and implicates a world of norms and values.

It follows that good philosophy and science of happiness will need to track differences in meaning of folk terms such as "happy," "happiness," and "satisfied." It will also need to track how "I," "my," "mine," and "you" are used. One familiar use of "I" is as an indexical. It points to or indexes this sociotemporal particular "this-individual-that-is-me." Second- and third-person pronouns serve the same indexing function from other perspectives.

Psychologists and philosophers have shown that the way "I" is used and the way norms attach to I's are not always individualistic.[29] In some usages, "I" refers to more than a spatiotemporal particular individual. When the self is conceived as interdependent, when flourishings, satisfactions, and dissatisfactions are attached to social units, one's friends and family, one's community, and the world, then there are norms in place that prohibit answering a question about my individual happiness or satisfaction in an individualistic way because "my" is not used to mean "only mine." Such interdependent usages are available, although somewhat rare, in individualistic countries. If someone is asked about her happiness or life satisfaction in North America, it would be unusual, but not incomprehensible, for her to say, "I am very dissatisfied with my life; how could I be satisfied/happy with my life when my brothers and sisters in Ukraine, Yemen, South Sudan, and Myanmar are at war, dying, and suffering?"

One cannot take for granted that happiness or life satisfaction standards are individualistic. The cognitive neuroscience of the emotions is neutral on how happiness is conceptualized and normatively structured. This means that it is entirely possible that the identical objective social conditions could coexist with entirely different happiness or satisfaction assessments depending on what "happy" or "happiness" means and whether "I" is understood as narrow or wide in meaning. Finally, it is by no means obvious that it is best if people learn to assess and evaluate their happiness and well-being individualistically rather than as dependent on the happiness and well-being of more-than-me, possibly on the happiness and well-being of all.

HAPPINESS: A BASIC EMOTION?

Happiness in the emotional state sense often appears on lists of basic emotions, of emotions that come with the equipment. But not always.[30]

One thought is that perhaps happiness is just pleasure. To be happy is just to be pleased. The idea has currency among hedonists, who come in high church forms, where value is attached to the quality of pleasures, and low church forms, where the pleasures of sex, drugs, rock n' roll are just as good value-wise as life, liberty, love, and human rights.[31]

It's possible that a culture could decide to build the language of emotions that way and corral all pleasant feelings under the superordinate term *happy*. We might say that *happiness* is just the general term for the positive or pleasant outputs of the five senses or the positive or pleasant outputs of the senses plus all the higher cognitive systems (imagination, disciplined problem solving, etc.). If we go down this road, then we are very far from identifying a basic emotion of happiness. But that search might be futile. It might be best to think that emotional happiness is not basic but rather emergent from some more basic pleasure systems inside forms of life that build the emotion with the conceptual anchors and the norms and scripts it abides.

Without resolving this question of whether happiness is basic or not, it is almost certainly correct that happiness is not a simple unified state. It is a complex emotion, and the meanings of the word "happiness" are many. Furthermore, and entirely unlike fear, there is no known happiness circuitry that supports the multifarious states that we call *happy*. If *happy* were just one way we hive off pleasant experiences in ordinary language or folk psychology from unpleasant ones, then one might look for the pleasure circuitry or one might be satisfied that moment-to-moment pleasure tracking indicates that that circuitry is activated whatever and wherever it is. But insofar as there is such a thing as happiness circuitry, it involves multiple brain and body systems and is not simply a pleasure registering system. There is nothing for happiness remotely like the amygdala-based danger response circuitry of the unconscious "fear system."

BEHAVIORAL CIRCUITS?

Still, one might be impressed by the fact that babies do smile and laugh, which speaks in favor of basic in the "comes with the equipment" (or really early in ontogeny) sense of basic. Since other basic affect programs allegedly produce distinctive behaviors, including facial expressions, perhaps happiness is simply the emotion revealed in smiling and laughing. This link may be behind the fact that some theories list joy or amusement rather than happiness as basic, since joy and amusement as understood in English typically come with smiling and laughing. So instead of looking for general pleasure circuitry—there is none—one might look for dedicated smiling and laughter circuitry.

But clearly that will not work. Even if there were such dedicated circuitry, it would not begin to capture what researchers concerned with human happiness in either the emotion state or evaluative senses are interested in. One reason is that happiness even in the emotional state sense is often of a serene or contented sort, and involves no smiling or laughing, nor any dispositions to smile or laugh. Finally, there are questions about whether happiness, or the kind of happiness being studied, is short-lived or long-lived. Dispositions to smile or laugh pass quickly. Happiness of certain important kinds is lasting.

UNIVERSAL CAUSES? UNIVERSAL BEHAVIORS? UNIVERSAL PHENOMENOLOGY?

We argued above that danger is universal, fear—conceived as a self-identical inner emotional response to danger shared by us with some common ancestor or with other extant descendants of that common ancestor, with great apes, chimps, bonobos, and orangutans— is not. Fear is the human emotion, nurtured into existence and then sculpted in linguistic communities that teach what fear is, what situations call for fear, how and when to respond to danger appropriately, and so on. This involves vast amount of social and cultural learning. None of this means that other primates, or other mammals lack emotions. Methodological barriers prevent us from knowing what they might experience.[32] But whatever that is, it is not what the human brain, with its language infused capacities and cultural shaping, does to our emotions.[33]

What universal and original cause of happiness is there that corresponds to the danger that the fear circuits were designed by natural selection to be activated by? Perhaps it is something very general like "things are going very well." But that's vague and requires a culture to specify what falls under the concept. Pleasant experiences feel good. That's analytical. But what makes one happy depends on personal history, context, and culture. How does a happy person act? There is no particular way a happy person behaves. Sometimes there is smiling and laughter; but often not. Sometimes there is kindness and generosity, sometimes not. Sometimes there is spiritual bliss, but usually not.

What about universal phenomenology? Something pleasant, perhaps? Once again, that's too thin to pick out happiness from a warm glow, a nice sensation or perception, a series of such sensations or perceptions, a good dream, the reaction to a good joke, a profound religious experience, and so on.

One emerging view in the science and philosophy of emotions is that valence and intensity as well as typical causes and effects are how we identify our own emotions, not by some proprietary phenomenological feel that is—take your pick—the amusement, the joy, the happiness, the elation that is, the subjective doppelganger of some distinctive neural substrate that instantiates that very inner emotional state.[34]

The social-cognitive view of human emotions posits that phenomenological feel, insofar as emotions have them, are not raw or intrinsic or the main defining feature of an emotion. An emotion like happiness is defined by a schema comprising typical causes + inner phenomenal features/feelings + characteristic content + typical dispositions to act + typical action.[35] This schema is especially important for theories that aim to appraise whether an emotion is apt, fitting, or moral. Even if fear is normally unpleasant in the valence sense, it can be, often is, entirely positive in the evaluative sense. I see the rattlesnake and run. Good for me, good for the rattlesnake. Likewise, if I am happy that my rival in business died a painful death or because I feel a warm glow for being in solidarity with my fellow neo-Nazis, the feelings are positive valence-wise but evaluatively bad. I am happy perhaps, but I am not good.

SOLUTION SPACE

There are several practical solutions to the polysemy of the word *happiness*. The best is to just accept that there are multiple meanings in both folk psychology and scientific psychology of concepts such as happiness and subjective well-being. The cognitive sense of happiness in judging one's life satisfying or, what is different, satisfactory is different from the hedonic sense for which one might measure and sum happy moments, and these are all different from the concept of happiness that infers it (or thinks it results) from the ratio of positive to negative emotions. And all these are different from the conception of happiness as a stable emotional state.

There are several models in well-being studies that offer theories of what happiness is and consists in and that offer instruments to measure it, and that, in addition, operationalize how it is conceived according to some particular theory or other. For example, Sonja Lyubomirsky and Heidi Lepper and Dan Haybron offer theories of happiness in which happiness is not identified with all of well-being but is considered a good in its own right, a desirable component of a good life.[36] Nor does either theory even try to operationalize the concept happiness in a way that captures all the variance in folk and scientific understandings of that concept; if it tried, it would likely be incoherent.

Haybron's empirical-philosophical view is that one of the things—not the only thing—we care about is an emotional condition plausibly identified as being happy. The stable condition of happiness (emotional well-being, EWB) is more important than the sheer number of smiley face or happy-happy-joy-joy-click-your-heels experiences. The condition is complex not simple, and it is anchored (at least in Anglophone precincts) to six factors: cheerful, energetic, tranquil vs. sad, lethargic, and stressed. Its causes are multifarious. Some might be constitutional (see chapter 5 of *World Happiness Report* 2022 for chapter on the genetics of happiness).[37]

Whereas life satisfaction measures (subjective well-being) call for a cognitive judgment about whether one's life is good or good enough according to some normative standard, self- and social expectations, EWB measures one's emotional condition as favorable or unfavorable according to plausible standards for what emotional state happiness consists in.

Happy people, according to the emotional well-being account, are cheerful (they endorse how they are living, how their life is going) and energetic (they are engaged with making things happen in their lives), and they are not stressed or frazzled (they are attuned to the flow of their lives, secure, largely in equanimity). It remains to be seen how well this view generalizes: there is some reason to think that some people in some subcultures and some personality types (such as extroverts) favor somewhat frazzled lives.

In any case, measures will need to be adjusted for different cultures. For example, Haybron's preferred questionnaire asks about "feelings of loneliness." In Tibetan, there is no linguistically simple way to express the relevant feeling! And, in any case, emotional well-being as the multidimensional cheerful, energetic, engaged state is neutral about the whys and wherefores of that state. This is fine if one wishes simply to measure this state on the assumption that everything else equals this state is good, all things considered. But since the all-things-considered condition is not assessed, we do not know for any particular high emotional well-being state that it is good, all things considered.

Two lessons are these. First, there are no known simple, easily identifiable happiness circuits in the brain. This is not due to the immaturity of brain science but to the fact that happiness on every conception is a culturally and cognitively complex emotion. There is no one brain state that is happiness. Second, there are several reasonable theories and measures of happiness, conceived as a psychobiological state. For example, Haybron's multidimensional theory of emotional state happiness seems promising. It might come to serve as a consensus cross-cultural view; it's too early to know for sure. But Haybron is 100 percent clear that his theory is a theory of happiness as an emotional state. It is not also a general theory of well-being. Happiness is good on his view. But it is not the *summum bonum*. And it is not the aim of government policy.

THE UPSHOT

In this section, we have taken up the narrow issue of what the emotion of happiness is. The emotion of happiness, whatever it is, is not the same as a judgment that one's life is satisfying, or what is different still, is satisfactory. Happiness is not a simple hedonic state shared across animals. What happiness means is language- and culture-specific. It abides norms and embeds values. Whether happiness is an unmitigated good or not, which kinds of happiness are associated with well-being and which kinds are superficial or unworthy, are matters subject to constant normative assessment and negotiation. Is happiness a good? Should emotional state happiness be an aim of public policy? It depends on what the sources and components of happiness are, including whether it is grounded in or caused by circumstances of justice, as well as what individuals and their cultures are happy about.

The happiness agenda as currently promoted operates with a thin theory of happiness, conceived mainly as subjective life satisfaction. Subjective life satisfaction is indifferent to whether the satisfied state is grounded in good values, worthy meaningful aims, and circumstances of justice.

Two final points: First, Bartels and colleagues have a chapter in the *World Happiness Report 2022* devoted to the genetics of happiness in which it is claimed that "about 30–40% of the differences in happiness between people within a country are accounted for by genetic differences between people."[38] It hard to see how anyone could surmise the genetic contribution to happiness without a very precise and univocal conception of happiness, which at the moment doesn't exist.

Second, chapter 5 of the *World Happiness Report 2022* contains an odd speculation that associates unhappiness with activity in the brain's default network.[39] The only charitable interpretation is that activity in this network is correlated with worrying and perseverating. At any moment when people are worrying and perseverating, they are not happy. Worrying and perseverating are unpleasant activities at any given moment (although doing so is sometimes necessary for problem solving and thus for a good life overall). But this teaches nothing, exactly zero, about brain mechanisms for happiness or unhappiness. Fear is also unpleasant at the moment. But no one would infer that amygdala activation associated with fear is unhappiness circuitry. The standard view is that on pretty much every conception, neither happiness nor unhappiness is highly localized or modularized.

4

WHY AVERAGING HAPPINESS SCORES AND COMPARING THEM IS A TERRIBLE IDEA

We have emphasized the normativity of all concepts of happiness, the distinctions between various conceptions of happiness, true happiness, and well-being, and a host of reasons not to elide these concepts; and we have emphasized the extraordinary cultural diversity in the meanings of happiness, well-being, and the ideals and goals for good human lives.

One response to all this from the fans of the happiness agenda would be to say: "That's fine, all measures of happiness recommended for policy use—asking directly about how happy one is, experience sampling of pleasant-unpleasant experiences (U-scale), subjective well-being at the moment, overall life satisfaction, positive-negative emotions ratios—are indifferent to these weighty substantive issues. We only want to know how well you are doing in achieving what you conceive as happiness however you conceive it."

In this section, we take up an issue that is of overwhelming importance, even if one thinks measuring value neutral happiness is smart for public policy, beyond its obvious instrumental advantages to a regime whose power normally depends in part on people being satisfied.

The issue can be divided into two parts: first is averaging individual happiness scores and presenting them as country scores, and second is comparing and ranking countries based on these average scores. We take them up in order.

Happiness on most every view is an individual psychobiological state. Cultures differ on whether they conceive the causes of happiness as individualistic, a matter of my achievements, satisfaction of my preferences, or communal, as matters of how and what we collectively do. Speaking of happy couples or happy villages or happy countries is meaningful, but largely metaphorical. Put another way: an individual's happy state might be entirely the result of how she as a monadic individual is feeling or faring, or it might require that some wider group be feeling or faring well for her to feel happy or judge herself happy. In both cases, the happiness is an individual state, whereas its causes and criteria, depending on cultural norms, might not be.

Several prominent happiness measures average individual happiness scores and produce country averages. The annual *World Happiness Report* is the most famous instrument that does this. It computes averages for countries and then ranks countries based on these averages.

What does average happiness mean? Does it matter? If so, how does it matter? One thing average happiness doesn't and cannot mean on any view of happiness is that there is a state of the heart-mind that nation-states have, the state's happiness, which is inherited from the happiness of individuals. Nation-states do not have mental states, emotional or cognitive.

Second, regarding the value of average happiness scores (and setting aside all worries about accuracy, adaptation, and cultural practices pertaining to self-reporting), they conceal all facts about its distribution. A potentially infinite number of distributions of any feature, property, or state (height, weight, food, money, happiness, well-being, etc.) is compatible with any average. The average salary could be $100 because everyone makes $100, or because there is a normal distribution of incomes from $0 to $200, or because there is a twin peaked bimodal distribution where half make $0 and half make $200, and so on. But all the interesting information relevant to everyday life and to justice is in the distribution, not in the averages. Furthermore, all the actionable information is contained in the distribution.

Every averaging account of happiness or any other good that does not take a clear moral position on constraints and priorities on distributional matters is open to what is known as the "repugnant conclusion."[1] If one is concerned only about total or average happiness, then one logically ought to be indifferent to how it is increased. If it is easiest to increase the average of the whole by increasing the happiness of those already moderately happy as opposed to those who are unhappy, this will work, and, in addition, there are practical reasons in its favor. There are moral reasons against it, of course, but they come from the deontological traditions in ethics, not from consequentialist ones or from ones that favor maximizing pleasure or happiness and minimizing pain or unhappiness.

This matters greatly to computing average happiness scores, especially in countries where we know antecedently that there are gender, racial, ethnic, and religious inequalities in freedom, rights, and justice and, because of these inequalities, differences in subjective happiness. Suppose the American state of Mississippi was impressed by happiness as a political goal in 1860. At that time the population of Mississippi was 350,000 enslaved people against a population of 300,000 free white people (54 percent slaves). Virginia had the largest number of enslaved people, 490,000 against a population of 1.1 million free white people (about 30 percent slaves). It is easy to imagine that state officials in Mississippi concerned with happiness—perhaps they noticed that Virginia planters were both richer and less worried than they were about the free to enslaved ratio—might seek to increase state happiness overall by decreasing the number of slaves in Mississippi (and possibly working to increase the efficiency of the smaller population of enslaved people), not because it is wrong to enslave other human beings but because it would reduce the slaveowners' precarity due to worries about slave revolts. Thus would work to increase Mississippi's average happiness; but it is disgusting, repugnant.

These considerations suggest that average happiness measures conceal almost all the interesting information about happiness, which insofar as happiness is important, will be contained in information about the distribution.

The second issue is averaging and then comparing and ranking nation states based on happiness averages. This is a terrible idea for a host of reasons. One reason against it, but not the one we are most interested in, is this: rankings can produce unwarranted pride and complacency in high-ranking countries and humiliation in low-ranking countries. International status seeking and international envy have little to be said in their favor, especially because nation-states are normally already trying to figure out what is best for them. Because of variation in how happiness is conceived, and because what produces it is often local, copying what other nations with different populations and different problems do to secure their average happiness is not easily transportable outside of widely shared and commonsense knowledge of basic needs.

Another reason against averaging and ranking is related to a point discussed earlier: average happiness scores might make one think that there is an actual property that a collective, culture, subculture, village, municipality, nation-state has that is its happiness. But there is no such property. As Grant Duncan writes, "Aggregated scores from national surveys of happiness, therefore, may not be the best way to estimate the well-being of Belgian or Japanese society—because whole societies are not the grounds upon which the feeling of happiness has content or practical meaning."[2] But suppose that advocates of the happiness agenda do not make this mistake, and that no one is misled. There are still serious problems.

The main reason that comparing and ranking nation-states in terms of average happiness scores is a terrible idea is this. The truly interesting and important features of happiness, insofar as it matters at all, are almost entirely in the distributions, not in the average or mean, nor in the median, the middle value in the distribution, or in the mode, the most common value, each of which can be computed. One can give a distribution for a nation-state, but not as a single numerical quantity, only as a graph. If there is agreement inside the state about priorities, then the distribution revealed in a graph could be actionable.

But distributions between countries are not easily compared. There is no numerical quantity that can be found to compare distributions across nation-states. One can assess multiple distributions morally and practically, but not by comparing averages (or mean or mode), because once again these do not provide any reliable information about distributions.

One could decide that one wants distributions evaluated by the shapes of the distributions or by percentages occupying certain locations on the two axes. For example, if any distribution shows that any gender, racial, ethnic, or religious group is in a low happiness group, we mark it down as *prima facie* racist and/or sexist. If a distribution is bimodal (half happy, half unhappy), we mark it down for being non-egalitarian. If everyone is high we mark it up as super-duper, and so on.

But here we are not comparing countries ranked by average numerical scores, we are evaluating them by ethical and political norms. And evaluated in that way, there will be no consensus about which country ranks highest happiness wise. The United Arab Emirates and Saudi Arabia rank higher by average happiness score than Spain, Italy, and Japan. Think about this. Suppose you must leave your homeland. Which among these countries would you prefer to live in, assuming (as some implausible data suggests) that you will quickly reach average happiness there? Whatever your answer, it will almost certainly reveal that you don't care about the average happiness, even expecting that that number represents your future happiness score. If you are a woman you will be rightly worried about gender injustice in the Emirates and Saudi Arabia. Likewise if you favor democracy, and so on. Weather and cuisine aside, your future happiness as measured by these methods it not what you care about the most, not what matters.

Finally, there is this serious problem: different metrics will give you entirely different rankings based on averages. This is easiest to see by comparing the WHR with the *Global Emotions Report*, both issued annually and both based on Gallup data. The WHR measures and ranks according to subjective life satisfaction (even though they measure and discuss positive/negative emotions, trust, and so forth, and in the 2022 report they measure balance and harmony as well as peace and calmness). The *Global Emotions Report* averages and ranks based on positive/negative emotions ratio. The results are entirely different (see table 4.1).

If one weighted and averaged the three measures and rankings, the results would be different still, although different in which direction would be indeterminate until one decided on how to weight subjective life satisfaction and positive/negative emotions. What is the right metric? What are the right weights

Table 4.1

Metric	Questions Asked	Top Five "Happiest" Countries
Life Satisfaction	Please imagine a ladder, with steps numbered from 0 at the bottom to 10 at the top. The top of the ladder represents the best possible life for you and the bottom of the ladder represents the worst possible life for you. On which step of the ladder do you feel you personally stand at the present time?	(2019–2021) Finland Denmark Iceland Switzerland The Netherlands
Positive Emotions	Did you experience the following feelings during a lot of the day yesterday? 1. Laughter 2. Enjoyment Did you learn or do something interesting yesterday?	(2021) Panama Indonesia Paraguay El Salvador Honduras
Negative Emotions	Did you experience the following feelings during a lot of the day yesterday? 1. Worry, 2. Sadness 3. Anger	(2021) Estonia Kyrgyzstan Latvia Russian Federation South Africa
Balance	In general, do you feel the various aspects of your life are in balance, or not?	(2020) Finland Malta Switzerland Romania Portugal
Peace	In general, do you feel at peace with your life, or not?	(2020) The Netherlands Iceland Taiwan Finland Norway

(continued)

Table 4.1 (continued)

Metric	Questions Asked	Top Five "Happiest" Countries
Calmness	Did you experience the following feelings during a lot of the day yesterday? [Followed by a series of feelings, including . . .] How about Calmness?	(2020) Vietnam Jamaica Philippines Kyrgyzstan Finland

(and why only these three metrics) over which to average and rank? No one knows. But we do know this: by the first way of ranking, Nordic social democracies are benchmarks for happy nation-states; by the second way of ranking, positive emotions, Latin American states are the benchmarks and exemplars; and by the third way of ranking, the balance and harmony measure, the top exemplars include Portugal, Romania, and Lithuania, countries that do not rank at the top of any other list. There is more: if one favors "feeling at peace," then Taiwan and Saudi Arabia are good places to be, whereas as if one prizes "feeling calm," Vietnam, Jamaica, Philippines, and Kyrgyzstan lead the list.

The point is that different metrics embed different norms that yield entirely different rankings. There is no international consensus that happiness is the *summum bonum*. There is no international consensus that happiness metrics should guide policy. And there is no international consensus on which measure (if any) is the best one to track happiness.

II

CULTURE AND HAPPINESS

5

POSITIVE AND NEGATIVE EMOTIONS

Culture, Content, and Context

Many measures of subjective well-being take positive and negative emotions (surpluses or favorable ratios) to be an indicator of a person's happiness and well-being.[1] Some think it is a the best indicator for both. A large body of research suggests that positive emotions, such as joy, interest, contentment, and love, are positively correlated with beneficial outcomes, such as high life satisfaction, workplace success, healthy interpersonal relationships, healthy immune response, and longevity.[2] Negative emotions such as fear, anger, disgust, and sadness are correlated with bad outcomes, such as prolonged infection and delayed wound healing, increased suicide rates among veterans and college students, and low job satisfaction.[3]

Yet there are many unanswered questions about the nature of positive and negative emotions.[4] These include: What exactly separates positive from negative emotions and which emotions are on each list? What is the relationship between positive/negative emotions and happiness and well-being?

One common and influential answer to the first question is that positive and negative emotions can be distinguished by hedonic tone. As Barbara Frederickson and Michael Cohn explain, positive emotions are pleasant emotional responses to a situation, while negative emotions are painful.[5] Some take this distinction to be part of the defining characteristics of positive and negative emotions, meaning that positive emotions are those emotions that are, by definition, pleasing, while negative emotions are those that are painful.[6] This sort of view is expressed by Frederickson and L. E. Kurtz, who remark, "positive emotions, by definition, feel good."[7]

If the hedonic tone criterion was right and feeling good is good, then there would be a straightforward answer to our second question, namely, given that positive emotions are pleasant and feeling good is good (and feeling bad is bad), they contribute to our well-being by making us feel good, while negative emotions harm our well-being by making us feel bad.

This sort of reasoning is intuitive, as expressed by various popular positive psychology publications, such as PositivePsychology.com: "Most people like to feel good, and positive emotions just plain feel good. They don't necessarily need a reason or cause behind them for us to enjoy them; we just do. Experiencing emotions like happiness, excitement, joy, hope, and inspiration is vital for anyone who wants to lead a happy and healthy life."[8] Further if positive emotions contribute to our well-being by making us feel good, and if negative emotions make us feel bad, then we should seek to increase or maximize the frequency of positive emotions and decrease or minimize the frequency of negative ones.[9]

But there is a rub, actually several rubs. First, not all positive emotions feel good, and not all negative emotions feel bad. Happiness over another's suffering can feel off, unpleasant, incongruous, morally disgusting; and appropriate sadness over a loss can feel soothing, consoling, and fitting. Second, there is a well-established view in psychology of the emotions, philosophy of mind, and ethics that emotions have aptness or fittingness conditions.[10] Emotions have conditions of legibility; they are to be expressed only when warranted, where warrants involve cultural scripts and permissions. Even if positive emotions "don't need a reason or cause behind them for us to enjoy them; we just do," their reasons and causes can matter a lot. A person who is always happy but insensitive to the weal and woe of others is a dolt, and a person who is always vicariously wounded because others are might be a moral grandstander. Emotions are normative and feeling and expressing them abides by moral ideals. Emotional experience and expression are supposed to abide culturally specific doctrines of the mean (Confucius defended the doctrine of the mean before Aristotle) and thus not be excessive or defective in intensity and expression. When emotions with normally positive valence are not apt, then they can feel bad, as in the case of happiness at another's misery. The same is so with negative emotions. Emotions like sadness, even extreme sadness, can seem like exactly the right response to tragedy, and both express and convey a realistic, properly mature assessment of things. Something would be off, not right, frivolous, or superficial if one did not experience and express the negative emotion given the circumstances. Sadness, as well as fear and anger, normally have negative valence, but they feel right when they fit the situation.

THE MULTIPLE DIMENSIONS OF EMOTIONS

So the first point is that the hedonic tone of emotions might be a rough and ready indicator of how pleasant an experience seems. But whether an emotion or set of emotions is good or bad, positive or negative, in balance, and fitting, depends on much more than its hedonic tone. It depends on whether it is apt, and aptness involves assessing the emotion's context and content, whether it is warranted, what it is about, and its overall value in a person's life, not just its hedonic value.

One kind of fittingness pertains to the intensity of a felt emotion. Emotions are set to have intensities of feeling and expression that track value, the quality of what is desired, lost or gained. It makes sense to be very distressed about not having enough income to pay rent, but not to be very distressed over not having enough money to upgrade to the latest iPhone. It makes sense to be very angry over being racially profiled by the police, but not over there being no more cookies in the cookie jar. It makes sense to be elated about the birth of a child, but not equally so about one's haircut.

We will want an excellent theory of happiness and well-being to be able to reflect such qualitative differences. It is not outside the realm of possibility that a culture might have very superficial, low, or misguided values about what ought to make one happy. If so, there are people—individuals or members of some community or nation-state—who are happy by their standards but are not living well by other standards.

These points are a version of John Stuart Mill's famous point about higher and lower pleasures. Some positive emotional experiences are qualitatively better than others. This fact is true, Mill maintains, even if the lower pleasure comes in a larger quantity (eating ten bonbons) than the higher ones (one hug from a dear friend). This fact has two consequences. First, some types of pleasure are qualitatively distinct from other types, and they cannot (or cannot easily) be averaged together and placed on the same scale. Second, a set of experiences with extremely high hedonic tone might not be better than a hedonically mixed, but distinctly human set of experiences. As Mill famously put it: "It is better to be a human being dissatisfied than a pig satisfied; better to be Socrates dissatisfied than a fool satisfied."[11]

These observations might shed light on disparities between the 2021 *World Happiness Report* and 2021 *Global Emotions Report*. The *World Happiness Report* gives pride of place to life evaluation judgments, whereas the *Global Emotions Report* favors positive and negative emotions measures. One might think that either indicator is a reliable indicator of the (presence or absence) of the same phenomena: happiness or subjective well-being, or one might think each simply measures what it claims to measure: the answer to the life evaluation question(s) in *WHR* and the answer to the positive-negative emotions questions in the *GER*. On the first hypothesis, we should expect to see similar rankings on both reports. We do not. For example, the top five on the Positive Emotions List—in order, El Salvador, the Philippines, Norway, Nicaragua, and Paraguay—are ranked at 61 (El Salvador), 74 (Philippines), 8 (Norway), 46 (Nicaragua), and 67 (Paraguay) on the World Happiness Rankings. From this evidence, we are best advised to take the view that the two measures are not indicators of the same underlying phenomena, although they might be both thought to be indicators of features of the same underlying phenomena. But what those underlying features are, is not entirely understood or carefully theorized.

CULTURAL VARIATIONS OF EMOTIONS

One concern about happiness or subjective well-being measures that depend on parsing specific emotions as positive or negative (remember that some positive and negative emotions measures do not actually measure emotions at all; they only or mostly measure behaviors—smiling and laughing—that tend to accompany certain emotions) is that not all cultures emphasize emotions as aspects of subjective well-being to the same degree, nor, when they do emphasize emotions, do they emphasize the same emotions as components of subjective well-being. Here are a few examples:

- The Oriya Hindu women of Bhubaneswar, India, have a view of well-being that does not depend on positive emotions, but rather on a mature fulfilling of one's social obligations as a married woman.[12] Oriya Hindu women think that emotions like happiness are associated with irresponsibility and immaturity. Well-being, by contrast, is associated with a kind of maturity characterized by dominance (having control over oneself and others), centrality (being responsible for managing a household's productive activities), and coherence (a kind of emotional or moral coherence appropriate to one's age, neither of which depend on experiencing transient, pleasant emotions).
- Many Muslim cultures make a distinction between happiness as a pleasant emotional state and true happiness as inner peace derived from devotion to God and define well-being in terms of the latter, not the former. This distinction has important implication for the desirability of certain positive and negative emotions, as Mohsen Joshanloo and Dan Weijers explain: "Generally speaking, Islam is critical of people that are perceived to be very happy (best understood as experiencing regular and intense positive emotions and few, if any, negative emotions in this context). Prophet Muhammad is cited as saying that "were you to know what I know, you would laugh little and weep much" and "avoid much laughter, for much laughter deadens the heart." Ever since the 1979 Islamic Revolution in Iran, under the influence of the Shiite ideology, happiness has been associated

with shallowness, foolishness, and vulgarity. Happy people are also seen as being distracted from God, making them morally and spiritually deficient (in Islamic cultures, true happiness is considered to be an inner peace derived from devotion to God). In contrast, sad people are often defined as serious and deep. Since Islam is relatively widespread, aversion to happiness for the reason that it can make you a bad person is likely also to be widespread. In particular, happiness as an emotional state is thought to be superficial and experienced only by people who are shallow and foolish, and sadness is seen as the more serious and deep emotion."[13]

- Bhutan, the small Buddhist country that has played an oversized role in enthusiasm for the study of Gross National Happiness, explicitly endorses an ideal of happiness that cannot be achieved by being a happy individual. The government says that no one is happy unless everyone is, which although empirically false, is ethically true for Bhutanese Buddhists. "We know that true abiding happiness cannot exist while others suffer, and comes only from serving others, living in harmony with nature, and realizing our innate wisdom and the true and brilliant nature of our own minds."[14]

- Furthermore, the Bhutanese government tracks emotional balance by studying the positive emotions of calmness, empathy/compassion, forgiveness, contentment, and generosity and the negative ones of anger, fear, worry, selfishness, and jealousy.[15] In is unlikely that intergovernmental agencies in different countries would come up with the same list of wholesome and unwholesome emotions. In general, just as different cultures emphasize different virtues, so too do they emphasize different emotions.[16]

- European Americans value high-arousal positive emotions, such as excitement and elation, while East Asians prefer low-arousal positive emotions, such as peaceful and serene feelings.[17] Moreover, in each cultural context the lack of preferred emotions is associated with depression (i.e., low subjective well-being).

- East Asian cultures look less favorably on excessive expressions of positive emotions, viewing them as arousing feelings of envy in others and leading to social disruption.[18] A similar difference is reflected in popular children's books—best-selling story books in the United States portray characters with more excited expressions, wider smiles, and more arousing activities than do Taiwanese best sellers.[19]

- In individualist cultures, positive emotions that are ego-focused, such as pride, are valued more than those that are other-focused.[20] One reason for this is that ego-focused emotions have as their content one's own internal attributes, such as one's needs, goals, desires, and capacities, which serves to validate oneself against others.[21]

- In more collectivist cultures, other-focused emotions such as goodwill, friendliness, and compassion are valued more because their objects are the qualities of others, which further serves to promote interpersonal dependence.[22] Moreover, other-focused emotions are an important predictor of subjective well-being.[23]

- Anglophone cultures view positive emotions and negative emotions as polar opposites. The aim is maximizing the former and minimizing the latter.[24]

- In East Asian cultures, positive and negative emotions are seen as mutually dependent and coexisting.[25] It is partly for this reason that East Asians are found to be more suspicious of positive emotions, more tolerant of negative emotions, and more comfortable with having mixed emotions or emotional complexity.

- East Asians are less likely than Europeans or Americans to down-regulate negative emotions when something bad happens to them, since what is bad could lead to future well-being.[26] Similarly, Joshanloo and Weijers find that East Asians are suspicious of excessive positive emotions, associating them with future ill-being.[27] Koreans report that if one experiences positive emotions now, then she is less likely to experience them in the future.[28] Japanese report that excessive positive emotions make one inattentive to her surroundings, which leads to future unhappiness and suffering.[29] Chinese report that excess happiness inevitably leads to suffering, a view suggested by the Chinese proverb "extreme brightness begets tragedy."[30]

The upshot is this: theories and measures of happiness and well-being that highlight the importance of positive and negative emotions need be sensitive to the widespread findings in cross-cultural philosophy, cultural psychology, and anthropology that there is vast cultural variation in what emotions are prized, the norms and scripts of feeling and expression, the settings on hedonic tone, and even which emotions are considered positive and negative.[31]

6

HAPPINESS AND WELL-BEING AS CULTURAL PROJECTS

Immigration, Biculturalism, Cultural Belonging

In this chapter, we emphasize the importance of cultural belonging for subjective well-being, for feeling okay about oneself, for correctly judging that one's values and aspirations are normal, and so on. The adjective "subjective" matters because although people who culturally belong will correctly experience themselves as well-adjusted, as belonging to the group they seek membership in, as sharing values with their community, they might still nonetheless lack conditions of objective well-being. The group to which they belong could be a den of thieves, Nazis, or Incels. Such an individual experiences subjective well-being, but not objective well-being. They do not, due mostly to very bad luck, have all-things-considered well-being. They are happy perhaps, but for the wrong reasons.

The key point for present purposes is that subjective well-being is in many ways better considered a cultural project than merely an individual project. Culture provides individuals with ideas and beliefs of what is "good," "right," and "true," as well as what it is to "be well."

Take value-fulfillment theory, which says that subjective well-being is not mere desire satisfaction but comes from fulfilling a person's central ideals and reflectively endorsed values: Value and goal priorities converge within cultures, and diverge between cultures.[1] In some cultures, subjective well-being means in the first place "affective autonomy" (e.g., to have a life filled with variety, pleasure and positive excitement); in other cultures, subjective well-being means to be "embedded" (e.g., live life in the security of the family and the social order, respect tradition, be polite and obedient, and protect your social image).[2] What makes for subjective well-being depends on the cultural value priorities.[3] Life satisfaction measures conceived as happiness measures will embed such differences without revealing them. That is, if one person is an 8 because he or she is happy about or satisfied with their life of pleasure, another person is an 8 because he or she is happy about or satisfied with a serene family life, and a third is an 8 because he or she is a member of a beloved community of fellow neo-Nazis, these facts about the causes and components of the three kinds of happiness are not revealed. Each is simply an 8 as far as happiness goes, and each is thriving.

Consistent with the idea that value-fulfillment is a "cultural project," a large cross-cultural study yielded that subjective well-being was better predicted by the relative preponderance of positive over negative affect in "individualist" countries, whereas it was better predicted by the life satisfaction of "a highly respected person living a good life" (a possible proxy for "embeddedness") in "collectivist" cultures.[4] The Oriya Hindu women of Bhubaneswar, India who thought well-being was a mature fulfilling of one's social obligations would fit this collectivist profile. In a similar vein, a cross-cultural longitudinal study found that individuals' well-being could be predicted from their progress made toward goals during the preceding month; however, fulfillment of culturally valued goals better predicted well-being than less central goals. In this particular study, white American students reported more well-being when they had made progress with respect to their personal goals (i.e., goal pursuit for fun and enjoyment) and Asian American and Japanese college students when they had made progress toward their social goals (i.e., goal pursuit to please parents and friends).[5] Again, the findings resonate with the idea that across cultures value fulfillment is conducive to well-being, but that the most significant values differ by culture.

Taking other theories of happiness and well-being, such as hedonic and emotional well-being theories, it becomes equally clear that achieving happiness or well-being, however conceived, is a "cultural project." These theories suggest that well-being is associated with (or even consists in) having certain emotions: the maximum of pleasure, or the right ratio of positive to negative emotions. The science is clear in this regard: this particular theory holds in some cultures, where well-being is in fact associated with these particular emotions or emotional patterns, but this association is far from universal.

Cultures differ in the normative and habitual ratio of positive over negative emotions, and consequently in the level of pleasure that is thought to be desirable.[6] In some cultures boundless happiness and a high positive to negative ratio of emotions are valued; in other cultures, a surplus of positive emotions is a sign of imprudence and naivety. In the latter cultures, research has established more of a balance between positive and negative emotions or, depending on measurement, more neutral states; and also less savoring of positive and less dampening of negative emotion.[7] What this means for hedonic and emotional well-being theories is not entirely clear. They don't talk about it. On the one hand, it seems that the preponderance of positive over negative affect does not enter as much as a criterion for the assessment of well-being.[8] On the other hand, individuals in cultures where positive emotions are valued do tend to report higher life satisfaction, and this seems to be the case because these cultures promote positive emotions.[9]

At an individual level, the case of subjective well-being is even more complicated: individuals who experience negative emotions have considerably less subjective well-being to the extent that their culture values positive emotions.[10] The cultural value on positive affect may thus serve individuals who manage to meet the cultural ideal but leave behind those who do not.[11] In that sense, the value on positive affect may maximize the well-being of some while not serving the "common good."[12] The individual pursuit of happiness is most strongly associated with ill-being in cultures where happiness is derived from individual success rather than engagement with others.[13]

In sum, subjective well-being is a cultural project. Culture plays a role (1) in how judgments of well-being are made (and thus whether hedonism or positive emotions theories or life satisfaction or psychological or philosophical eudaimonistic theories or some hybrid closely describe individual's assessments of well-being), and (2) in codetermining the precise objectives for well-being (which values or goals, what objective lists) as well as the scope (e.g., maximizing well-being, or maximizing harmony and the common good, or satisfying some perfectionist moral requirements).

WHAT EMOTIONS ARE CENTRAL TO WELL-BEING DEPENDS ON CULTURE

Now we elaborate on an emotions theory of well-being that goes beyond predictions of the link between specific culturally certified emotions and subjective well-being, suggesting that the cultural fit of emotions contributes to well-being. Emotions themselves can be seen as goals, since they prepare individuals for action.[14] Individuals seek to have emotions that are useful to them in the situation—that prepare them for the tasks at hand—rather than merely seeking to feel good.[15] For example, participants in psychological experiments cognitively prepared (mostly, unconsciously) to be afraid when they were about to enter a task that required avoidance, and they cognitively prepared to be angry when they expected a confrontation.

Emotion selection or promotion can be seen as a "cultural project" as well: emotions that serve central cultural tasks are promoted at the expense of emotions that are less useful, given cultural values and goals.[16] For example, anger promotes personal boundaries, which is positively valued in many individualist contexts, but is considered a taboo emotion in cultural contexts that value relational harmony. Conversely, shame helps to acknowledge failure to meet the social norms and seeks acceptance by others. It may be less compatible with some culture's value placed on high self-esteem and independence, but conducive to social cohesion, which is valued in other cultures. Consistently, anger is sought after in independent, and avoided in interdependent cultures; for shame, the reverse pattern is found.[17]

Taken together, research shows that people seek emotions that further central cultural values and cultural tasks; difference in cultural values comes with cultural differences in the emotions sought.[18] The alignment of actual emotions and emotions sought is substantial, though of course not perfect.[19]

Subjective well-being is connected with emotions that further cultural values and prepare one for cultural tasks; and conversely, is negatively associated with emotions that interfere with these values and tasks.[20] For instance, in white American contexts, a high value is placed on high-arousal positive emotions, since these states prepare them for controlling one's environment (a culturally valued goal); in Hong Kong Chinese contexts, value is placed on low-arousal positive emotions, since these states prepare one for the culturally valued goal of adjusting to one's environment.[21] Ill-being (or in this case, depression) is associated with the failure to have the valued emotions in the respective cultures: high-arousal positive emotions (e.g., excitement) among white Americans and low-arousal positive emotions (e.g., calm) among Hong Kong Chinese.[22]

Finally, achieving the culturally normative emotions is associated with greater subjective well-being, while not achieving culturally valued emotions is associated with ill-being.[23] This also means that emotions that are associated with well-being (or indicators of good health) in one culture may not be (or not to the same extent) in another culture and that emotions that are associated with ill-being (including poor health) may not be in another culture.[24]

Why is cultural fit of emotions associated with well-being or health outcomes? There are several hypotheses, but the evidence is still limited and often indirect.[25] First, if emotions prepare for action, then culturally normative emotions may be the ones that lead to "good" or "right" outcomes on the culturally central tasks; importantly, these include relational tasks. Second, if emotions themselves can be considered goals, then achieving those goals will be proper and desirable and as such be conducive to one's sense of self and social reputation. Third, emotions that fit with the cultural norms may garner social support and social capital, given that they make for smoother relations and a better social reputation. All of these effects of the cultural fit of emotions are likely to contribute to subjective well-being (and have been suggested to benefit physical health too).

WELL-BEING WHEN ONE IS PART OF MULTIPLE CULTURES

By sharing the emotions of their culture, individuals align themselves—often unwittingly—with the values and goals of this culture. Having the "right" emotions —i.e., having high *cultural fit* of emotions— is key for social inclusion and subjective well-being. This raises the question of subjective well-being for an increasing segment of the world population who partake of multiple cultures or who have moved to a different culture from the one in which they are socialized. What do we know about their cultural fit(s) of emotions? And what does subjective well-being look like for them?

The subjective well-being of individuals who move between cultures does not exclusively depend on how they fare in majority settings, but also on how they manage in minority settings. In fact, by some measures, individuals who live largely segregated lives among other immigrants from their own heritage culture have better "psychological well-being" than individuals choosing any other path. It is possible to be well and "get by" in immigrant communities.[26] Yet, by other measures, their subjective and objective well-being is limited.

Immigrant minority individuals who want to "get ahead" in society will have to navigate the educational and occupational settings of majority society. Minorities' relationships with majority individuals are indispensable bridges to these settings: they give minority individuals access to opportunities and help them make use of these opportunities when they occur.[27] As cases in point, minority students who have at least one majority friend in school are less likely to drop out of school and perform better, and minority individuals who report strong ties with majority individuals are more likely to earn a better salary.[28] Generally speaking, then, minorities' educational and occupational outcomes are dependent on their access to majority networks, which is maximally provided by close (positive, frequent, reciprocal) relationships with majority individuals.[29] Emotional fit with the majority plays an important role in establishing and maintaining these relationships.

The cultural fit of the emotions of recent immigrant populations to the majority norm grows with exposure to majority groups.[30] Second-generation immigrants to both Belgium and the United States have higher emotional fit than first-generation immigrants; yet only the third generation of immigrants becomes indistinguishable from the majority pattern of emotions.[31] It takes immigrants more than a generation to achieve cultural fit. This means that, at least within majority cultural contexts, first- and second-generation minority individuals are likely to be less efficacious: less "competent" in central cultural tasks in majority contexts and less agile in interactions. They are also judged abnormal, different, less reputable by majority standards.

In this chapter we have been bracketing questions of fairness, and substantive, hermeneutical, and affective injustice: Could a culture or subculture be so corrupt that the fit it requires for happiness and subjective well-being is objectively awful? Imagine it requires that happy, well-adjusted people believe in natural slavery as Aristotle did. (Yes). Might it be fairer, and possible, to create a society or an organization in which majority culture does not have the power to define what is normal or socially competent? (Yes.) And would this break the association between emotional fit and well-being? (Quite possibly.) Given the prevalent power differentials however, lack of cultural fit has consequences for subjective well-being. In fact, immigrants to the United

States whose emotions were more different from the majority's reported greater somatic symptomology.[32]

Within any generation of immigrants, there is substantial variation in emotional fit as well. The best predictor of cultural fit in emotions is intercultural contact. Minority individuals who have more opportunity to meet with the majority, and especially those with majority friends, are more likely to show emotional fi and this is true longitudinally as well.[33] The association between intercultural contact and cultural fit of emotions is bidirectional, which suggests that less segregated societies provide better chances for emotional fit and therefore might offer better opportunities for the well-being of immigrant minorities in majority contexts.

Most immigrant minority individuals spend their lives switching between majority and minority contexts. It is abundantly clear that in-group relationships protect minority individuals when engaging in majority settings, and as stated before, they are an independent source of subjective well-being as well.[34] Emotional fit with the minority emotional norms is therefore just as important as fit with the majority norms. Importantly, individuals' fit with majority emotions does *not* preclude fit with heritage culture emotions in individuals from groups with a recent history of immigration.[35] Especially individuals who have heritage culture friends are found to fit the heritage culture emotions.[36] Some research suggests that individuals flexibly adjust—like bilingual children—their emotions to the norms of the current cultural context. Emotional fit with the majority culture is high when engaging in situations scripted by the majority culture, but emotional fit with the heritage culture is high when engaging in situations characteristic of the heritage culture.[37] Successful frame-switching itself may be a predictor of subjective well-being, but there is no research substantiating this as yet.

THE COMPLICATED PICTURE OF WELL-BEING

Many factors may affect the well-being of people who are part of multiple cultures; the focus here is on cultural fit of emotion as an important aspect of being part of the cultural fabric, but other factors (e.g., discrimination, lack of resources) undoubtedly play a role as well. Migration and multiculturalism have always existed but affect an increasingly large segment of the population. Researchers should be concerned with their subjective and objective well-being. With some available pieces, we tried to piece together the well-being puzzle of minoritized immigrants groups. The puzzle is far from complete. In a sense, this part of the book can be seen as "agenda-setting" based on preliminary research. Against the background of "well-being as a cultural project," we ask what happens when individuals or groups move to a new culture or move between cultures.

Real life is endlessly more complicated and dynamic than can be captured in data on relatively recent immigrant groups. Individuals move between hybrid and changing cultural contexts, and the fit within any particular one of them is hard to measure.[38] The overall well-being for people who move between cultures is partly an emergent property of their fit, and thus their well-being depends on the dynamic of fit, belongingness, and what is lost and what is gained in the interactive process. What this looks like for particular individuals is dependent on the acculturation trajectory.

7

HAPPINESS AND WELL-BEING IN CONTEMPORARY CHINA

The American writer Lydia Davis has a short story called "Happiest Moment." Someone teaching English in provincial China asked his students when "the happiest moment" was in their lives. A student answered that "his wife has once gone to Beijing and eaten duck there, and she often told him about it." For him, "the happiest moment of his life was her trip, and the eating of the duck."[1]

When one is asked about happiness or well-being in survey research, the focus is usually on one's subjective experience. But to answer questions about subjective experience, one first must evaluate feelings or emotions to offer a self-report, in which these feelings are labeled and categorized as "happy," "angry," or "sad." But under what conditions would one say, "I am happy" or "I am angry?" Subjective feelings are experienced through social relations of which we are a part, in ecologies alive with ethical values we hold dear, as well as social norms that we are expected to follow. They all come into the mix as we assess, classify, justify, and evaluate our own emotions. As Joseph LeDoux defines it, "human emotions are autonoetic conscious experiences that are cognitively assembled, much like any other autonoetic conscious experience," and they are contextualized and interpreted differently over time through "accumulation of memories" as well as "self-narrative revision."[2]

In light of such reorientation of focus, we need to see self-reports of feelings and emotions as not self-evident, but as interpretations made in specific personal, social, and cultural contexts. The internal process of evaluation and interpretation of feelings is a profoundly social process. These interpretations have complex cultural meanings, and researchers have found significant cultural variations in the way emotion terms are used in psychological self-reports.[3]

Different inquiries have different aims and different methods. One can study and compare contemporary Chinese happiness, and what is different, contemporary Chinese subjective well-being—a more capacious category—with China in the past, or with other nation states. One can compare the happiness or well-being of minority groups in China with minority groups in the United States. One can compare the happiness or well-being of people in Beijing with those in Xinjiang. One can use subjective well-being indicators or emotional well-being indicators, or one can use the methods of the human rights theorist, or one can proceed with the tools of the sociologist or ethnographer. Each is informative in its own way. What matters, however, is to place our methods in social, historical, and cultural contexts, and to be explicit about what they can reveal, and what they can't reveal.

China's changing moral landscape has been examined by philosophers as well as social scientists in recent years. How do contemporary Chinese conceive a good life? What is the moral psychology of ordinary people in contemporary China, especially after the end of the Mao era? What are the main personal, moral, and political ideals in twenty-first-century China? The focus of this chapter is to locate some of the cultural resources for the envisioning, interpreting, and labeling of a life of well-being in contemporary Chinese society, with feminist movements in China as a case study.

In order to understand people's accounts of their emotions or subjective experiences, we need a framework akin to what Flanagan calls "anthropological realism" in ethics: "the right unit of attention for ethics is the whole person-in-communal relations, not person parts, say genes, or the emotional centers of the brain, or the relational parts of the brains, not brains, period, but persons who seek to live well in relations with other persons in particular natural and social ecologies with histories."[4] This is where our discussion of happiness and well-being should be located as well.

In her analysis of ancient Greek ethical theories, especially the ethics of Aristotle and the Stoics, Julia Annas makes the bold statement that the ancients do not lack theories of morality.[5] Rather, their theories about how to live a good life through seeking *eudaimonia* (true happiness or flourishing) is guided by moral concerns about the good of others and the good of the world around them. In other words, the ancient concepts of happiness and morality are intimately connected. She remarks:

> There are many reasons why ancient ethics should appear as a source of fresh insights in areas neglected by most of twentieth-century academic moral philosophy. Ancient ethical theories are concerned with the agent's life as a whole, and with his character. Concern with character and choice, with practical reasoning and the role of the emotions, is central rather than marginal. This has seemed to many to be a useful corrective to modern theories which operate with a narrow and abstract notion of what is relevant to morality, and which are frequently criticized for producing theories which are seriously at odds with our conceptions of what matters in our lives.[6]

This connection between individual flourishing and collective well-being is a shared characteristic of classical Greek and Chinese philosophies, as well as ancient and contemporary China. The Confucian concept of well-being is not based explicitly on a religious framework, even though there is a religious dimension to it, which is to be aware of the presence of something higher than us, the presence of the heaven (*Tian*) above. It also emphasizes the cultivation of virtues through social action aimed at perfecting oneself, improving family, supporting community, and benefiting all humanity, all without a theory of morality that is explicitly stated and argued. The Confucian sources are arguably becoming increasingly significant and central in the articulation of this discourse, especially in the past two decades.[7]

CONTEMPORARY CHINESE HABITS OF THE HEART: FOUR DISCOURSES

What does the discourse about happiness, well-being, and the good life look like among contemporary Chinese people? Does it align or not with happiness as conceived by proponents of the happiness agenda? The short answer is that the thick Chinese conceptions of true happiness and well-being embed an ethical form of life as a necessary condition. And thus a Chinese person can feel happy, even be happy or satisfied in the narrow psychological sense, without being truly happy, without having well-being or living a good life.

China has undergone a tremendous change in the past thirty to forty years in its transition into a thriving market economy, and it can indeed be argued that Confucian ethical values have grown stronger rather than weaker. One may speak of a rediscovery or renaissance of Confucian ethical life in the past twenty years.⁸ However, there have also been growing concerns over the loss of values in China's rapid transition to a market economy, with its emphasis on competition, profit-making, and individualized risk taking.

In the seminal 1985 sociological study of systems of meaning in contemporary America, *Habits of the Heart: Individualism and Commitment in American Life*, Robert Bellah and colleagues focused on the seemingly impossible question about the social meanings of a good life.⁹ What are the major moral and ethical discourses that inform the definition of happiness for ordinary Americans if any do (it was possible of course that American style happiness had been entirely de-ethicized and was entirely a matter of me and my feelings/satisfactions)? The answers came from extensive interviews in urban and suburban America. There is a system of discourse of meaning that defines what a good life is. It consists of four major components: the biblical religious tradition, the civic republican legacy, the language of utilitarian individualism, and the language of expressive individualism. These discourses of meaning form a resilient "web of significance" that define what happiness and/or well-being are for ordinary Americans in their everyday life. They not only inform action but also make possible the many narratives people might use to talk about their lives: narratives about work, politics, religion, love, marriage, and other commitments and activities.

What are the possible "habits of the heart in China" that define what a good life is and what well-being—subjective and objective—consists in? Do contemporary Chinese people offer evaluations of their lives in terms of happiness or well-being; and, if so, how do they do so? What are the moral resources of different conceptions of a good life? What are the major moral or ethical languages about happiness and well-being that exist in China today? How do people pursue the kind of well-being they deem valuable? We propose that the following discourses of meaning in contemporary China are what defines well-being, as well as serving as both motivations and justifications of action:

1. The *official moral discourse of "the common good of the people"* offered by the Chinese government, which today is deeply influenced by the Confucian political theory of benevolent politics;
2. The *neoliberal moral discourse of the marketplace*, which prioritizes the pursuit of individual self-interest and the privatization of risk;
3. The *Confucian moral discourse of filial piety and the cultivation of other virtues*, which emphasizes the centrality of the virtues such as benevolence (*ren*), justice (*yi*), ritual propriety (*li*), wisdom (*zhi*), and trustworthiness (*xin*), with filial love and care (*xiao*) as the foundation of all human virtues;[10]
4. The *religious moral discourse* about the meaning and purpose of one's life that may come from multiple religious traditions, such as Confucianism, Daoism, Buddhism, Christianity, and Islam.

The first discourse of meaningful life and well-being offered by the Chinese government can be seen and heard daily in China. Through official national newspapers and television stations, the Chinese state systematically promotes a particular definition of well-being. It adopts a Confucian language of benevolent politics (*ren zheng*), suggesting that citizens are receivers of well-being made possible by the state, and emphasizes the importance of the common good as well as social stability. The political nature of the official discourse complicates the already multifaceted systems of meanings of well-being and a good life in China.

The second discourse comes from the emergence of capitalism, which could well be termed as representing "sensualists without spirit, specialists without heart," the disturbing state of being described by Max Weber in his critique of modern capitalism.¹¹ Scholars have been arguing whether China has become a neoliberal state, politically or economically, but what is relevant to our study is whether neoliberal—or simply raw capitalist—values have become one of the dominating ideologies affecting people's lives today in China.¹² Lisa Rofel describes it as follows: "A sea-change has swept through China in the last fifteen years: to replace socialist experimentation with the 'universal human nature' imagined as the essential ingredient of cosmopolitan worldliness. This model of human nature has the desiring subject as its core: the individual who operates through sexual, material, and affective self-interest."¹³ Such individuals care a great deal about their satisfactions; it is every ego for itself.

The third discourse is the ancient Confucian language of filial piety and familial devotion, which places the centrality of the family—relations between parents and children, between other familial relations, and between oneself and one's ancestors—above all other values. It is an ethical language spoken on all levels of Chinese life, followed by people from vastly different social, religious, and economic backgrounds. This Confucian ethical tradition governs the realm of family life and social relations, affecting people's conduct in everyday life, in China as well as in Asian countries and regions where the influence of Confucianism is still strong.¹⁴

The fourth discourse is the religious formation of one's narrative about oneself and what it means to live a good life in the world. This may be called "the religious reason to be," and it refers to the various religious values that inform people's narratives about the meaning of one's life. For instance, the Buddhist concept of karma may be central to a Buddhist lay believer's effort of making sense of her own life, as well as being the reason behind her choices of future actions.

It is important to note that having a religious system that informs one's personal values does not necessarily contradict following the other systems of meaning, even though contradictions or even conflicts may well be part of the daily struggle for many. For example, a Catholic whose moral imagination is formed by Christian theology may still follow Confucian values such as filial love and care; and although she might not be able to entirely stay away from the neoliberal ethos, she might have a different attitude toward it, compared to her non-Catholic or nonreligious friends. This complex system of religious values and multiple religious engagements, with its endless individual configurations, forms the Chinese religious moral imagination about what a good life should be.

THICK VALUES IN PLURALISTIC TRADITIONS

We will say a bit more about this fourth language, since it can be missed if one starts with the assumption that China is largely irreligious and assumes that religious beliefs and values are irrelevant to Chinese happiness and well-being. Who are the "religious people" in China? Chinese religious life is a puzzle to any observer from the West. In survey data, we learn that the Chinese are not particularly religious: 93.9 percent do not "belong to a religious denomination."[15] Yet once we ask questions about religious practice—ancestral worship, burning incense in temples, and other ritual activities—we get an entirely different picture: 73.8 percent have conducted some combination of religious practice in the past year.¹⁶ In 2016, the number of people who engage in ancestral rituals is even higher: at least 80 percent surveyed have conducted "tomb-sweeping" activities "in the past year."¹⁷

The standard survey questions about religion—involving self-identification, membership in religious communities, and frequency of "attendance of services"—are deeply problematic in the Chinese context. Religious life in China is for the most part lived through rituals and practices rather than membership and self-avowed identity, with Christianity and Islam as exceptional cases rather than the norm.¹⁸ As a result, if the survey questions are not sensitive to these specific conditions, the findings cannot be counted on to reflect empirical reality.

As recent data demonstrate, the majority of Chinese people who practice religious rituals regularly nevertheless do not claim any religious identity.¹⁹ This is especially true for the Confucian tradition. Since there is no official initiation process for someone to "convert" to Confucianism, to become a Confucian is—in theory and in reality—a lifelong process of practicing the cultivation of virtues as well as commitment to rituals. Empirically, ancestral rites remain the most practiced religious rituals in China today, as they have been for thousands of years. Their centrality in the Chinese religious system is made possible by the fact that one doesn't need to be a "card-carrying," self-avowed member of Confucianism to be the person who takes seriously the ritual duties stipulated by the Confucian tradition and performed in the Confucian mode.

"Implicit identity" is salient in people with certain religious rituals, beliefs, and ethics that are significant or even central to their identity and conception of a meaningful life, yet they do not necessarily acknowledge it as the source of a religious identity. "Explicit identity" is manifested in people who recognize and acknowledge one or more religious traditions (although rarely more than one) as central to their identity. This is most markedly demonstrated in monotheistic religious life. The notion of a singular and exclusive religious identity is very much rooted in a monotheistic imagination, and it does not have much explanatory power in the cases where pluralistic religious life is the norm.[20]

The most salient finding from fieldwork in China is that no matter where or to whom people are praying, there are shared moral sentiments and moral beliefs expressed through their narratives of prayer. The terms we hear most frequently are "doing good deeds" (*xing shan*), "being a good person" (*zuo haoren*), "filial piety is the root of all virtues" (*baishan xiaoweixian*), "divine retribution" (*shanyou shanbao eyou ebao*), and "heaven has eyes" (the god/gods are always watching us) (*laotian youyan*).

These expressions, sentiments, and beliefs motivate as well as regulate people's actions in everyday life. They also inform the ongoing development of individual identities, condition people's relations with one another, and offer a context in which one may find meaning in one's life. Although there is no singular religious system guaranteeing morality in Chinese life, as there is in societies with the dominant presence of monotheistic religions such as Judaism, Christianity, and Islam, China's religious moral imagination is no less central to people's moral understanding, moral character, and moral behavior. Happiness depends on excellence in both ritual performance, which involves sustaining relations with a treasured lineage, and on moral excellence. On such a view of happiness, one's wife's trip to Beijing, where she enjoyed a duck, might well be the happiest day in her husband's life.

In an interview in Shanghai in the spring of 2017, a woman in her early fifties, a well-educated magazine editor, said that she had a lot of worries about the future for herself and her family:

"We are ordinary people who have no power to affect the currents in the world," and her worries often kept her awake at night. "However," she said: "whoever are corrupt or unethical today might think that they can get away from being punished. But they cannot. We are all under the watchful eyes of heaven. What the wicked ones have done will sooner or later catch up with them. It's the same with good deeds. If you act with kindness and generosity, you have a good life, no matter how badly the world might be treating you. The unethical ones do not live a good life, no matter how successful they might be right now with their schemes, and no matter how well the material world is treating them today."

Although a self-avowed nonreligious person, she said that she took ancestral rites seriously, following her mother's example who would spend days getting ready for the offerings to the spirits of deceased family members on important Confucian ritual dates such as Qingming and Chinese New Year's Eve. In her own words, she described herself as someone who was thoroughly rooted in Chinese traditions in everyday life. She clearly cared about divine retribution in her conception of a good life: moral deeds will eventually be rewarded, and the crooked ones will be punished, for this is the working of the heaven above, which is always watching over all of us.

The Chinese phrase she used, "Heaven has eyes (or 'we are all under the eyes of heaven')" comes up frequently in interviewers with people in urban China. It refers to *Tian*, a term referring to the divine force of heaven in the Confucian tradition, as the giver and enforcer of moral values, and its never-wavering presence is an imperative for us all to behave morally. The heaven evoked in her statement is not an abstract transcendence, but a higher divine force that cares about the morality—and the lack thereof—of human beings.

There have been many controversies over how to understand the Chinese term *Tian*, from the Jesuit rites controversy in the seventeenth and eighteenth centuries to Protestant missionary debates in the nineteenth century, to contemporary scholarly discussions about the Chinese high god or deity. Recently, Kelly Clark and Justin Winslett have argued that, in early China (pre-220 BCE), there were texts "rife with depictions of the High Deities," which are "often represented as moralizing agents that punish vice and reward virtue."[21] Edward Slingerland similarly suggests that the *Tian* that Confucius refers to is an andromorphic god that administrates moral commands.[22] These interpretations resonate with the main thesis of "Big God," which maintains that Big Gods, in their watchfulness, foster cooperation in increasingly diverse and fragmenting societies.[23]

Under the great shadows cast by innumerable skyscrapers in metropolises like Shanghai, Beijing, and Hong Kong, sacred sites from diverse religious traditions are sought out by people who have inherited this complex religious world both culturally and ritually. If we look for religion by examining the rich system of interconnective religious practices that emerge, interact, and evolve in social time and social space, a new landscape of Chinese religious life becomes visible. Even though most people may not be able to articulate a clear theology, the sacred values and beliefs shared by people—such as divine retribution and filial love as the foundation of all virtues—become strong reasons for people to act morally. These commands and values are essential to what it means to live a good life, and the Confucian conception of well-being is inseparable from this moral imagination.

To conclude, in order to comprehend the moral imagination that is the foundation of the conception of well-being in China, we need to take into account the challenges of negotiating shared as well as conflicting values in a highly diverse society.

Whenever we speak of a moral imagination in the singular, we risk not doing justice to the plural values and traditions in any given society. That said, across various conceptions of a good life on offer in contemporary China, they almost all share some combination of ethicized, ritualized, and religious roots, and conceive happiness as accruing, if it does, from success at living according to values and virtues of the relevant traditions that are in certain respects, and despite interacting with nonindigenous sources, distinctively Chinese.

CHINESE FEMINISM: A CASE STUDY

With the four discourses of meaning in hand, we provide a case study of feminist movements in contemporary China where the four discourses intersect and interact on the ground. Chinese feminism can be understood as a contestation between liberatory languages (with sources in socialist feminism and the Western enlightenment), which conceive well-being as requiring gender equality and justice, and the traditional Confucian discourse, which prizes a certain conception of a well-functioning family as the basis for the good life. These contestations are first and foremost about equality and rights, not about happiness.

Socialist Feminism

After the CCP came to power in 1949, Mao rallied women to join the labor force, proclaiming that "women hold up half the sky." For the first time, women were released from traditional kinship patriarchy and allowed to enter the public domain of production. To promote the rights and interest of women and mobilize them in the socialist construction efforts, the all-China

Women's Federation (ACWF), a state-sponsored organization, was founded in April 1949.[24] This commitment to gender equality was further translated into legal principles. The Common Program approved by the first plenary session of China's "People's Political Consultative Conference," which became the de facto legislature from 1949 to 1954, promised to "abolish the feudal system which holds women in bondage" and promote women's equal rights "in political, economic, cultural, educational, and social life."[25] The Marriage Law passed in 1950 also emphasized free choice of partners, outlawing arranged marriage, child-adoption marriage, polygyny, and prostitution.

Gender Inequality in Contemporary China

The socialist feminist movement launched by the state in the Mao era improved women's conditions in certain aspects, such as their access to education and employment.[26] However, China's early gains for women have not been maintained with the decline of centrally planned socialism and the launch of market reforms since the late 1970s. In its embrace of global capitalism, China has seen rapid economic development and growth over the past forty years. However, men and women continue to secure uneven gains from it.[27] In fact, gender gaps have worsened over the last decade or so. According to the Global Gender Gap Report 2021 report, China ranks 107th of 156 countries in the global gender gap rankings, slipping from 57th of 130 countries in 2008.[28]

Here are a few examples of gender inequality in contemporary China:

- The gender gap in labor force participation between men and women has widened, rising from 9 percent in the 1990s to almost 15 percent in 2020.[29] So has the gender wage gap: in 2000, women's earnings were approximately 84 percent of men's earnings, but by 2013, this figure has dropped to 65 percent.[30] This situation has further been exacerbated by the COVID-19 pandemic, which has had disproportionate impact on women's employment opportunities and has widened existing gender gaps in labor markets.[31]

- Chinese women have limited presence in the political sphere. Only 24.9 percent of parliamentarians and 3.2 percent of ministers are women.[32] There has not been a single woman who has ever sat on the seven-member Politburo Standing Committee, the nation's top ruling body.
- Chinese women fall victim to domestic abuse and sexual harassment. One-quarter of Chinese women have suffered from intimate partner violence according to a government's statement in 2010, a figure that is likely understated.[33]
- China continues to have a wide sex ratio at birth: 88.8 girls for every 100 boys in 2018, a result of "strong son preference and gender-biased prenatal sex selective practices."[34]
- State-sponsored media campaign's denigration of "leftover women (*shengnü*)"—urban, well-educated, professional women aged over twenty-seven who are unmarried—browbeats women into hasty, ill-considered marriages in the interests of safeguarding social stability.[35] In the rush to marry, women often fail to insist on joint ownership of the marital property, despite jointly financing the purchase, and thus are "shut out of the biggest accumulation of real-estate wealth in history."[36]

Recent Feminist Movements in China

In recent years, there has been a growing feminist awakening among young, urban, well-educated women in China, who have begun to raise challenges to the patriarchal underpinnings of the regime:

- Online communities have been built on social media such as Weibo, WeChat, and Douban, where women could share the injustice that they face in everyday life.
- On Valentine's Day of 2012, a few leading feminists organized the "Bloody Brides" action against domestic violence, in which they paraded down a busy commercial area in Beijing, wearing "blood" spattered wedding gowns.[37]
- On February 19, 2012, volunteers in the southern city of Guangzhou started the "Occupy Men's Toilet" campaign to protest against a lack of sanitation facilities for women.[38] The Guangzhou government responded to the activists' demand by launching a plan to increase the level of toilet parity from a ratio of 1:1 to 1:1.5.
- In March 2015, five young feminists planned to protest against sexual harassment on International Women's Day (March 8) by handing out stickers on public transportation. They were arrested in Beijing on March 6 before the plan was carried out and were detained for thirty-seven days.[39]
- In January 2018, thousands of Chinese women and men signed #MeToo petitions, calling for action against sexual harassment, although many of the petitions were soon removed from social media by censors.[40]

Feminist Awakening and the Contestations of Discourses

China's feminist awakening can be seen as a contestation among different discourses of meaning, in particular between the traditional Confucian discourse and the liberatory discourses of socialist feminism and Western feminism, which advocate gender equality.[41]

In particular, Confucianism has long been associated with sexism. Confucian scholars and statesmen since the Han dynasty explicitly weaved oppression against women into the Confucian virtues.[42] Dong Zhongshu, the Han dynasty statesman who promoted Confucianism as the official ideology, for example, first articulated the three core relationships (*sangang*): "The lord is *yang*, the retainer is *yin*; the father is *yang*, the son is *yin*; the husband is *yang*, the wife is *yin*. The way of *yin* cannot proceed anywhere on its own. . . . Therefore, the retainer depends on his lord to gain merit; the son depends on his father; the wife depends on her husband; *yin* depends on *yang*; the Earth depends on heaven (Chapter 53)."[43] The three core relationships, which were essential to structuring human social life in imperial China, were deeply hierarchical. They especially contributed to the subjugation of women, who stood at the bottom of the hierarchy and were confined to the patriarchal family.

Despite the vicissitudes of Confucianism after the fall of imperial China, Confucian concepts about social structure and relationships still loom large in the fabric of people's life, perpetuating gender inequality in today's China. Cultural norms still regard the son as the heir who could pass on the genealogy of the family. Raising a daughter is considered to be an economic burden: once married, she is like spilt water, and belongs to the family of her husband. Also, the Confucian ideal of "men manage outside; women manage inside (*nan zhu wai; nü zhu nei*)" still pervades. As a result, women bear the burden of household work disproportionately and are the first to sacrifice their professional career to fulfill their obligations in the domestic sphere.

To combat gender inequality, Chinese feminists attempt to reconstruct Confucianism in a way that is compatible with the liberation of women.[44] To do so, they not only contest the sexist ideas in Confucianism, but also selectively appropriate elements from liberatory discourses such as socialist feminism and Western feminism. In particular, socialist feminism, understood as the whole discourse of women's liberation in the Mao era, has created the legitimacy of the CCP's rule in part by describing it as the savior of Chinese women. As Wang points out, although this discourse is not fixed, its major tenets include: (1) women's oppression is a part of class oppression; (2) "women's participation in socialist and communist revolution is the only way to their eventual liberation;" (3) "the socialist state implements gender equality, but women's thorough emancipation can be achieved only at a higher stage of human history—communism."[45]

The discourse of socialist feminism has become a major source of strength for Chinese women and has given them some political leverage in negotiating with state leaders who are less committed to gender equality than the early CCP founders.[46] However, it is not without its problems. First, socialist feminism sometimes removes gender as a distinct social category that defines individual identity, which can result in reducing gender politics to class politics.[47] Honig thinks that this amounts to the "masculinization of women," since women are included in a masculine state order with the expectation that they act like men.[48] Second, socialist feminism emphasizes the primacy of top-down regulation, with the state-sponsored all-China Women's Federation (ACWF) monopolizing the representation of women. This leaves little space for Chinese women to take their matters into their own hands.

Since the 1990s, Chinese women have also turned to Western feminism for inspiration. The United Nations Fourth Women

World Conference and its parallel NGO Forum held in China in 1995 first introduced to Chinese feminists the transnational feminist concept of gender. This concept is attractive to Chinese women in that it highlights their autonomy and agency, and acknowledges their right to take control of their own destiny "without subjecting themselves to the demands of a patriarchal state."[49] It further provides them with an analytic tool to interrogate both the Confucian discourse of gender hierarchy, which finds its way into the postsocialist discourse of femininity, and the socialist feminist discourse, which effectively erases gender as a distinct social category. In this sense, Western feminism empowers Chinese women with a new conceptual framework and creates a new space for feminist movements, even as it struggles to be reconciled with preexisting discourses rooted in China's distinct social, political, and cultural reality.

To conclude, feminism in China takes a hybrid form and appropriates elements from different sources. On the one hand, it is embedded in preexisting traditions, which are contested, reconstructed, or revitalized to undermine the subjugation of women. On the other hand, it is inspired by Western ideas and practices, which await reinvention to be able to grow on foreign soil. Also, theory-building in Chinese feminism is a "highly dynamic process," as the different discourses are flexibly used under particular historical and structural conditions to address particular theoretical or practical challenges faced by particular groups of women.[50] It should be noted, however, that the feminist quest in China is not about happiness or subjective well-being. Rather, it is about justice and equality, which are regarded as intrinsic goods and essential to Chinese women's flourishing.

III

RACE, RACISM, RESIGNATION

8

HAPPINESS, RACE, AND HERMENEUTICAL JUSTICE

The Case of African American Mental Health

The conviction that social and political institutions and policies should promote human well-being is at least as old as Plato's *Republic*. Equally well established is the idea that we cannot advance well-being without a deep understanding of what it consists in, and reliable information about how to produce it. Aristotle rejected the idea that subjective reports could teach what *eudaimonia* consists in, although it could reveal (as it does in the opening sections of *Nicomachean Ethics*) the relative distribution of false views about *eudaimonia*, for example, that it consists in fame, reputation, money, or pleasure. In contrast, many contemporary thinkers argue that governments and their citizens need a comprehensive understanding of subjective, as well as objective, indicators of well-being if they are to make sound decisions about social policy.[1]

Yet, getting a reliable picture of happiness, subjective well-being, and objective well-being (which are different and ought not be elided) can be more challenging than some researchers have thought. The interpretive challenges are especially pronounced in societies with histories of persistent discrimination against some groups. In an illuminating recent example, when the

National Study of American Life seemed to reveal unexpectedly high subjective well-being among African Americans, some researchers explained the findings by positing greater "resilience" among African Americans.[2] But critics might plausibly wonder whether its findings simply reflect African American *resignation* in the face of persistent inequality.[3] What if the responses from African American subjects reflected lowered expectations and adaptive preferences in the face of persistent disadvantage rather than a stronger sense of subjective well-being? In societies shaped by persistent discrimination, defensible interpretations of subjective reports about well-being virtually always require going beyond the reports themselves to analyze the conditions in which the reports are made. For example, findings that African Americans living in Atlanta and St. Louis have high life satisfaction despite living in objectively unsatisfactory conditions indicate a serious problem with the reliability of life satisfaction measures and are not cause for celebration about human resilience or as evidence that the causes of happiness are endogenous, that is, inside people and largely under the control of each individual.

One sees the word *resilience* a lot in the happiness literature. We mark two uses that need be kept apart, but that often are not. First is *resilience* as shorthand for saying that some measure didn't change or that people didn't change their answers on some metric, for example, on overall life satisfaction. Second posits *resilience* as a character or personality trait that enables one to carry on and not suffer much the "slings and arrows of outrageous fortune." Normally, the second sense is insinuated as a compliment (sometimes in the language of "grit") but is often patronizing and condescending ("I sure am glad she didn't make too much of a fuss over that. Resilient Lass!"). When one says that life satisfaction metrics were resilient during COVID-19 in the first sense, one is just asserting the fact that they held stable. One is not explaining why they held stable. If, however, one says that the African American community was resilient during COVID, they might mean that despite suffering more disease and death during COVID than whites, African Americans have, on average, more of the character trait of resilience. Used this way, resilience is conceived as playing a causal role in the stability of life satisfaction reports among African Americans. It is offered, perhaps, as an alternative to other candidate causal surmises: African Americans are beaten down and have realistically low expectations for how their lives will go, or life satisfaction is an insensitive detector.

Societies with histories of serious discrimination present a second and more serious difficulty for any study of subjective well-being. This is because, in these contexts, interpretive resources available for describing and understanding subjective experience are too often shaped by discriminatory and stigmatizing stereotypes and prejudices. When this occurs, interpretive systems can produce a phenomenon that philosopher Miranda Fricker has described as "hermeneutical injustice."[4] This is a species of what Fricker calls epistemic injustice, which involves various wrongs to others *as knowers* that result from our epistemic practices. In hermeneutical injustice, deficiencies in society's interpretive resources both limit what "external" inquirers can understand about some subjects but also obscure from some of those subjects themselves the full truth about their subjective experiences.[5] Fricker uses the example of the concept of "sexual harassment." Sexual harassment existed before the 1970s, when the concept gained currency. But it was hard for victims to speak about it and for the culture to appreciate the depth of the harm it caused before the concept was formulated, established, and widely shared.

In zones of life where hermeneutical injustice exists, relying on standardized questions and measures will not merely prove uninformative, but it may be likely to support policies that sustain or even worsen social injustice. This means that hermeneutical injustice is virtually always linked with social injustice.[6] If one aim of research is to promote subjective well-being, researchers have a duty to explore the possibility that some subjective reports may have been dangerously constrained by hermeneutical injustice.

One well-known example of the phenomenon involves theorizing and measuring the well-being and ill-being of African Americans. Studies have revealed three disturbing trends in the treatment of this population: (1) the underdiagnosis of depression, (2) widespread misdiagnosis of depression as schizophrenia, and (3) widespread inattention to the growing incidence of suicide, especially among young African American males. One obstacle to addressing these problems is that the language in which African Americans talk about their mental health sometimes masks the true nature of their experience—sometimes even from themselves. Still further, African Americans sometimes assent too quickly to misdiagnoses because they lack the interpretive resources to resist mischaracterization of their symptoms. This does not mean that the subjects are unreliable. Rather, these subjects have become accustomed to thinking about their own experience by reference to unreliable systems of interpretation.

Hermeneutical justice, as Fricker and we describe it, is primarily epistemic. The conceptual and discursive resources needed to describe a phenomena (sexual harassment, sexism, racism) are not available or are available but recessive or discouraged ("That's just being friendly," or "That's just the way marriage works," or

"I just chose the best job applicant").[7] There is also "affective injustice," which involves asymmetrical norms of emotional expression, what Arlie Hochschild calls "feeling rules." Blacks or women who demand equal rights are being "uppity" or "shrill." Amia Srinivasan describes norms that ask oppressed people to count their blessings, to be grateful, satisfied, patient—"cool, calm, and collected"—as "a second order injustice that is parasitic on first-order injustice, a psychic tax that is often levied on victims of oppression."[8] Affective injustice matters for the happiness agenda because it means that oppressed groups cannot be expected to speak forthrightly about their dissatisfaction and anger. In 1961 James Baldwin said: "To be a Negro in this country and to be relatively conscious is to be in rage almost all the time."[9] But this rage is something many contemporary citizens and politicians would prefer not to acknowledge, questioning its legitimacy given alleged advances in civil rights law.

In addition to this kind of affective injustice, where members of an oppressed group have reason to be distressed, but are strongly discouraged from expressing their distress, there is a further kind of affective injustice that African Americans suffer: misreading and misinterpreting resignation for resilience, misinterpreting depression as psychosis, and treating anger as a character defect rather than a natural response to racism.

The existence of hermeneutic injustice and affective injustice for certain populations, in the present case African Americans, require that life satisfaction reports be read in the light of an antecedent evaluation of whether or not circumstances of justice obtain (e.g., that racism is absent, jobs plentiful, mental health systems are in place, families are strong, etc.), and not with an inference from high happiness or subjective satisfaction scores to the conclusion that things are well among African Americans.

HERMENEUTICAL INJUSTICE AND THE AMERICAN MENTAL HEALTH CARE SYSTEM

Some readers will find it hard to believe that hermeneutical and affective injustice in America's mental healthcare system is as severe as we have suggested. But one clear sign of its severity is that, in January 2021, the American Psychiatric Association (APA) issued a formal apology to Black, Indigenous, and other People of Color for its historical support of and silence regarding "direct and indirect racism in psychiatry."[10] The apology acknowledged that the effects of the APA's racism have been broad and deep and that, from the beginnings of American psychiatry, the profession created structures of misinterpretation, unequal treatment, and unequal access to treatment, that not only affected how some marginalized and stigmatized groups were "understood" but limited and constrained their freedom and undermined their quality of life.

Ironically, the American approach to mental health began with an unexpected concern for hermeneutical justice when the "father" of American psychiatry, Benjamin Rush, became the first American physician to argue in print that mental illness was a "disease of the mind" rather than a sign that one was possessed by demons.[11] But, regrettably, despite being in favor of the abolition of slavery, Rush also believed that black skin was caused by leprosy and needed a cure.[12] This claim ended up aligning his stance with some dangerously racist practices and beliefs. Moreover, from the mid–nineteenth century forward, concern for hermeneutical justice in mental health care was rarely extended to African Americans. In an especially sinister example, an 1851 article by University of Louisiana professor Samuel Cartwright claimed to find two "diseases of the mind" that were peculiar to "the Negro race." The first was "*drapetomania*," the "troublesome practice" that many enslaved persons had of running away from their captors. The second was "*dysaethesia aethiopica*" which, in enslaved persons, was manifested as a tendency to "seem to be insensible to pain when subjected to punishment."[13]

To be sure, even in the nineteenth century, Cartwright's claims were challenged by medical professionals in non–slave states, and his categories have been officially rejected by the profession of psychiatry. But, as Jonathan Metzl argues, the tendency to pathologize the African American desire to be free from discrimination—and all too often to treat it as evidence of schizophrenia—continued well into the late twentieth century.[14] Moreover, in a trend that has continued into the twenty-first century, one outcome of the consistent misinterpretation of African American affect has been the overdiagnosis of schizophrenia. Epidemiological surveys have consistently shown that schizophrenia affects all racial and ethnic groups at the same rate, approximately 1 percent. But one 2005 study established that African Americans were four times as likely to be diagnosed with schizophrenia as whites.[15] In 2015, another comprehensive study reiterated the depth of the problem, noting that for African American populations, diseases such as manic-depressive illness and major depression disorder are often misdiagnosed as schizophrenia.[16] When misdiagnoses are given, patients end up getting the wrong treatment, often with medications that have dangerous, life-altering side effects. When depression goes undiagnosed and untreated, it becomes a risk factor for potentially life-threatening behaviors and conditions such as alcoholism, drug abuse, and suicide attempts.[17]

One cause of these diagnostic failures is that, in a holdover from the nineteenth century myth of the "happy slave," it was assumed well into the twentieth century that African Americans were not intellectually complex enough to be depressed. Moreover, widespread resistance to diagnosing depression—often due to persistence of the belief that African Americans do not get depressed—continues to this day. Regrettably, rates of misdiagnosis around depression and schizophrenia are high even among African American mental health professionals if they have not learned to question the deficient interpretive resources they still learn in much of their training.

Of course, most mental health professionals would acknowledge that psychiatry is not an exact science. Reliable diagnoses of mental illness can be made only after obtaining a precise and detailed history, and the history and the resultant diagnosis can be only as good as the clinician making the diagnosis. But the process also requires time and sensitivity to the variety of ways in which various illnesses may "present" in different populations due to differences in education, culture, gender, and socioeconomic status. The most recent revision of the *Diagnostic and Statistical Manual of Mental Disorders* (DSM-5) finally acknowledges just how complex the diagnostic process can be.[18] But for many the training process still lags far behind the "state of the science" described in the DSM-5. More important, African Americans have been consistently unlikely to get the kind of diagnoses and care that come anywhere close to the DSM-5 ideal.

It will not be surprising that these developments have helped to create suspicion and mistrust of the mental healthcare system among African Americans. They have also increased the likelihood that the stigma associated with mental illness in all populations will be especially potent in African American communities. This is one reason that some African Americans talk about their mental health in language that downplays or sometimes even seeks to deny the existence of depression.

African Americans—perhaps especially African American males—are deeply resistant to admitting that they feel sad or depressed. In a critical example, there is evidence that Martin Luther King Jr. attempted suicide at least twice before the age of thirteen and that despite the bouts of severe depression as an adult, he consistently refused to seek treatment.[19]

Another source of the difficulty in diagnosing depression among African Americans is that their depression sometimes has a distinctive "presentation." For instance, some African Americans present with more somatic symptoms—such as sleep disturbance, appetite disruption, and weight loss—than people in other populations.[20] The psychiatrist F. M. Baker, with extensive experience diagnosing African American patients, has also identified some distinctive personality "styles" or traits that can also mask depression in African Americans.[21] One common phenomenon is that some African American patients present as "stoic believers"—that is, as less likely to *report b*eing depressed because they believe that this is what sincere religious faith requires.[22] Other patients present as "John Henry Doers," harking back to the legend of John Henry, an African American man famed for an almost inexhaustible capacity to drive steel pins in order to set railroad track.[23] "John Henryism" leads the depressed patient to try to avoid being perceived as depressed (and even to avoid thinking of themselves as depressed) by taking on more and more challenges and tasks in a frantic effort to prove their continued ability "to cope." All this is best explained by the social-cognitive theory of the emotions: The language of emotions is introduced alongside traditional specific, often subculture specific norms and scripts for enacting, expressing, suppressing, and explaining them.

By far the most problematic of the distinctive styles affecting presentation of depression among African Americans is the phenomenon whereby a patient seems to be dealing with depression by letting anger and hostility essentially "take over" the personality. A growing number of studies suggest that this presentation may be especially common in young African American males.[24] But Baker believes that the syndrome is not confined to this group and thus advises that any clinician who confronts an angry African American patient must take special care in preparing the patient history. It is important to explore "recent stressors" in the patient's life, decreases in energy levels and constructive plans for the future, and plausible evidence of suicidal ideation.[25] Unfortunately, depressed African Americans who present as extremely angry are often misdiagnosed with schizophrenia. Moreover, the diagnosis will be challenged only when patients or their family members are knowledgeable enough to seek a second opinion (and have the means to do so).[26] Many patients are unlikely to protest a diagnosis of schizophrenia—and some may in fact actively assent to it—since very few feel empowered to challenge historically developed patterns of misinterpretation and posit the possibility of hermeneutical injustice.

But nowhere have hermeneutical and affective injustice been more destructive than in the failure to address increasing rates of suicide among young African American males. Epidemiological studies had long suggested that suicide is less prevalent among African Americans than among other populations. But even if these past studies were reliable, a report produced by the Congressional Black Caucus has shown the emergence of a disturbing new pattern. From 1991 to 2017, suicide attempts by Black adolescents (generally) rose by 73 percent, and among young Black males serious injury from lethal suicide attempts rose by 122 percent.[27] Especially disturbing trends now appear among elementary school age children: among American children ages

5–11, there were more suicides among African American children than among non-Black children.[28] There is also good evidence that while suicide declined overall in the United States in 2020, the rate of suicide rose among African Americans and may even have doubled.[29]

These figures would be troubling in their own right. But considered in the context of some happiness and well-being research that too quickly posits the resilience of African Americans, the figures are especially concerning. Equally concerning is the tendency for some subjective well-being researchers to argue that "objective indicators such as income" may not be as important to subjective well-being as we might think.[30] For, as one journalist who writes about patterns of suicide has recently argued, while there is rarely any one cause for suicide, "research shows that there is a connection between people's ability to pay their rent each month and their mental health."[31] Moreover, to the extent that COVID-19 had disparate effects on people's economic well-being, it seems likely that the 2020 increase in suicides among African Americans was at least partly a function of increased economic insecurity and deprivation. Subjective well-being research which overlooks—or even denies—this possibility is deeply problematic.

THE IMPORTANCE OF SEEKING THE "WHOLE TRUTH"

This exploration of hermeneutical and affective injustice in mental health care has shown that misinterpretation, unequal treatment, and lack of access to quality care are a source of ill-being for many African Americans. Two implications of this discussion are especially relevant to happiness and well-being research.

First, some of the ways in which African American populations have adapted to hermeneutical injustice cast doubt on the idea that the kinds of "standardized" questions included in most contemporary happiness and well-being research can get at the truth about subjective indicators of well-being for African American subjects. The problems of "presentation" that are relevant here go beyond concerns about lowered expectations and adaptive preferences. But second, if the quality of some subjects' lives is at least partly—sometimes even largely—a function of lack of access to material resources, subjective well-being research may be dangerously uninformative if it fails to acknowledge that fact. Being unable to afford a secure roof over one's head, or to afford necessary medicine and nutritious food at the same time, constitute the kinds of stressors that make one more prone to poor mental health and sometimes even to suicide. Well-being research that does not, or cannot, acknowledge the connection between well-being and just social conditions seems to be seriously lacking in reliability and credibility.

A partial solution to the problems identified here would be to include questions in subjective well-being studies that provide better opportunities for subjects to concisely identify sources of "ill-being" in their lives. A survey instrument would not need to be excessively long to elicit better data in this domain. Indeed, this might require only a handful of additional questions, such as (1) Do you have any major sources of economic, social, or family stress in your life (although see the next section for the difficulty of getting reliable stress reports)? (2) Do you feel able to cope with these stresses? (3) Do you feel confident about being able to make constructive and realizable plans for the future? (4) If not, are you prevented from doing so by circumstances beyond your control or under your control?

If the goal of subjective well-being research is to inform policy decisions meant to improve the quality of life in a given region, we cannot accomplish that goal unless we know in some *detail* what the quality of life really is, and specifically whether circumstances of justice obtain. This requires more nuanced information than most surveys provide about how the quality of life might differ, substantially, from one social group to another. To be sure, the relevant information must include both subjective and objective measures of well-being, but those measures must enlighten us about the well-being of every major social group. If well-being studies simply reproduce familiar myths that some groups are just more "resilient" than others, we are failing to meet the desired objectives. We cannot determine how to promote human well-being, until we understand how many ways in which it is possible to produce—and to mask or ignore—human unhappiness and ill-being.

These facts matter to subjective well-being research for two reasons. First, where hermeneutical injustice of this sort exists, there will be social groups whose subjective reports consistently mask the extent of their actual unhappiness and ill-being. That fact seems likely to taint some of the data on which research about happiness depends, and some of the conclusions based on that data. Second, when conclusions about happiness or well-being rest on tainted subjective reports they may lead policy makers to support institutions and policies that ignore, reinforce, or even worsen, the conditions that give rise to unaddressed unhappiness and ill-being. It follows that happiness research intended to be relevant to or to guide public policy is fully defensible only when it satisfies two conditions: (1) it presumes a deep connection between happiness, well-being, and social justice, and (2) it recognizes that we cannot promote happiness and well-being unless the information we gather allows us to get "behind" responses that reflect distorting effects of hermeneutical injustice. If these conditions are not met, we should be agnostic about what the happiness or well-being data mean or indicate.

According to some theories of well-being, e.g., desire satisfaction theories or subjective well-being theories, the theorist ought not impose her own views or the views of any particular comprehensive normative theory on what happiness *should be* like or about.[32] If one thinks there are no constraints of the kinds of happiness that ought to be promoted, only that it ought to be promoted, one holds a libertarian view. Many normative theories—for example, psychological and philosophical *eudaimonistic* theories as well as classical, Enlightenment-inspired, liberal ones, and Marxist-Leninist-Maoist ones—permit and invite historical discoveries about necessities for a good human life (respect, dignity, and recognition of rights) to be used, as it were, to *correct* judgments or preferences and to constrain and guide policy. Conditions 1 and 2 are offered as a proposal to regulate the conduct of subjective well-being research, as well as policy promotion of happiness by principles of justice.

9

INTERPRETING SELF-REPORTS OF WELL-BEING

Even if happiness is not the *summum bonum*, and even if well-being is not only about how people feel, happiness and well-being matter in a host of ways. Happiness is correlated with political stability, and misery and ill-being always deserve attention. The growing interest in well-being metrics for policy might represent a welcome step toward helping it be more sensitive to people's values and voices when making decisions on their behalf. People care about rights, duties, and obligations, and they care about the distribution of resources and opportunities. They also value outcomes, including how well their lives actually go for them—well-being, that is. Whatever else matters, it is plausible that policymakers should not be oblivious to whether policy makes people's lives go better or worse. Well-being instruments can take a variety of forms from physiological measures of stress or hypertension to measures of ratios of positive to negative emotions to objective list measures.

In this chapter, we develop the analysis from the previous chapter and assess one aspect of well-being and focus on self-report measures, specifically measures in the broad area of subjective well-being, which encompasses people's judgments about their lives, as well as their emotional responses to their lives.

While such measures may enjoy a good degree of validity in some contexts, more work needs to be done to understand how they work in different contexts, especially across culturally dissimilar groups. Otherwise we risk failing to grasp what the data are really telling us and thus, ironically, basing policy on a distorted understanding of people's experience of their lives—perhaps even worsening the situation of the most vulnerable groups.

SELF-REPORT MEASURES AND THEIR VALIDATION

Self-report measures of well-being can take many forms, from asking if one is happy, to asking about life satisfaction to eudaimonic questionnaires eliciting reports about matters like the participant's relationships or sense of meaning in life.[1] But the most widely used measures, especially in policy circles, assess subjective well-being. As usually understood, subjective well-being has two basic components: life evaluation (how satisfied are you with your life?) and emotional well-being.[2] The latter, affective side of subjective well-being is often characterized as "affect balance" or "hedonic balance," but measures in this area typically focus on emotions and moods as opposed to physical pleasures or pains.

Subjective well-being is sometimes deemed "hedonic" as opposed to eudaimonic. But this framing is misleading. As we have insisted throughout, life evaluation instruments are fundamentally cognitive, not affective measures, capturing respondents' judgments about how well their lives are going by their standards. A social worker with a stressful job, for instance, might not have a very pleasant time of it but still be satisfied with her life, since she values doing good more than feeling good. Life evaluation measures are valuable, in part, because they are *not* hedonic. They are capable, in the best circumstances, of measuring life satisfaction by whatever standards a person judges their own life. These could be hedonic, eudaimonic, ethical, or theological or admixtures of these. No one can tell from the life satisfaction scores what the standards used are, since that information is not sought or reflected in the measure. Whatever life satisfaction measures, it is not happiness in any ordinary sense. But it seems plausible to think that life satisfaction measures gauge something important about well-being, assuming they are valid.

Are they valid? A variety of factors go into the validation of self-report measures, for instance, evidence that questionnaire items hang together well enough and correlate well with related measures but not too strongly with unrelated items.[3] But for our purposes the most important factor is how closely the instrument tracks the bit of reality we are using it to measure. For example, does an anxiety scale track how anxious a person really is? Maybe not, if people don't answer the questions accurately, or if the items reflect a misunderstanding of what anxiety is. If not, then that's a reason to doubt that it is a valid measure of anxiety. The trick here is that we usually lack an independent handle on the construct we're trying to measure—there is no "true anxiety" register in a person's brain to which survey responses can be compared to see if they're correct. Anxiety is like happiness in this respect; there is no reliable brain state of either, and mature neuroscience does not expect to find one. Both are person-level states. So researchers validate the measure indirectly, seeing whether it correlates appropriately with other sorts of evidence, like friends' reports, physiological indicators, and life conditions that are related to the construct. With a life evaluation measure, for instance, we look to see if it tracks things like quality of relationships, employment status, and so forth, that we would expect to be important to how people see their lives going for them. Likewise for emotional well-being measures: do they correlate appropriately with indicators we believe to be emotionally impactful, like financial stressors or conflict in relationships?

One difficulty is that we don't usually know exactly what correlations would be "appropriate" or plausible: commonsense is all over the map about many questions regarding happiness and subjective well-being, so lots of results are liable to seem plausible. We will return to this point. There is also a chicken-and-egg problem here, since we often want to use the measures we are validating precisely for the purpose of determining how important such things are for happiness and well-being. For instance, life evaluation measures have been employed to argue that income significantly contributes to well-being, if less so than many have supposed.[4] But the fact that income predicts life evaluation has also been taken as evidence for the validity of life evaluation measures in the first place, because we might expect income to predict how favorably people see their lives. There need not be a vicious circularity here, since construct validation is a holistic process and income is just one of many variables that have been used to assess the validity of life evaluation and other subjective well-being measures. And in fact for subjective well-being measures generally, many lines of evidence suggest that they do in fact correlate plausibly, to a considerable extent, with the sorts of things we would expect them to. Among subjective well-being researchers, the more common measures of both life evaluation and emotional well-being are widely taken to be well established as valid, or more cautiously, to enjoy a good degree of validity.[5]

Three cautions are in order. First, it is not always clear what a measure is supposed to be a valid measure *of*. A life satisfaction instrument, for instance, would normally be deemed valid if it accurately measures how satisfied people are with their lives. But such measures are widely used largely because they are thought to be good indicators of happiness or well-being, or some major aspect of happiness or well-being. And arguments for their validity often focus on their utility as indicators of happiness or well-being. This may not turn out to be a problem, but we should note that a valid measure of attitudes of life satisfaction may not tell us much about happiness or well-being if life satisfaction itself is only weakly related to happiness or well-being. Perhaps people really are satisfied with their lives, as the self-reports suggest, but only because they have resigned themselves to a hard lot in this world, as we suggested in the case of African Americans in the previous chapter. We will return to this sort of possibility shortly.

A second caution is related to the first. In the context of well-being studies (although perhaps not in the context of happiness studies) it is arguably less important that we get information simply about this or that mental state than that we find how we (think we) are doing in the things that matter to us. To the extent that a measure is intended to serve as an indicator of well-being, then it needs actually to track well-being (or at least, whatever aspect of well-being it is meant to track). So one aspect of validity, for many instruments, is *normative validity*: the extent to which a measure tracks the values—the matters of importance—that it is purported to track.[6] Of course, the nature of well-being is hotly contested, so there is no simple test for the normative validity of a measure. But there is widespread agreement that certain things do matter—friends, family, a rewarding occupation, pleasure or at least not suffering intensely, being ethical by the lights of one's culture—so that a well-being instrument that was completely insensitive to all such matters would lack normative validity and hence not be a valid well-being measure by any reasonable standard. This could be the case even if the instrument perfectly tracked the mental state it was created to measure, and hence was a valid measure of that state of mind, happiness, say. That state may just not be meaningfully related to well-being.

Third, validation is not an all-or-nothing affair. It is an ongoing process so that validity comes in degrees and is generally relative to certain contexts. In this realm, at least, there is no such thing as a measure we can just deem valid. In most studies, for instance, life evaluation measures are employed in contexts not too different from the ones in which they were validated and seem to yield plausible results that cohere with what other indicators tell us. Likewise for emotional well-being measures. But as we are emphasizing in this book, "most studies" may not examine some very important contexts—perhaps even most of the important contexts. Questionnaires that perform well among Western undergraduates may not yield valid well-being data in other populations, like their less privileged neighbors. And even if a scale passes the usual validation protocols in multiple cultures globally, it is another question whether it allows valid comparisons of well-being *between* those cultures. Perhaps culture A skews negative relative to culture B, or just does so on certain sorts of items. Will that fact have turned up in studies looking just at one of those cultures at a time? We will return to such questions.

DIFFICULTIES: THE CASE OF LIFE EVALUATION MEASURES

The issues come into sharpest relief regarding the most popular sort of subjective well-being measure, global life evaluation surveys that ask people to rate how well their lives are going or how satisfied they are with their lives. Such measures appear to have a decent degree of validity, correlating in plausible ways in many populations with variables such as relationships, material sufficiency and so forth. In the global rankings of the annual *World Happiness Report*, for instance, the happiness metric is the Cantril Ladder, which asks people to rate how well their lives are going from 0 (worst possible life) to 10 (best possible life).[7] On its face this seems a good way to get a sense of how well people's lives are going by their standards, especially when aggregated over large samples so that individual oddities and random errors are liable to wash out. And in fact the scores on this question correlate reasonably well with plausible items like having social support, perceptions of corruption, income, and so forth with worldwide rankings also making some intuitive sense: stable and affluent Nordic countries tend to top the list, while countries at the bottom, like war-torn Afghanistan, do not appear to be misplaced.

An often-noted concern is that different people may answer life evaluation questions differently, especially across different cultures. How might a Yiddish speaker answer such a question? In *Born to Kvetch*, Michael Wex observes, "*Gants gut* [Real good]—if you're not afraid to say it, you have no business speaking Yiddish."[8] Plainly, the norms here are different from those in Utah or Costa Rica, raising the question: does a Yiddish speaker's 6 mean the same as a Costa Rican or Utahn's 6? Perhaps, but it would be surprising if it did. While these are not unfamiliar worries, for the most part the community of well-being researchers seems not to have appreciated the depth of the challenge.[9] Responses to such concerns tend to note such points as how well the measures generally seem to have performed across tens of thousands of studies; that globally, even across diverse cultures, the measures seem to deliver plausible-looking rankings, and that one can find a wide range of responses in the culture of concern. Where a population registers surprisingly high life satisfaction, for instance, it might be noted that they aren't generally Pollyannas, since they give negative answers on some items like financial satisfaction.

The problem is that lots of different correlational profiles are bound to seem plausible, making it challenging to tell good from not-so-good performance. Income could be strongly or weakly related to well-being, and either result would fit with some large strain of commonsense (and in fact there is ongoing controversy about which it is). Many kinds of studies also seem unlikely to be strongly affected by cross-cultural and other differences in reporting. Even when not limited to samples of Western undergraduate students, studies about, say, the relationship between life evaluation and unemployment or marital status may either involve relatively homogenous populations or variables that aren't likely to track relevant cultural differences. And when aggregating worldwide, we may encounter the same "washing-out" effect that occurs at the individual level: just as life evaluation trends across many individuals might be plausible even if any given person's rating is completely untrustworthy, trends across 140-plus countries may be plausible in aggregate even when dubious in particular cases, for example, comparing the United States and Bhutan. To the best of our knowledge, there has been no serious attempt to validate subjective well-being measures between, say, Japan, Bhutan, Israel, the United States, and Paraguay, or between any other countries.

It may seem plain on its face that life evaluation and other subjective well-being measures *must* be valid, since it is plausible that people generally know what they care about and how things are going by their own standards. But, in fact, there is considerable controversy about whether, because of hermeneutic injustice, affective injustice, adaptive preferences, self-deception, performance demands, limitations of introspection and memory and so forth, we are epistemic experts even on our own lives.[10]

But let's suppose for the sake of argument that people are good judges of how their lives are going by their own standards. The problem is misunderstanding what people are actually telling us when answering life evaluation questions. It isn't what most researchers seem to think. Self-reports do not simply convey information about how well people see their lives going for them. They also contain lots of other information besides, for instance about how people prefer to interpret the facts about their lives.

Let's illustrate with a very simple example: suppose a carpenter needs fifteen nails to complete a task properly, though twenty would be ideal. Fewer than fifteen can be managed but with substandard results, though at some point there are too few to be useful at all. She in fact has sixteen nails. Should the carpenter be satisfied with her nail situation? Here there are natural "good" and "satisfactory" points—namely, fifteen nails in both cases, since "good" and "good enough" seem likely to coincide. With sixteen nails, it seems a reasonable answer on a 0–10 scale might be in the positive range, above neutral (5), but below 10 since the situation could be improved. So, somewhere between 6 and 9. It is possible, and indeed seems likely, that the carpenter has no preferences that would decide among these four values: the answer is bound to be somewhat indeterminate or arbitrary *by her own standards*. Anything from a 6 to a 9 would represent her perceived preference satisfaction equally well: it's a coin toss. But there are other factors that can help determine the answer she will give. For instance, perhaps we're talking about P, who lives in a positive-thinking culture (Utah), or alternatively less positive-thinking Yiddish speaker N. P tries to put things in the best reasonable light, and so rates her nail situation a 9, while N, always careful not to be too smug, rates it a 6 ("How close I came to not having enough nails"). This is quite a large difference in response, but in terms of what they care about, each is doing equally well. Their feelings could be equally pleasant also—it's just nails. They differ only in how they think and talk about it: how they make the conversion from perceived preference satisfaction to a judgment about the goodness or satisfactoriness of that state of affairs. They differ as the "glass half-full" person differs from the "glass half-empty" individual.

This is about as simple a case as one could get: two people have clear, quantitative preferences about a situation with only one dimension of evaluation. Yet, while doing equally well by their standards, they rate the situation very differently, and *neither is making a mistake*. Now suppose we want to compare whole *life* evaluations between N's and P's. One could sympathize if the persons making the evaluations felt lost in a sea of apples and oranges. Consider all the incommensurables in a person's life, across the dimensions of work, of leisure, of family life, of friends and community life, of moral or other personal accomplishment, of health, of happiness, and so on. Placing any one subdimension of just one of those dimensions on an 11-point scale is, we've seen, something of a coin toss: to a significant degree, arbitrary. Still more arbitrary is it to take the totality of what one cares about in one's life, add it all up, and assign a number to it. Since any of a range of answers would be consistent with one's experience of life, one is free to let other factors play into one's judgment: for instance, focusing more on the positives for comfort when times are hard, or more on the negatives when extra motivation is needed. Or giving the most culturally acceptable answer one can truthfully get away with: if, for instance, the local expectation is that you're supposed to be positive about your life and you aren't clearly doing badly, why not conclude that you're doing fine? It should be plain that the cultural differences between N's and P's will have abundant scope to play out, yielding substantial differences in their reported evaluations of their lives even if, as best even God could make out, their lives are going equally well relative to what they care about.

In fact, the most popular life evaluation instruments, life satisfaction measures, add a further dimension of arbitrariness to the picture: not just how good one's life is, but whether it is good *enough*—satisfactory. That is, life satisfaction judgments take a somewhat arbitrary summing-up of how one's life is going overall and add to it a further judgment about whether that level of goodness is good enough. One needn't be satisfied with a merely good life (you aspire to a great life), nor dissatisfied with a bad life (it beats being dead). When slum dwellers in Cairo were asked to explain why they were satisfied with their lives in one study, for instance, typical responses suggested that they did not think life was going well, a representative answer being, "One day is good and the other one is bad, whoever accepts the least lives."[11] Since there is no reason to think that many people have firm ideas about where to set the "good-enough" point for their lives, or that they should—unlike undercooked food at a restaurant, you can't send a middling life back—life satisfaction judgments introduce a further element of arbitrariness. Thus it can be natural to feel less satisfied with one's life after attending a high school reunion with highly successful peers, and more satisfied after attending the funeral of one of those peers, not because one's life is better or worse in either case but because we can reasonably adopt different perspectives on our lives depending on the situation. When the judgment is a coin toss, one might as well bias it in whatever way serves one's purposes.

Obviously, there will need to be caution when comparing life evaluations inside and across nation states among socially and culturally dissimilar populations. Perhaps it will be possible to determine a reasonably accurate function allowing us to translate scores from one culture into equivalents in another—to take a crude example, adding 1 point to Japanese life evaluations versus the United States—allowing us to make comparisons.[12] Simply noting that the measures generally correlate well with other variables, even in these two cultures, won't cut it: all that may be true, consistently with N's reporting much lower life evaluation scores than P's even when both groups are doing equally well by their own standards.

The same issue can arise within cultures as well. The surprising findings, in multiple studies, that life evaluation reports did not decline through the COVID-19 pandemic, for instance, do not clearly establish that people's lives were no worse by their standards in 2020 and 2021 than 2018 and 2019. Rather, perhaps the world changed so radically that what counted as "just a part of life," and hence not worth being dissatisfied about, may have changed—thus obscuring a very real decline in quality of life as people recalibrated the scales they used to assess their lives. In the United States, for instance, essentially unchanged life evaluations are juxtaposed against a staggering increase in symptoms of depression and anxiety disorder, from 11 percent to an exceedingly grim 41 percent of the adult population in one study.[13] People will reasonably ask, in light of these data and their own experience, whether they should really believe that the pandemic made life no worse on balance. Certainly the disproportionate negative impact of the pandemic on communities of color both globally and in the United States, along with the devastating global effects along lines of socioeconomic class, could call these findings into question.[14] Such challenges require answers.

EMOTIONAL WELL-BEING MEASURES

While we have focused on life evaluation instruments (how satisfied are you with your life on a scale of 0–10?), the basic issues arise for self-report measures of happiness and well-being generally, and thus for emotional well-being (EWB) measures as well as other subjective well-being measures. For example, differences in positivity biases can affect how likely people in different cultures are to report negative or positive emotions, and cultures notoriously differ widely in norms about the expression of emotions, and even in the types of emotions they experience.[15]

How far such issues complicate emotional well-being measurement compared to life evaluation is not a simple question, and we will not attempt to settle it here. Offhand it is plausible that life evaluation measures benefit from greater uniformity in understanding the question(s) posed, where emotion terms like "stress" or "depression" may take different meanings or have no counterparts at all in some cultures. Different cultures often have different norms (Arlie Hochschild calls these "feeling rules")[16] regarding the expression of specific emotions, for instance, depression and anger, whereas such norms may be less pronounced in the case of life evaluation. On the other hand, affect items tend to be more specific and less cognitively demanding to answer, and hence perhaps more "reality-constrained" than global life evaluation judgments, where arbitrariness allows irrelevant factors to play a greater role in responding. Perhaps emotional well-being scales can reduce cross-cultural difficulties by avoiding items that are most prone to trigger distorting effects from local norms, like anger and shame.[17] (Then again, this is a bad idea if the "distortions" are informative about a particular culture or subculture.) Some scales employ only positive items, for instance, avoiding altogether widespread norms against negative emotion expression.[18]

There has been some concern that emotional well-being measures largely track transient concerns rather than important life conditions, but this is not clearly the case, and it has been argued that emotional well-being actually functions well as a kind of global life evaluation.[19] Several studies have found that emotional well-being items better track "psychosocial prosperity" items like relationships, stressful life conditions, competence, respect, and autonomy than life evaluation measures, which better predict material conditions.[20] The three earlier studies all employed the Gallup World Poll data, and together these findings suggest that emotional well-being measures might give better evidence for overall well-being than life evaluation instruments, at least on the plausible assumption that standard examples of psychological needs being met are more important signs of well-being than matters like material prosperity. The pandemic results noted above may be a poignant case where emotional well-being metrics better depict overall well-being than life evaluations. But that is an unusually stark case, and again the issues are complex. Suffice to say that emotional well-being measures do appear to be sensitive to important life conditions, even if less so to the sorts of social and material circumstances that have traditionally interested policymakers. Perhaps that is not an undesirable result for a policy agenda that takes seriously the call to move "Beyond GDP."

How might we solve this sort of problem—and do so in a way that allows us to take seriously the reasonable concerns among the public about the comparability of self-reports? Various methods will likely be needed, and quantitative approaches can help, but there is probably no way to do this without actually talking to people and letting them speak for themselves. "Why did you rate your life this way?" "Do you think your life is better this year?" "Tell us what's going on in your life these days." Qualitative and ethnographic methods aren't practical for every study, but they are essential to use in select cases so we can develop a better understanding of the quantitative instruments and calibrate them for use across populations with different reporting styles. What are the stories behind the numbers? How do narratives compare between, say, Black and white Americans reporting the same life evaluations? Even a small number of studies can tell us a lot.[21]

It may be challenging to incorporate such information into quantitative assessments, but it would be irresponsible not to gather such readily available data at all, thus ignoring a large part of people's perspectives on their lives and refusing to show people the respect of taking their reasonable concerns seriously. That would be ironic, to put it mildly, in the context of an effort to let people themselves be the authorities about their well-being. When some Han Chinese patients began exhibiting serious side effects with Carbamazepine, an anticonvulsant used to treat bipolar disorder, investigators did not brush off the concerns on the grounds that the drug seemed benign in all the other studies.[22] Just because something is a safe drug (valid measure) in lots of contexts, we cannot assume that it must be safe (valid) in all contexts.

STRESS AND RACE IN ST. LOUIS

The stakes are high, especially as the groups for whom it is most important to get accurate well-being assessment are often among the most vulnerable and marginalized. When that vulnerability results from centuries of intense, pervasive racial discrimination and terror, social, cultural, and political differences in how people think and talk about their lives (and to whom) are bound to arise. Additionally, the experience or threat of discrimination and terror themselves shape how people think and talk about their lives. Regarding life evaluations, it appears that Black Americans report modestly lower scores than white, while Latinos are slightly higher than whites and Asians report most negatively.[23] All of these groups have not just different preferences and fates; they also have different norms and scripts for talking and thinking about their lives. For example, Asians generally have lesser positivity biases than the other groups. Additionally, cultural prohibitions against "airing one's dirty laundry" may affect how much and what kind of detail respondents offer. Can we assume a well-being score of 7 from a Black American means the same as a well-being score of 7 from a white American? Given the foregoing considerations, this assumption may not be justified. At the very least, these considerations provide an opportunity for deeper exploration.

As discussed earlier, Black Americans report high levels of optimism.[24] But perhaps the optimism numbers themselves point to a problem: perhaps they point to pressure to embrace a narrative of resilience, regardless of how one actually feels (see our remarks about resilience in the previous chapter). Or maybe they evince an admirable resilience forged over centuries of oppression, an unwillingness to be bowed by hardship. And maybe that resilience causes Black self-reports to tend toward the P end of the spectrum, whereas whites—even American whites—tend more, relatively speaking, toward the N end of the spectrum, more prone to disappointment and grief when hopes aren't realized, and perhaps more entitled or at least accustomed to a more agreeable lot in life. If that were the case, then perhaps the right translation function would reveal that Black life evaluation scores should be *much* lower than those of whites. If governments are allocating resources partly or wholly on the basis of such self-reports, the ill effects of getting this wrong would be hard to understate. It would be dubious, for instance, to distribute aid away from poor Black citizens toward poor white citizens simply because the latter's relative sense of entitlement makes them more prone to complain about their lot.

There is good reason to suspect that at least some self-report measures are skewed by such effects. In an analysis of Gallup daily surveys for the St. Louis metro region from 2008 to 2015, for instance, we found self-reported stress to be lowest not in affluent white municipalities but in predominantly Black neighborhoods that would appear to be among the most distressed parts of the region from metrics of health status and healthcare access, violent crime, life expectancy, poverty and so forth.[25] (The prompt was "Did you experience a lot of stress yesterday?") A resident from one of those zip codes suggested to one of the authors that the issue isn't a lack of stress, but that it's seen as just a part of life—not something to remark on. Various lines of evidence suggest that stress may in fact be very high among African Americans. For example, high rates of hypertension among Black populations are not readily explained in terms of ethnicity or diet, and the phenomenon occurs mainly in countries with large white populations and an ongoing history of racism such the United States and South Africa as against Nigeria and the Caribbean. In St. Louis, low-birth-weight births run two to three times higher among college-educated Black than white women, and emergency room and hospitalization rates for mental health conditions among African Americans are 64 and 121 percent higher, respectively, than among whites.[26]

While these findings are not conclusive, they lend credence to the idea that Black and white respondents exhibit substantial group differences in how they report on stress. Given the notorious racial problems in this city, to take such results as showing that poor Black St. Louisans lead relatively stress-free lives without closely scrutinizing what might be driving these results could be a grave mistake, especially in policy settings. Again, multimethod studies can help us look under the hood and see what's behind the reports. The reports might yet be eminently useful even in problematic contexts, but we need to understand what they signify and why.

CRUDE UNDERSTANDINGS OF ADAPTIVE PREFERENCE-LIKE PHENOMENA

For the sake of argument, assume there are certain objective values, and objective standards of acceptable achievement regarding those values. Suppose group G reports higher well-being than might be expected given deficiencies in those values, so that Group G's reports suggest higher than actual well-being. For example, Group G reports a well-being score of 7, when all things considered, researchers might have predicted a lower score, perhaps even a *significantly* lower score. What might one make of this result? In what remains, we consider a few possibilities. To be sure, these possibilities are not exhaustive; nor are they mutually exclusive. However, they can provide examples of much-needed nuance in order to make sense of adaptive preferences.

1. *Judicious positivity.* Skewing positive where it is helpful and the costs/risks are low (e.g. optimism) might lift spirits, motivate effort, or dampen disappointment. Perhaps people report

INTERPRETING SELF-REPORTS OF WELL-BEING ◌◌ 181

satisfaction with objectively unacceptable circumstances as a reasonable self-regulation device.

2. *Sincere value divergence* (divergence not due to distrust of interviewer, desirable responding, etc.). Our attitudes are not inert data readouts that simply track the facts. People reasonably disagree about the best attitudes and courses of action to play the cards they have been dealt in life. Individuals (and even groups of people) may choose to engage life on terms that others may not understand, e.g., fostering virtues of appreciation and gratitude even if fully aware of the negative aspects of life.

3. *Judicious negativity.* Skewing negative (e.g., lowering expectations) where it is helpful and costs/risks are low might enable one to prepare for the worst even as they hope for the best.

4. *Low standards.* Accepting less of what is valuable than should be accepted can also moderate disappointment. We exercise caution when considering this possibility, as it could be used to justify distributing fewer resources to those who are already vulnerable and/or marginalized. In other words, if one perceives a group as having lower standards and expectations than others, then one might think that it does less harm to deprive them of resources than it would to deprive another group of resources.

5. *Sour grapes.* Devaluing something that one would otherwise value because it cannot be attained. Sour grapes can lead one to give up on efforts to improve one's lot in life, whether the improvements could be a result of individual, communal, or social/political efforts.

6. *Pollyannas* exhibit excessively positive beliefs about one's situation. This is distinct from judicious positivity in that Pollyannas exhibit a degree of positivity that may exceed the cost of such positivity.

Recognizing the variety of psychosocial and cultural factors that could influence self-reported well-being is an especially urgent matter, especially when thinking about disadvantaged and other vulnerable groups. Positive-responders in difficult circumstances are often characterized in disparaging terms as Pollyannas or broken spirits who gratefully accept what's doled out to them and take comfort in "small mercies," but perhaps a group reports surprisingly high subjective well-being out of stoic fortitude and self-discipline. Or perhaps they have high standards and high expectations but still tend toward "glass half full" answers for a complex mix of reasons of gratitude, faith, a habit of confronting hardship with humor, or a simple aversion to complaining. In other words, a positive attitude does not necessarily signify a lack of problems or a lack of awareness about the gravity of those problems.

Such mechanisms illustrate just a tiny slice of the many factors that can influence the transformation from lived experience to reported well-being. When people—especially the most vulnerable among us—complain that the conclusions we've drawn from subjective well-being data don't match up with their experience, we must take seriously the possibility that we've misinterpreted the results. Let's talk to people and find out if the stories behind the numbers are or aren't what we thought. Even if researchers were in consensus that there isn't a problem, the issue isn't purely scientific: people deserve a voice in how their lives and well-being are represented in the public forum, and to be given reason to believe that their interests have been fairly represented.

IV

CONCLUSIONS

10

RECOMMENDATIONS FOR POLICY USE OF HAPPINESS METRICS

It is time to sum up. There are theoretical lessons and practical consequences for the conduct of happiness and well-being science and its policy arms.

- There is vast intercultural and intracultural variation in standards and conceptions of happiness and well-being.
- All the standards and ideals, both scientific and philosophical, as well as those internal to specific cultures, traditions, and subcultures are normative, involving views about what matters, variation about which emotions are prized, at what intensity, with what expressions, about what emotional balance consists in, about whether happiness is an important thing or not, and if so, what kind is important, what a good life consists in, and so on.
- Most indexes and measures of well-being and happiness, and ill-being and unhappiness, are based on snapshots of how well people are faring, or judge they are faring, according to some standard or other, and should not be mistaken as revealing anything very fine grained or deep about how people in fact feel or are actually faring.
- Metrics, measures, psychological studies, and ethnographies can provide starting points for explanation and policy

consideration. We should not think any social scientific surmise captures the way life is or is going at the level of grain, at the level of complexity that life is lived.

- There is principled disagreement among theorists who work on happiness and well-being (and unhappiness and ill-being) about what happiness and well-being are or consist in. And there is no conception of either happiness or well-being that enjoys a consensus among specialists in this area. For researchers to assume a particular theory of happiness or well-being without acknowledging that they are taking a stand on contested matters is not best practice, especially when addressing nonexperts who aren't aware of the controversies and may thus be misled about what the evidence shows. Some theorists working in this area certainly endorse a life satisfaction theory of happiness, for example, but it does not appear to be a majority view among either the experts or the public.[1] Neither a life satisfaction view of happiness nor any other, such as an emotional state theory, can simply be assumed as if alternative views were not worth taking seriously. The same situation holds for views on well-being. Some think well-being is independent of goodness, others think moral goodness is a necessary condition of a life well-lived. Some think well-being is independent of discovery and development of one's talents, others that well-being is primarily a matter of discovering and developing one's potential excellences.

- Work in philosophy of language and logic, linguistics, and philosophy and psychology of the emotions definitively shows that emotion terms are not semantically equivalent across even the best translation manuals.[2] This means that there is guaranteed to be a certain incomparability across even the best measures that try to control for meaning across linguistic communities. To make the point in stark terms: The best translations of emotion terms from say, English, of *fear, anger, happiness*, etc. or that translate the question "how *satisfied* are you" to any other language are guaranteed not to preserve or secure synonymy between the languages. Why? Because it is independently known that such emotion, affect, evaluative terms cannot be translated across languages without semantic loss or gain.

- The abundant evidence of adaptation, under- and overestimation, and different and highly variable performance expectations on responses to self-revealing questions about life satisfaction, happiness, positive or negative emotions, and emotional well-being for different sexes, genders, ethnic groups or depending on particular social roles, statuses, and religions, is not elided or smoothed by large data sets. It is covered up. And this warrants skepticism about aggregated results for any population that we antecedently know is comprised of sub-populations that differ along such dimensions.
- There is too much inequality, discrimination, and injustice inside many nation-states and between nation-states to use happiness averages in these snap shots for policy making. Average income and average happiness might show a people to be rich and happy, when many subgroups are poor and unhappy.
- There are serious conceptual problems with averaging and ranking based on any single happiness metrics. Insofar as any kind of happiness and well-being matters, it is the distribution that matters.
- Measures of subjective well-being intended to be relevant to or to guide public policy is fully defensible only when it satisfies two conditions: (1) it presumes a deep connection between well-being and social justice and (2) it recognizes that we cannot promote well-being unless the information we gather allows us to get "behind" responses that reflect distorting effects of hermeneutical injustice and affective injustice. If this is not done

and controlled for, we ought to be agnostic about what the well-being or happiness data mean or indicate.

- Policy ought, first and foremost, to be focused on gaining information about the pre-conditions, causes, and locations of ill-being and working to eliminate it. We need fine grained data and thick descriptions that depict accurately how worst-off groups are faring, and why. It would be empirically and ethically best if scientists and public policy researchers did not in any way suggest that they have measured *overall* happiness or the well-being of a people by any snapshot or set of snapshots using one or a few common tools or indicators.
- We should be especially wary of cross-cultural comparisons. We know for certain that cultures vary in terms of their substantive ideals for a good life, well-being, and happiness. Many metrics abstract away from particularities (by, for example, asking that *whatever* your view of the good life is, how satisfied are you living *that* life?). This kind of bracketing, abstraction and indifference to the particularities of the background ethno-theory (more like ethno-theories) of well-being and happiness, might allow us to get a clear, simple and informative snapshot, a single numerical score that expresses how well an individual or nation state thinks it is doing according to its own standards of happiness or well-being whatever those are. By explicitly abstracting away from distinctive, identity constitutive local views on well-being and happiness, it avoids the messy business of evaluating very different, possibly incommensurable forms of life.[3] This can be considered a good, practically wise thing, because it simplifies measurement. Or it can be considered a bad thing because it is deliberately superficial and fails to even try to gather the data that many scientific and philosophical theories think is required to assess accurately well-being and happiness (including according to many normative theories

questions about the ethics of happiness, whether what a people are happy about *is* valuable). More sensitivity to cultural and subcultural diversity would have a salutary effect of how happiness and well-being studies are received. It will lead to the recognition that there is no basis for comparing (and ranking) nation states according to any international standard of what happiness and well-being are or consist in. That said, there are widely shared standards, an overlapping consensus, of what ill-being and suffering consist in. This is where policy should be focused for the foreseeable future.

• Insofar as there is any cross-cultural consensus across philosophical and religious traditions about what matters, about the order of goods, it is a consensus that being morally decent is more important than being happy or satisfied with one's life. Insofar, as there is any cross-cultural consensus across political philosophies, it is that respect for human dignity, equality, and justice and meeting basic human needs are the primary duties of a good society. Meeting these conditions enhances well-being. Does it also make people more happy, more satisfied with their lives? The record so far is ambiguous. Many people say they are happy when they live in very unjust societies (both "fat cat" exploiters and billionaires and oppressed people); and some people become very unhappy when their societies make egalitarian and progressive social policy (think opposition to universal medical care, progressive tax policy). Tracking justice is significantly more important than tracking how people feel.

11

UNIVERSAL RIGHTS, SUSTAINABLE DEVELOPMENT, AND HAPPINESS

Two out of Three Ain't Bad

Our aim is this book has been to honestly assess the happiness agenda, a highly visible segment of happiness philosophy and science that claims that happiness is the *summum bonum* and that happiness ought to be the aim of government and international policy.

We have insisted that happiness is a conditional good. Whether it is good all things considered depends on its causes, its character, and its content. We have focused on intra- and intercultural disagreements about the nature of happiness and its status in the order of goods. And we have discussed some problems with the use of conflicting indicators of happiness, each with limitations of its own, and that point to different success stories depending on the conception of happiness deployed and measured.

We haven't taken a position on how valuable happiness, in any of its guises, is in the order of goods. But we have taken a position that it does not have the status of the first thing in a "first things first" policy regime. Rights, justice, eradicating poverty, and promoting sustainable development come first. If these things are in place, then maybe—assuming the weather within one's soul cooperates—one might be happy and satisfied in ways that embed moral decency, meaning, and the development of excellences.

FIRST THINGS FIRST: JUSTICE, EQUALITY, DIGNITY

Universal rights, recognition of human dignity and equality, the eradication of poverty, and sustainable development are goals about which there is substantive international agreement. Two United Nations agreements speak specifically to them: the UN Declaration of Universal Human Rights of 1948 and the seventeen Sustainable Development Goals (SDGs) of 2015.[1] Universal rights and sustainable development are widely thought to be basic conditions for human well-being. Neither universal rights nor sustainable development alone or taken together is guaranteed to produce happiness.

Still some think that universal rights and sustainable development are necessary conditions for happiness. But this is not true if one is talking about ordinary happiness as measured by life satisfaction or positive/negative emotions. First, such measures are indifferent to whether the happiness is entirely self-centered or arises in conditions where rights are respected, or among people who are benevolent and respect rights, or in situations where sustainable development is an end.

Second, happiness research itself reveals that happiness, conceived as life satisfaction, can exist in circumstances where rights are not respected. Countries like Saudi Arabia, the United Arab Emirates, and Bahrain have high life satisfaction but weak human rights records. The same is true of emotional happiness, which is sometimes high in countries that have not eradicated poverty or are not on the road to satisfying the SDGs.

A community or a country, even the international community, could stipulate that the kinds of happiness it deems worthwhile—"true happiness," human flourishing, *eudaimonia*—and thus worth policy energy must exist in political circumstances that respect universal rights and that aim at gender, racial, ethnic, and climate justice, that promote sustainable development and the eradication of poverty and other forms of suffering and ill-being. Such a normative conception of happiness would be like a conception of healthy food, which stipulates that the most otherwise superhealthy food overall is just not healthy if it contains even a little lead or a small amount of known carcinogens.

This is not a stipulation that fans of the happiness agenda have made. But it might be smart. It would make it clear that the only kinds of happiness worthy of policy attention are not just feeling happy or being satisfied with one's life. That is, the good is not simply judging that people think or are of the opinion that they are faring well or are feeling happy, but that they are faring well or are happy because they are living good human lives according to norms and standards that have been discovered and accepted as the right ones over world historical time. And we should allow the possibility that these norms, values, and standards have developed in tradition specific, path-dependent ways.

But if happiness theorists went in this direction, they would not even try to evaluate happiness so conceived in countries that do not respect all human rights and that are not committed to the eradication of poverty and to sustainable development because people in those countries can't really be happy in the stipulated normative sense. This will not appeal to scientists who rightly think that most conceptions of ordinary happiness are worth tracking, although perhaps not for policy purposes, because ordinary happiness is an interesting *prima facie* phenomenon in its own right, even if it doesn't have reliable causal or constitutive relations with rights and sustainable development. There are happy narcissists and selfish creeps and unhappy saints; there are unhappy billionaires and happy peasants. As much as one might hope that karma would align happiness with decency and make a just society a necessary condition of quotidian happiness, it doesn't.

In closing, it's worth looking more closely at the bases of the agreements reached in the two UN resolutions on rights and sustainable development, alongside the rationale for one that was passed in 2011 on happiness. The Universal Declaration of Human Rights begins its "Preamble" this way: "Whereas recognition of the inherent dignity and of the equal and inalienable rights of all members of the human family is the foundation of freedom, justice, and peace in the world." The Preamble culminates four short paragraphs later in a proclamation: "The General Assembly proclaims this Universal Declaration of Human Rights as a common standard of achievement for all peoples and all nations." Then the enumeration of the thirty rights follows.

Article 1 reiterates, "All humans are born free and equal in dignity and rights. They are endowed with reason and conscience and should act towards each other in a spirit of brotherhood" and, as we would now say, of sisterhood.[2]

The thirty human rights protect the freedom, dignity, and equality of all human beings. Only Article 1—All human beings should act towards each other in a spirit of brotherhood," and Article 29—"Everyone has duties to the community in which alone the free and full development of his personality is possible" mention what one ought to do. We should act in a spirit of brotherhood and sisterhood, and we have special, unspecified, duties to our own community.[3]

Article 25 states that there is a universal human right not to be poor, to have health care and protection from unemployment, and so on: "Everyone has the right to a standard of living adequate for the health and well-being of himself and of his family, including food, clothing, housing and medical care and necessary social services, and the right to security in the event of unemployment, sickness, disability, widowhood, old age or other lack of livelihood in circumstances beyond his control."[14]

There is no right to be happy, no right to happiness. Article 25 is not it. It is a right to be free of ill-being and preventable suffering. Nor are the articles devoted to rights to education and various civil and political freedoms happiness rights in disguise. They are rights to develop capabilities, to make free choices, and to exercise one's reason in ways that allow one to live a good life.

The seventeen Sustainable Development Goals adopted unanimously by the UN in 2015 are updates of the Millennium Development Goals (MDGs) of 2000. This "Preamble" reads:

> This Agenda is a plan of action for people, planet and prosperity. It also seeks to strengthen universal peace in larger freedom. We recognize that eradicating poverty in all its forms and dimensions, including extreme poverty, is the greatest global challenge and an indispensable requirement for sustainable development. All countries and all stakeholders, acting in collaborative partnership, will implement this plan. We are resolved to free the human race from the tyranny of poverty and want and to heal and secure our planet. We are determined to take the bold and transformative steps which are urgently needed to shift the world onto a sustainable and resilient path. As we embark on this collective journey, we pledge that no one will be left behind. The 17 Sustainable Development Goals and 169 targets which we are announcing today demonstrate the scale and ambition of this new universal Agenda.

They seek to build on the Millennium Development Goals and complete what these did not achieve. They seek to realize the human rights of all and to achieve gender equality and the empowerment of all women and girls. They are integrated and indivisible and balance the three dimensions of sustainable development: the economic, social and environmental.[5]

The Universal Declaration of Human Rights and the Sustainable Development Goals reflect a consensus about values and norms. What grounds or justifies the thirty universal rights and the seventeen SDGs? The answer provided in both texts is that the inherent dignity and equality of persons grounds the universal rights, and that these same universal rights ground the SDGs. The SDGs "seek to realize the human rights of all."[6] The right to be relieved of ill-being, poverty, suffering, and precarity in Article 25 of UDHR reappears as the most urgent unmet goal, the eradication of the tyranny of poverty in the SDGs.

These two international agreements have been signed by all 193 members of the United Nations (the UDHR over the years since it was adopted by majority vote) and the SDGs at the time they were adopted unanimously in 2015 (to be achieved by 2030). The UDHR and the SDGs are admirable accomplishments. Furthermore, these agreements have yielded numerous methods for assessing and tracking how well different nation-states do on respecting human rights and where different nation states are in the process of achieving various benchmarks (169) for the SDGs.

HAPPINESS

There is a third UN agreement that pertains directly to happiness and well-being. On July 19, 2011, the United Nations'

General Assembly unanimously passed resolution 65/309, entitled "Happiness: Towards a Holistic Approach to Development."[7] Here is the resolution in its entirety:

The General Assembly,

Bearing in mind the purposes and principles of the United Nations, as set forth in the Charter of the United Nations, which include the promotion of the economic advancement and social progress of all peoples,

Conscious that the pursuit of happiness is a fundamental human goal, Cognizant that happiness as a universal goal and aspiration embodies the spirit of the Millennium Development Goals,

Recognizing that the gross domestic product indicator by nature was not designed to and does not adequately reflect the happiness and well-being of people in a country,

Conscious that unsustainable patterns of production and consumption can impede sustainable development, and recognizing the need for a more inclusive, equitable and balanced approach to economic growth that promotes sustainable development, poverty eradication, happiness and well-being of all peoples,

Acknowledging the need to promote sustainable development and achieve the Millennium Development Goals,

1. Invites Member States to pursue the elaboration of additional measures that better capture the importance of the pursuit of happiness and well-being in development with a view to guiding their public policies;

2. Invites those Member States that have taken initiatives to develop new indicators, and other initiatives, to share information thereon with the Secretary-General as a contribution to the United Nations development agenda, including the Millennium Development Goals;

3. Welcomes the offer of Bhutan to convene during the sixty-sixth session of the General Assembly a panel discussion on the theme of happiness and well-being;

4. Invites the Secretary-General to seek the views of Member States and relevant regional and international organizations on the pursuit of happiness and well-being and to communicate such views to the General Assembly at its sixty-seventh session for further consideration.[8]

The happiness resolution differs from the Universal Declaration of Human Rights of 1948 and the Sustainable Development Goals of 2015 in several ways. First, the UDHR and the SDGs involved deliberation over many years. The happiness resolution was an inspired and inspiring public relations exercise that attempted to express some common or folk truths about happiness without similar sustained inquiry and to draw some conceptual connections among the struggles to eradicate poverty and other forms of ill-being, human rights, sustainable development, and happiness, the last of which is not mentioned or discussed in the other two documents. Second, the happiness resolution was motivated especially by the perfect coincidence of Bhutan's widely discussed commitment to gross national happiness over gross national product, with a contemporaneous groundswell among economists to move away from single-minded emphasis on GDP. In fact, the resolution says this: "Recognizing that the gross domestic product indicator by nature was not designed to and does not adequately reflect the happiness and well-being of people in a country."[9] Third, the resolution takes the opportunity to suggest a unified justification for the UDHR and the SDGs (by way of linking happiness to the MDGs, the predecessor of the SDGs), which it had previously justified as advancing human rights, eradicating poverty, and securing and healing the planet.

This all makes a certain amount of rhetorical sense, and it works inspirationally. But upon close examination it doesn't work logically, empirically, or philosophically. One reason is that this assertion: "[Cognizant that] happiness as a universal goal and aspiration embodies the spirit of the Millennium Development Goals" doesn't quite pass inspection.[10] First, as we have emphasized throughout, what happiness is or what the word "happiness" even means is contested. Second, the claim about happiness "embodying the spirit" of sustainable development is vague. Third, a universal goal better be determinant if it really is so, but the concept of happiness lacks determinacy; it is an exemplar of a polysemous concept, albeit an almost universally positive one; in fact, the positivity of the word is one reason it so easily passes by without the slightest inspection. Fourth, how valuable happiness is, on every conception, comes into dispute. It is rare across philosophical traditions, and across cultures for happiness to be considered the *summum bonum*. Fifth, the Millennium Development Goals of 2000, like their successor, the Sustainable Development Goals of 2015, are not grounded, and need not to be grounded, in the universal quest for happiness. Sustainable development and human rights are right and good. But they are not right and good because they produce happiness. Sometimes they do; sometimes they don't.

The resolution nonetheless is inspiring, and it contains much wisdom. First, before it claims that happiness is a "universal goal and aspiration" it states that "the pursuit of happiness is a fundamental human goal."[11] This is plausible. The indefinite article is correct. Happiness is a fundamental human goal, not the fundamental human goal, so long as we grant that the kind of happiness, well-being, or good life that humans aim at is highly variable, culture-, subculture-, and tradition-specific.

Second, the happiness resolution does not endorse "the happiness agenda," which says that happiness is the *summum bonum* and that advancing happiness should be the aim of public policy. It endorses something much weaker and thus more plausible: member states are invited to develop better measures and indicators of happiness and well-being "with a view to guiding *their* public policies."[12] The invitation is not to develop some cross-cultural metrics or indicators, although it does not preclude doing so. What is clear is that the development of better theories and measures and sharing them is so that member states can use it to "guide *their* public policies." There is no suggestion that the aim is to develop universal standards as, for example, the international community succeeded in doing with the thirty universal rights and seventeen sustainable development goals.

This opens space for a concluding thought, perhaps a fantasy. Conceptions of happiness and well-being are normative through and through. There are contestations inside cultures and communities, as well as across cultures and nation-states, about what makes for a good life and what importance, if any, feeling happy or being happy or satisfied contributes to such a life. Many conceptions of well-being require goodness; some don't. Among those that require goodness, there are variations in the ethical conceptions in terms of virtues and values that are most prized, and in terms of how demanding the ethical conception is. Insofar as the UN happiness resolution encourages scientists to develop quick and minimalist measures of happiness, we think those scientists miss an opportunity.

Conceptions of happiness, well-being, human excellence, and flourishing are thick, complex, and richly textured. Standard happiness and well-being metrics are thin, simple, and spare. Some people in some cultures are encouraged to be articulate about what they value and why, including which mental states they prefer. Such people can sometimes provide the relevant thick descriptions. But often norms and conceptions of what kind of happiness one pursues, if any, and its relation to the kinds of happiness that are valuable are left in the shadows of the unarticulated, taken-for-granted background of everyday life.

Global communication, massive amounts of forced and unforced immigration, travel, education, and the increasing number of people who live in multicultures make this an opportune time to take advantage of the extraordinary variety of conceptions and contestations about true happiness, well-being, and flourishing and to reflectively explore some of the historical and contemporary possibility space for living good human lives. Considering what is of value and why is a noble way of using some uniquely human capacities of empathy, imagination, intellect, and reflection. If one's conception of happiness, well-being, flourishing, and the good life pass reflective inspection, then one may well feel more secure in the conviction that all the work to live well is worth it. Engaging in this sort of reflection will require psychologically, sociologically, and anthropologically rich descriptions of what we ourselves are doing and why, as well as what others are doing and why. Such capacities for attentive perception of the other; for thick description of one's own and others' values, practices, and ends; and for critical reflection on the quality of our aims and values can be lost. Humans are not only capable of reflective agency, but we are also great imitators, capable of blowing whichever way the prevailing social winds blow. There is no guarantee that a superficial and unworthy conception of happiness won't win the day. Some think it already has won the day in some precincts.

One small intervention might be this. Instead of—or in addition to—a worldwide movement to develop metrics for countries to use for advancing happiness in their public policies, let's think of it this way: Teach the children well. In particular, encourage children and teenagers to begin the lifelong practices of reflecting on what makes for a good human life and defending their value commitments and goals. Whether, and if so how, happiness figures in a good life will be one of many matters that will need to be thought through, constantly revisited and reassessed. Wait a few generations and see what people raised in these sorts of reflective cultures have to say about happiness and its worth. In the meantime, there is all the work that needs to be done to protect the rights, dignity, and equality of all human beings, to eradicate poverty, to assure good education, good health care, including mental health care, to rid ourselves of the scourges of deaths of despair, epidemics of addiction, poor mental health among young people, of sexism, racism, and all variety of discrimination and ethnic hatreds, and to achieve sustainable development and prevent ecological disaster. Doing this will make the world better, much better. It will take an enormous amount of time and work. Remember the words of Martin Luther King Jr., "the moral arc of the universe is long, but it bends towards justice."[13] If happiness is eventually judged really important or the next right thing to bring us somewhere much further down that long arc, there will be plenty of opportunity to advance it after the demands of justice and equality have been satisfied.

V

RESPONSES BY FOUR CRITICS

12

ON ERSATZ HAPPINESS

JENNIFER A. FREY

I believe (and in some of my scholarly and popular essays I have argued) that the constitutive aim, goal, or purpose of human life is happiness. It is the source and summit of our practical lives. This places me in a long and venerable tradition that treats happiness as the highest good to which we might aspire, a tradition that stretches back to Plato and Aristotle, the great pagan philosophers, but also includes the great medieval scholastic theologian Saint Thomas Aquinas and the great Jewish philosopher Moses Maimonides. It is also a view held by some of the most influential moral theorists of the past fifty years, women such as Elizabeth Anscombe and Philippa Foot. According to this longstanding tradition, we cannot cease to want to be happy any more than we can cease to be human beings. Happiness defines who and what we are because it structures our practical reasoning and explains why we are subject to the demands of virtues like justice, fortitude, temperance, and wisdom.

Given that I align myself with this philosophical and theological tradition, one might suppose that I would be thrilled with the "happiness agenda" that is the target of this book. Yet I find myself fundamentally at odds with it, for at least three reasons.

First, the happiness it offers us is cheap, shallow, and unworthy of human aspiration, precisely because it is detached from the robust demands of virtue (or *any* objective standards for thinking seriously about flourishing human lives and societies). Second, its central metaphysical conception of happiness as a mental state or collection of mental states is deeply implausible. And third, it is far too individualistic to be a useful tool for addressing the needs of civil society.

On the first point, the problem is largely semantic. "Happiness" is a word that, especially in the English language, has become shopworn and coarsened. Terry Eagleton once quipped that happiness is "a feeble, holiday-camp sort of word, evocative of manic grins and cavorting around in a multicolored jacket."[1] Even in the philosophical literature on happiness, it is typically presented as some form of general good cheer. Happiness is attained, we are told, when a person has attained more positive mental affect on balance, or achieves more pleasure than pain, or judges their lives to be satisfactory on the whole. It should be plain that if this is all that happiness amounts to, serious people will find it unworthy of their time and attention.

Too many philosophers have followed the happiness agenda by conceding a conception of happiness that is entirely *subjective*—that is, subject to no robust, self-transcendent norms or measures that are tethered to the reality of the way things are or should be in flourishing human communities. Happiness is operationalized and measured by social scientists entirely in terms of an individual's first-person experiences and the subjective quality of those experiences, since these are conveyed through self-reports. This casts far too narrow a focus on the individual person and individual mental states, and it opens up a problematic dualism between the perspective of the individual and objective facts about human nature and human goodness.

After all, if all that matters is the way individuals feel (even in the aggregate), then rather than do the hard, political work of making such goods more accessible to all members of any given society, we may prefer to invest in technologies that manipulate people's mental states so that they *feel* good as individuals, regardless of whether this feeling tracks the reality of their lives or the nature of their society. This was the strategy of the happiness-obsessed governors of Aldous Huxley's *Brave New World*, who worked tirelessly to ensure that its citizens were "happy" in the subjectivist sense. How was this accomplished? By keeping everyone busy and distracted from the unpleasant realities of their society through participation in mindless, pleasure-seeking activities alongside a steady diet of psychotropic drugs. Of course, we now have virtual reality systems to keep people "happy" in the subjectivist sense and drugs Huxley could only imagine, which raises the question: why not just unplug from the real world altogether and live one's best fantasy life? If we can create happy illusions from a subjectivist perspective, that should more than suffice.

The problem is that happiness, in the subjectivist sense, isn't meaningfully tied to the possession of genuine human goods, like loving friendships, the discovery of new knowledge, or the appreciation of beauty. In fact, this may be preferable to the messiness and unpredictability of a real human life, where we cannot control outcomes. In real life, our loves might be unrequited or painfully demanding, our intellectual labors frustrated, and our deepest longings unfulfilled. Why bother with it at all?

Now, it is quite plain that if we think of happiness in any of the subjectivist senses on offer, there is no chance it is our highest good or the ultimate, defining end of an excellent or flourishing human life. To see this, we might ask ourselves whether we would raise our children to prioritize their own personal pleasures, to focus on feeling self-satisfied, or to strive for positive mental affect, come what may in life? Most parents think, rightfully, that their children should *feel* good only to the extent that *they are good and truly living well*. And so most parents raise their children to seek what they believe is really good in human life and try to instill in them the personal qualities necessary to attain such goods.

Furthermore, the people we tend to *admire* the most, whose qualities we tend to want to instill in others, are those who have fought and sacrificed for our highest ideals, those whom we are inclined to call *noble* or *virtuous* or *wise*: Martin Luther King Jr., Nelson Mandela, Saint Damien of Molokai, Mother Theresa, Abraham Lincoln, Michelangelo, or Johann Sebastian Bach. These are exemplars we put forward to young people because we believe that their ways of living and being are *worthy* of imitation. We admire these people because, in their time and place and according to their means and talents, they rose to the demands of virtue in order to preserve what is good, true, and beautiful, and not simply for themselves but for the societies they lived in. In short, we admire them because we think they were people of good character who lived exceptional lives.

Classical philosophy recognizes that our thought about happiness cannot be separated from our reflection on how we should aspire to live and what sort of human person we most wish to be. When Aristotle speaks of *eudaimonia* (often translated as happiness or fulfillment or flourishing) as the highest good, he recognizes that he is speaking about what it looks like to realize objective human excellence. Metaphysically speaking, happiness is an activity, not a state, and it has to do with the actualization of human potentiality into a characteristic shape or form. Happiness can never be attained through external manipulation, but only through internal transformation—that is, through the cultivation and expression of virtues, which are those stable dispositions of thought, action, and feeling that enable us to attain characteristically human forms of excellence. When Aristotle says that everyone wants to be happy, what he means is that like all living creatures, we seek our own condition of objective flourishing, given the kind of things we are.

In short, Aristotle recognizes that there is no way to think about happiness without thinking about human nature and human goodness generally, and he famously proclaims that man is a political animal whose flourishing happens in society with others. For that reason, happiness is never merely the possession of a single individual; after all, how could an individual be happy if his social conditions militate against it? In the Aristotelian tradition, happiness is a common good that is shared with others, not a private good or merely individual good. A common good, unlike a private good, is not competitive, which means that one person's pursuit of the good does not detract from another's pursuit of it. But even more fundamentally, a common good is participated in and enjoyed with others. I cannot really be happy, for Aristotle, at the expense of others, nor can I flourish outside the bonds and obligations of civil society. Like his teacher, Plato, Aristotle sees that happiness outside of the obligations of justice is no happiness at all.

And this brings us back around to virtue. If happiness is found in communion with other persons (for Aristotle, happiness is inseparable from various forms of loving communion he calls friendships), then we need the dispositions of thought, feeling, and action that make us good participants in relationships with others, the goods of which are greater than the goods that only redound to our individual selves. Virtue, then, orients us to the common good, and this is what our individual good consists in—being an excellent participant in the common good of the various societies that give shape to human lives.

Although I cannot argue the case adequately here, I think this tracks our practical reflection about our own happiness. When I stop to consider what makes me happy in the sense of being deeply fulfilled, I inevitably think of myself as wife, mother, daughter, sister, friend, colleague, parishioner, citizen, and perhaps even a member of the party of humankind, to borrow a famous phrase from David Hume. I am not happy outside of the forms of social communion that shape my life. But these social relationships require me to view my happiness as part of a common good that I participate in with others. Happiness in the deep sense necessarily involves a self-transcendent perspective in which I view my own life and actions in relation to a greater social whole. My happiness cannot be separated from the social world in which I operate.

For the tradition I locate myself in, there is no chance of being happy in the deep sense without becoming a certain kind of person who stands ready to act, feel, and think according to certain characteristic patterns. A conception of happiness divorced from the demands of virtue is an ersatz happiness that is not worthy of our admiration or political attention. There is no way to be virtuous except to become virtuous through a certain kind of habituation or training: just as you need to train your muscles to excel at sports or a musical instrument, so you need to train your mind and heart in order to excel at human life on the whole. Virtues enable us to experience authentic human happiness; they allow us to possess what is true, good, and beautiful from a human perspective.

We should not unthinkingly accept a "scientific" account of happiness that is shallow, selfish, and untethered from the demands of virtue and what is most excellent in human life. Philosophical and theological wisdom traditions give us a vision of happiness on which a person will be most satisfied or fulfilled with her life insofar as she is conformed to what is really and truly good for human communities. Social scientists would do well to work with philosophers, theologians, and literary critics to come up with a concept of happiness that is more substantive and serious. In the meantime, we should hit the pause on the happiness agenda, because the prospects that it will bring about true happiness are very dim indeed. If nations want to improve the lives of their citizens, they can start by working to create a more just social world, since there is no real human happiness apart from its concrete demands.

13

WHY THE ANALYSIS AND ASSESSMENT OF HAPPINESS MATTERS

HAZEL ROSE MARKUS

I am under the sun in a lounge chair at a beautiful spa. I have an hour before my massage, a birthday gift from a good friend. The weather could not be more perfect. The sky is an intense northern California blue framed on both sides by dark green cypresses. On my lap is a draft of *Against Happiness*. Not the best read for the situation, it seems. At this moment I am happy, even though the due date for this comment was imminent. Yet before I begin to read, other thoughts crowd my sunlit mind. My mood shifts. I can be happy in this privileged space, but I can't possibly *be* well. Less than two weeks earlier the Supreme Court had denied American women a right previously guaranteed for fifty years by the U.S. constitution. The well-being of millions had taken a hit. What am I doing luxuriating in a spa?

Dilemmas of happiness, life satisfaction, and well-being form the skeleton of *Against Happiness*. The book is a treat. With incisive examples and lively prose it creates and sustains a deep and wide-ranging multidisciplinary conversation. The book is a cautionary tale for both beginners and seasoned experts, and for anyone who has embarked on the well-intentioned and seemingly practical thought experiment of understanding happiness and well-being. The book's diverse team of authors, spanning philosophy, neuroscience, cultural psychology, sociology, religion, and ethics, detail the many challenges of defining happiness and the potential folly of designing policies to promote it.

Noting the problem of many types of happiness, they write: "Pleasant experiences feel good. That's analytical. But what makes one happy depends on personal history, context, and culture." I think good, I'm in. This book on happiness recognizes the challenge of reconciling my short-lived sun-kissed emotional state with my growing rage perpetrated by the Supreme Court. I am happy, but given my history, context, and culture, I can't really be happy. In the chapter "Recommendations for Policy Use of Happiness Metrics," the authors go further with a claim that "all the standards and ideals, both scientific and philosophical, as well as those internal to specific cultures, traditions, and subcultures, are normative, involving views about what matters, variation about which emotions are prized, at what intensity, with what expressions, about what emotional balance consists in, about whether happiness is an important thing or not, and if so, what kind is important, what a good life consists in, and so on." This is right, I believe. The statement makes me happy. My only problem is with the book's title: *Against Happiness*. I am not against happiness; I am all for it.

As a social psychologist and cultural scientist, I believe that happiness—as a placeholder term for good feelings or some general sense of being well as opposed to bad feelings or being ill *is* likely one of the answers to well-being. I make this claim in full agreement with the authors that the *World Happiness Report*'s view of happiness is too narrow and that philosophers and social scientists are still far from a consensus on shared standards of happiness and well-being. Later the authors write, "We haven't taken a position on how valuable happiness is. . . . But we have taken the position that it does not have the status of the first thing in a 'first things first' policy regime. Rights, justice, eradicating poverty, and promoting sustainable development come first." Measuring happiness is infinitely challenging. Yet I believe it is critical for well-being and public policy and that social scientists should continue to try to measure it.

Like the authors, I would like to see an emphasis on the implementation of policies that would guarantee rights, foster justice, eradicate poverty, and promote sustainability. This is essential for well-being, although I realize my idea of universal rights doesn't even accord with the ideas of many in my own nation. Yet, as a student of what moves people to action and why, I know the importance of an elaborated and detailed understanding of the varieties of feeling good and being well and how they are custom crafted to accord with what is normative and good in a given cultural context.[1] Cultures diverge in what matters to people, what they take to be good, and these commitments are reflected throughout the culture and affect all aspects of psychology and behavior. Since philosophers, social scientists and policymakers try to motivate and incentivize people to take up the pursuit of justice, equality, and dignity for all, this is crucial knowledge. Efforts to motivate people toward particular policy goals—for example, to wear a face mask—with a mismatched model of what is the good or right way to be in a given context are unlikely to succeed.

As the authors detail, ranking the happiness of nations and regions with very different histories, ideas, and practices, the majority of which have yet to be the focus of intensive study and sociocultural analysis, is certainly a problem. Measuring sticks are always inflected with culturally particular assumptions of what is good, best, and right. They fail to measure what those doing the measuring can't see or don't want to see. Policies based on these findings can inscribe stereotypes and prejudices. Here I find the book's chapter on hermeneutical and epistemic injustice to be particularly useful.

Yet a comparative happiness project, one that addresses the significant limitations revealed by *Against Happiness* could be a boon to science and to policymakers. The agenda has the potential to further multidisciplinary academic collaboration and to link researchers with practitioners. The ideal project would expand far beyond the current happiness agenda and would reflect new insights and findings by culturally aware philosophers and social scientists, index more dimensions and facets of good feelings and well-being, and include more and varied types of questions. While happiness and satisfaction rankings can homogenize and hide differences, they can also highlight differences and inspire hypotheses. They can raise fundamental questions of equality and justice. Why, for example, are people in Finland and other Nordic countries compared to people in the United States so satisfied with their lives?[2] Could it be that happy countries like happy families are alike in some ways? And if so what are the features of the sociocultural context that matter for happiness and well-being: health, sufficient resources, mutual respect, trust, social cohesion, safety and belongingness, autonomy? Do political rights, gender equality, and equality of income and wealth matter? What is my responsibility if I am happy and satisfied and others whether close or distant from me are not?

Comparative rankings of good feelings can also help underscore the foundational truth that there is more than one right answer to what is the good, true, right, beautiful, or efficient way to live.[3] Many Americans are culturally shaped to focus on the future and the pride of individual accomplishment as the source of well-being. Many Europeans are culturally shaped to concentrate more on the now and the satisfactions of community and everyday life. While East Asian cultural ideas and practices tend to focus on maintaining connections to others and fulfilling expectations, roles, and responsibilities, American cultural ideas and practices tend to emphasize expressing authentic selves and resisting the constraining influence of others.[4] These different ways of being happy and well are all valuable and viable. What are their sociocultural sources? One's own way of being well is not the only or the best way, and as individuals and nations, we have to find ways to adjust to each other and the reality of these differences as we try to understand what can sustain us all.

My culturally crafted American optimism for the potential utility of an enhanced comparative happiness project is grounded in the fact that many more researchers with non-Western-centric schemas for the world, for life, for the good and for themselves are being drawn to this comparative project.[5] In the best case, these researchers will draw on their own schemas for happiness and well-being and suggest new questions that reflect and capture different subjectivities and begin to reveal how our many cultures constitute a complex array of lived experience. They will also reveal how each person is shaped by many intersecting cultures, not just those of nation but also those of other significant social categories, including race/ethnicity, gender, social class, religion, and occupation. Further, as researchers develop and expand these happiness measures, they would be paired with parallel studies that unpack the individual responses and link them to the circumstances and lived realities of everyday experience, including institutional policies and practices, norms, patterns of sociality, and historically derived ideas and values.

The growing globalization of scientific research and collaboration on topics of culture and behavior has the strong potential to contribute to a comparative happiness project that is scientifically generative and relevant to policy. I will sketch two examples of empirical projects that compare the United States with Japan and that fuel my optimism for this possibility. Both programs of research find striking cultural variability of the type described in *Against Happiness*, yet given the extensive empirical record of U.S. and Japan comparisons, these differences are not anomalous, and they can be at least partially understood.

SOCIOCULTURAL VARIATION IN BEING

Among the many ways cultures can differ, how they conceptualize the relationship between self and others is one that has received considerable empirical attention.[6] The self or way of being a person takes on particular culture-specific forms depending on the mix of sociocultural contexts that the agent or being inhabits. These divergent views of the self and relationships lead to differences in a wide range of psychological processes, what motivates people, how people relate to each other, how they experience emotions and what it means to feel good, happy, well, content, or satisfied.

In the West, including North America and Western Europe, the person is often understood as an *independent* self—a separate, relatively stable, autonomous, free entity. According to this view, what is inside the self, a person's internal attributes, including attitudes, emotions, rights, goals, and preferences, is assumed to be the source of agency and to guide behavior. The respondents whose cultures have shaped them to construct and focus internally on their preferences, attitudes, and individual rights are well prepared to answer a question about their own feelings. Q: Are you happy? A: Yes, I like the sun. Q: How satisfied are you with your life? A: Not very at the moment; women's rights have been denied.

Outside the West, in Japan, for example, a person is more often understood as *interdependent*, as a part of encompassing social whole—a connected, flexible, committed entity, always *in relation* to close others. Agency arises from attending to and adjusting to close others. Good feelings, well-being, and life satisfaction are less about an assessment of one's own feelings, preferences, and attitudes and more an assessment of the state of one's relationships and whether the needs and perspectives of close others are being taken into account. Q: Are you happy? A: Well, it depends on the situation and how important others are feeling. Q: Are you satisfied with your life? A: Hmm, I am not really satisfied; I am trying to improve how well I am meeting the standard for the role of a teacher, employee, mother, etc. In Japanese social worlds, good feelings tend to require taking a disciplined, even a critical stance, to the self and trying to realize the sympathy of others.[7] Well-being then is collaborative project; it cannot be realized by oneself. Well-being also implicates others in the West, but the patterning of many Western worlds prioritizes the individual's rights, goals, and preferences.

So it is not just that different things make people happy in different contexts; it is that the ways of being well and the subjective experience of good feelings are different in different cultural contexts. Where Americans are pursuing their inalienable rights to happiness as mandated by their foundational Declaration of Independence, Japanese are doing something else; they are invested in realizing the sympathy of others. The problem with the "how satisfied are you with your life" question for the Japanese is that it fails to capture the relationality that is key to the motivation and behavior of the interdependent self that has been robustly theorized and revealed in empirical work.

MULTIPLE PATHWAYS TO WELL-BEING

For several decades, I have been part of a large and diverse team of researchers led by Carol Ryff of the University of Wisconsin. This team developed the parallel Midlife in the U.S. (IMIDUS) and the Midlife in Japan (MIDJA) studies. The goal of the project was to examine the interplay of sociodemographic, psychosocial, behavioral, and biological factors on physical and mental health in large representative samples in both nations. At the core of the project is a carefully constructed survey instrument: the Ryff Psychological Well-Being Scale that indexes well-being on six dimensions including environmental mastery, autonomy, purpose in life, self-acceptance, positive relations with others, and personal growth. These dimensions reflect a cultural model derived from multiple theories and empirical studies of well-being. The surveys also included measures of positive and negative affect, satisfaction with life and self, self-esteem, control and as well as multiple respondents' health and their social lives. The guiding hypothesis of this multiwave, multidecade project was that a sense of being well would matter for all aspects of life but could manifest in different forms and through different pathways. The Ryff scale is now often used by teachers and counselors to assess the effectiveness of various health and wellness programs.

Studies examining both MIDUS and MIDJA data find that well-being including both physical and psychological factors tends to correlate with what is normative and culturally sanctioned in each nation, that is, independence in the United States and interdependence in Japan.[8] In both samples, as many happiness and well-being theories predict, lower levels of negative emotions and higher level of positive emotions are associated with better self-reported health and fewer chronic health conditions.[9] Yet some clear and intriguing cultural differences have also emerged, however. Studies with the six factor Ryff PWB scale find that negative emotions are more strongly related to lower levels of well-being and to reports of more chronic conditions and limitations in the activities of daily life in the United States than they are in Japan.[10] Why might negative feelings have a much stronger impact on well-being and health in the United States than in Japan? The probable answers involve a variety of significant ontological concerns.

In East Asian contexts, negative feelings are understood as situationally afforded and grounded in specific relationships.[11] In contrast with the West, where emotions are thought to reside inside of people, negative emotions are seen as arising from external sources and as inevitable and transient elements of a natural cycle. As negative thoughts and feelings are more accepted as part of life, they are accorded less significance, and they appear to be less related to well-being and health. Many other findings from MIDUS and MIDJA data would be hard to make sense of without the foundation of in-depth studies of cultural variation.[12] There is a great deal to be understood about good feelings and well-being, but overall, the empirical picture emerging from this program of research is that on average people are happy and experience well-being to the extent that they experience a fit or a match with what is normative or culturally sanctioned. A cultural fit affords more easily available meaning and affirmation for one's actions as well as more social resources.[13]

HAPPY STUDENTS, HAPPY SCHOOLS?

In a project led by Jeremy Rappleye of Kyoto University, we examined the move by the Organisation for Economic Cooperation and Development (OECD) to include well-being as a factor in their work tracking comparative education and skills, the Programme for International Student Assessment (PISA).[14] The underlying PISA commitment is that student achievement is necessary for economic growth, and their stated aim is "better policies for better lives." The addition of a measure of well-being was in response to the criticism that PISA only tracked scores in reading, math, and science and that a single performance-based quantitative yardstick could harm students, many of whom hailed from a great diversity of educational traditions.

In 2017, the OECD published a report with academic achievement scores as well as well-being scores. While the report found most fifteen-year-olds were happy with their lives (average 7.3 on a 1–10 scale of life satisfaction), there was large variation among countries. Correlating life satisfaction and student performance, regional groups of countries were quite apparent. Countries of northern Europe clustered in the "High Satisfaction, High Performance" quadrant, Latin American countries in the "High Satisfaction, Low Performance" quadrant, countries of the Mediterranean in the "Low Satisfaction, Low Performance" quadrant, and countries of East Asia in the "Low Satisfaction, High Performance" quadrant. The United States posted average life satisfaction and average performance. The OECD report of the results contrasted the mostly very happy students of the Netherlands with their unhappy peers in East Asia.

One immediate conclusion from these correlations of achievement with well-being is that countries with unhappy students need policies and practices that will promote happy schools. The OECD claimed "Well-Being 2030: Individual and Societal" as the overarching goal for its education work in this decade.[15]

Are East Asian students unhappy? The OECD report briefly mentions the possibility of differences in educational practices and then cites the long study hours that are common in East Asia, even though life satisfaction did not correlate with time spent studying. Given these data, what is the next step? Do educators work to raise the low life satisfaction scores of East Asian students? Do they create a happiness curriculum or a pedagogy that focuses on helping these students develop their individual passions?[16] Or do they reassess the measuring stick?

Researchers Hidefumi Hitokoto and Yukiko Uchida took the last step. They developed an Interdependent Happiness Scale that was different from scales like life satisfaction that focus on individual subjective states. Their scale indexes happiness along with the feelings of close others. Sample items include: "I believe that I and those around me are happy," and "I can do what I want without causing problems for other people." Their goal was to capture some nuanced aspects of interdependent happiness, especially a sense of harmony with others. They confirmed the validity of the scale in other countries including the United States, Germany, Japan, and Korea. Their analysis shows that when happiness is conceptualized in terms of interdependence, these countries do not differ in happiness. Other studies show that in relatively interdependent nations, strong achievement is correlated with rating of support from others.[17] The point here is that additional culturally tuned items (indigenous or non-Western items) have the potential to capture aspects of happiness that are missing from widely used assessments. A culturally resonant understanding of happiness might be useful in the process of designing policies for better schools not only in East Asia, but also in the United States and Germany.

These two examples of efforts to measure well-being make the case that good feelings take different forms and have different functions. The authors of *Against Happiness* would not be surprised; this is their argument. Yet these studies also suggest that even limited measures or mismeasures of happiness and well-being can provide some answers, and most important, the next set of questions to be answered. "Good" feelings are not always positive feelings. Negative feelings are not equally consequential for health and well-being in the United States and Japan. When happiness is assessed in less individualistic ways, students in the United States and Japan do not differ in happiness. This is crucial knowledge for those who would strive first to foster justice, equality, and dignity and to build better policies for better lives.

CONCLUDING THOUGHTS

Against Happiness is a multileveled, necessary, and trenchant critique of a project that indexes happiness around the world with the question "How satisfied are you with your life?" and with ratings of positive and negative affect. It would be hard to read this book without becoming fascinated with questions of what happiness is and why it matters, and without reflecting more than usual on your own happiness, when and why you are happy, if you are satisfied, and what the relationship is between your well-being and that of others. I am happy with the sun and a massage. As this book makes clear, my well-being is a more complex matter, but an essential concern for researchers, practitioners, and policymakers.

I am convinced by a growing volume of research that a globally comparative project on happiness (one more broadly conceived and analyzed than is currently the case) could be very productive and useful. This type of project attracts scholars and researchers across disciplines and generates widespread interest and attention to the question of a good life and how to realize it. An expanded project needs to analyze the ideas and practices that give rise to particular patterns of good and bad feelings and to multiple ways of being well, and it needs to include more diverse ways to assess them. Without these more in-depth studies of the many styles of human flourishing and a better understanding of how cultures shape good feelings and ways of being well, efforts to successfully implement policies will be stymied before they begin.

The point of this commentary is to emphasize that this book of many perspectives is a major contribution to the analysis of happiness and well-being. But I also want to propose that we not throw out the baby with the bath water. Assessing happiness and well-being will always be a fraught endeavor, but there is value in a set of metrics that can capture both the more universal and the more particular and that expands to become more inclusive with more research. The *World Happiness Report* moves somewhat in this direction, but it could do much more.[18] Motivating people toward collective goals of rights, justice, less inequality, and sustainability will depend on a much more nuanced understanding what people in different cultural contexts understand as good feelings and what it means to be well. The analysis and assessment of happiness then is not sufficient for the understanding of well-being and policy, but it is necessary.

14

THREE OUT OF THREE IS BETTER

JEFFREY D. SACHS

Owen Flanagan and Joe LeDoux and their colleagues challenge the "happiness agenda," which calls on governments "to pursue the elaboration of additional measures that better capture the importance of the pursuit of happiness and well-being in development with a view to guiding their public policies."[1] Their conclusion is that our global focus should be on human rights (notably the Universal Declaration of Human Rights) and sustainable development (notably the 17 Sustainable Development Goals), but on not the promotion of happiness. As they put it, "Two out of three ain't bad." I will argue that the full triumvirate—human rights, the SDGs, and happiness—are a fitting, complementary, and important program of global aspirations.

Part of the problem is that Flanagan, LeDoux and their colleagues critique an exceptionally strong version of the happiness agenda, in which the goal of happiness *replaces* the other two goals (human rights, sustainable development) and serves at the *summum bonum* of public policy, based on one metric of happiness, the Subjective Well-being (SWB) of individuals as reported by survey data. One such SWB measure, reported annually by the *World Happiness Report*,[2] is the Cantril Ladder question asked annually around the world by the Gallup World Poll:

- Please imagine a ladder with steps numbered from zero at the bottom to ten at the top. Suppose we say that the top of the ladder represents the best possible life for you and the bottom of the ladder represents the worst possible life for you.
- If the top step is 10 and the bottom step is 0, on which step of the ladder do you feel you personally stand at the present time?

I wouldn't defend such a strong version either. Happiness, even when properly defined, is not the sole objective of society or a suitable *summum bonum*. Nor is any single empirical measure of happiness alone a sound basis for public policy. The UN General Resolution calls for *additional measures*, not for a single measure.

I want to defend a more moderate viewpoint. Happiness, interpreted as a "good life" (rather than as the flow of happy emotions or feelings), is a meaningful objective and an important one both for individuals and for society. It complements human rights and sustainable development, but it does not replace them. Moreover, it can be measured, at least imperfectly, but careful and imperfect measurement is better than no measurement (if the imperfections are recognized). The Cantril Ladder is one way to measure aspects of happiness (*qua* good life), but certainly not the only one.

First, let us face the challenge that occupies much of Flanagan, LeDoux, and their colleagues' argument: happiness means many different things, and the word is used in many different ways. Moreover, according to them, the happiness agenda is unclear or inconsistent in these uses. This is certainly true, the reason being that there is not one singular happiness agenda.

Even the *World Happiness Report*, of which I am proud to be a founding editor, is a compendium of diverse views and approaches.

My own views are the following. Happiness, for the purposes of public policy, should focus on helping individuals to lead "good lives," in the philosophical tradition that goes back to Aristotle's *Nicomachean Ethics* and *The Politics*. Moreover, I conjecture that happiness in this sense is a valid *global* goal alongside others, even taking into account the very real and pertinent differences across societies and cultures. Indeed, I believe that if we follow an Aristotelian program that examines the constituents of a "good life," we will find the possibility of forging an "unforced consensus" with other philosophical and religious traditions, enabling us to forge a global program on happiness that finds resonance in very different societies around the world without creating a straitjacket for any of them.

Flanagan, LeDoux, and their colleagues are correct that the folk use of "happiness" sometimes refers to emotions and sometimes to life evaluation. Much of their book critiques the use of emotions as the basis for public policy, arguing that emotional happiness is too little understood, too much socially constructed, and too ephemeral and fleeting to be a guide for collective action through politics. I agree.

My own focus is on a good life, which Aristotle termed "*eudaimonia*," and which unfortunately is sometimes rendered as "happiness" in English translation. Aristotle meant something much richer than mere emotional happiness. These days, *eudaimonia* is often translated as "thriving," which is a bit better than "happiness" from the point of view of common use but still not up to the job. *Eudaimonia*, for Aristotle, means living the kind of full life a thinking and reflective person should like to lead, taking into account human nature and the nature of living with others in a political and civil society (as a *zoon politikon*, or a political animal). Aristotle, like Flanagan, LeDoux, and their colleagues, and like myself, discounted the importance of fleeting emotional happiness. Yes, pleasures are important, but they are not the definition of a good life. As Aristotle famously wrote, "One swallow does not make a summer; neither does one day. Similarly, neither can one day, or a brief space of time, make a man blessed and happy."[3]

Aristotle's own famous formulation is that *eudaimonia* is "an activity of the soul in accord with virtue." In particular, *eudaimonia* is achieved through the cultivation of good character, including practical wisdom, fortitude, temperance, and justice. A good life is therefore a human excellence that is realized through a good upbringing, a sound moral and intellectual education, proper mentorship, and the habit formation of making wise choices. Aristotle recognizes pleasures, in moderation, are part of a good life. Moreover, a good life depends on adequate external goods, such as a good upbringing, financial security, a decent appearance, reliable friendships, and so forth. As Aristotle treats at length in *The Politics*, *eudaimonia* crucially depends on living in a healthy political community (*polis*) as well, indeed living as a participating citizen.[4]

Aristotle would not have signed off on an individual's subjective self-report of well-being (as in the Cantril Ladder) as a definitive measurement of *eudaimonia*. Unlike British empiricists, who regard one's own self-report of preferences or well-being as an unchallengeable bottom line, Aristotle (like Flanagan, LeDoux, and their colleagues) would view self-reports as subject to all kinds of biases. The self-judgments of an intemperate or cruel man, for example, would not be a basis for judging the person to be living a good life. Such evidence would be useful, but only partial, and full of potential pitfalls, as Flanagan, LeDoux, and their colleagues note.

Still, if an individual professes to be unhappy according to the Cantril Ladder, that self-report should alert others (e.g., a social worker, a legislator, a friend) to potentially serious concerns, such as the economic deprivation of the individual, their loneliness or social isolation, their possible mental illness (such as depressive disorder), or the corruption of the political system in which the individual lives. The aggregation of such subjective data for a country, based on a representative survey, can similarly tell us much about the conditions conducive to *eudaimonia* or lack thereof in the society. Thus, John Helliwell and colleagues have shown us that cross-country differences in average subjective well-being (SWB) relate to income, health, social connectedness, political corruption, and the expressed or revealed values of prosociality in the nation.[5] Aristotle, I believe, would have approved. Differences across societies in SWB are related both to external goods (economic, social, and political), and at least provisionally (since the evidence is weak) to individual character and values as well.

Measures such as the Cantril Ladder obviously have many shortcomings. A scale from 0 to 10 cannot really enable a detailed self-report on own's life conditions. Nor can it assure the meaning or accuracy of a self-evaluation, for example, if made by a sadist, a glutton, a crook, a fraud, or an individual who is afraid to give an honest answer. It cannot provide accuracy from a downtrodden individual who has been misled to believe that subservience and poverty are their inevitable lot in life. And it cannot account for differences across cultures in how surveys are answered. All of this is true. Yet the data are nonetheless interesting, informative, and less distorted by the various taints that are often supposed. Poor people really are less happy, and not in a stoical acceptance of their relative deprivation; people in poor health, or with clinical depression, report lower subjective well-being; people in social isolation suffer; and people living under the weight of corrupt politics feel the burdens. The data therefore tell us much that is of importance, even if imperfectly.

Aristotle would, I believe, offer an additional hypothesis that has not yet been well examined by modern happiness data. Suppose we could investigate in some real depth the character of the individual—his or her good or bad judgments, sense of fairness, fortitude under pressure, self-control over impulses and desires—the things that Aristotle identified as the main virtues. Aristotle would predict that such virtues are generally conducive to a good life, measured not only by the subjective assessments of the individual but also by objective evidence: reputation in the community, contributions to society, excellence in work and family life. He would also hypothesize that societies replete with individuals of high character would also display a higher social functionality, not only in a higher SWB but also in greater prosperity, social peace, less crime and violence, and more cooperation with other societies. These are important hypotheses yet to be tested.

Even if we somehow had a perfectly meaningful cardinal measure of eudaimonia for each individual in society, our work in politics would not be done. As Aristotle himself recognized in *The Politics*, the *distribution* of well-being matters as well, not merely the sum or average.[6] Flanagan, LeDoux, and their colleagues are right to emphasize that the average SWB (as measured by Gallup, for example) is not the end of the story, but they are wrong to throw out the information on averages altogether. Bentham proposed that the sum of well-being should be the bottom line. That is now widely understood to be wrong, since it could entail sacrificing some individuals for the sake of the rest in a morally reprehensible way. Kant's Categorical Imperative to treat individuals as ends, not means, is useful here.[7] So too is the human rights approach, which endows each individual with certain rights and economic endowments that cannot be taken away for others. John Rawls, of course, was on the same path in his *Theory of Justice*.[8]

Measures of *eudaimonia*, even if accurate, cannot help us much with regard to our responsibilities to other species, Earth's threatened ecosystems, and future generations. That is why the world community has adopted sustainable development as a new category of societal objective. Sustainable development addresses issues that are not well addressed in traditional philosophy and religious reflection because the challenges to Earth's ecosystems are something new, even if challenges of environmental stewardship are old. Pope Francis and Patriarch Bartholomew have shown us how to update ancient religious wisdom for the sake of modern sustainable development concerns.

My bottom line is this. Happiness, in the Aristotelian sense of good lives or *eudaimonia*, is an important objective for individuals and societies. A good life is not merely what each individual defines as a good life. A good life is based on a shared human nature (e.g., the ability to apply reason, to care for others, and to form friendships and political communities). Individuals have some sense of what constitutes a good life, but they can be helped—through a good upbringing, education, and mentorship—to have an even deeper and richer understanding. That's why we read, discuss, and debate Aristotle. He and other philosophers, neuroscientists, sociologists, and other thinkers help us to understand ourselves better. The happiness (*eudaimonia*) agenda is a work in progress, though an important one. In the Western world, it is roughly 2,400 years old, but it is still making progress. In other parts of the world, the lineage is similarly long and evolving.

Can one agenda fit all of the world? Certainly not as a rigid straitjacket. Cultures differ; geographies differ; individuals differ. But yes, as a reflection of a common human nature, with a common evolutionary origin, and in an increasingly interdependent global society. Flanagan, LeDoux, and their colleagues endorse two pillars of global cooperation: human rights and sustainable development. I'll opt for the three, including happiness (good lives), as shared aspirations of humanity.

15

WHAT THE GALLUP WORLD POLL COULD DO TO DEEPEN OUR UNDERSTANDING OF HAPPINESS IN DIFFERENT CULTURES

JEANNE L. TSAI

Do findings from the Gallup World Poll (GWP) tell us about people's happiness, well-being, and life satisfaction across the world, and if so, should they guide government policymaking? For the authors of the *World Happiness Report* (WHR) and at least some of its nine million readers, the answer is yes, and it is easy to see why.[1] First, these data capture people's feelings or subjective experiences, which have long been overlooked by economists and policymakers in their assessments of how nations are doing. Second, the GWP allows researchers to examine how people's feelings relate to environmental factors like GDP per capita, revealing that objective indicators like wealth do not tell the whole story about how people are feeling. Third, because the collaboration between the WHR and GWP has been going on for ten years, these data can reveal stability and change in happiness and well-being over time, particularly in response to life-changing events like the COVID-19 pandemic. Last, but certainly not least, the GWP samples 1,000 respondents from 150 nations to examine how people are doing in different parts of the world. As such, their data could reveal important cultural similarities and differences in people's values and experiences of happiness.

Given the strengths of the GWP, why are the authors of *Against Happiness* so concerned? I will not repeat their many excellent points here, but their main argument—based on evidence from anthropology, philosophy, religious studies, sociology, and cross-cultural psychology—is this: happiness and well-being as currently defined and measured by the GWP may matter to its creators but may not matter as much to people across the world. If this is true, GWP data are limited in what they can tell us about how people are doing across the world, and using GWP data to shape government policies therefore would be premature and potentially harmful.

As a psychologist who has studied culture and emotion for thirty years, I agree with the authors' points. The good news is that there are ways to address the weaknesses of the GWP, which underlie many of the authors' concerns. Here I describe six ways to improve the GWP for studying happiness across cultures, and I describe how we have addressed these issues in our own work. The first three concern the measurement of happiness and well-being, while the last three concern the measurement of culture.

MEASURE VALUES AND IDEALS

By asking people to rate how close they feel to their best lives and to indicate whether they smiled, laughed, did something interesting, or felt worried or sad or angry during the previous day, the GWP focuses on respondents' actual experiences (their "actuals"). In doing so, the GWP assumes that the people in the 150 nations have similar "ideals." More specifically, the GWP assumes that across the world, people want to lead their "best" lives, want to smile, laugh, and do interesting things and avoid feeling worried, sad, or angry. But what if many people in the study—and in the world—don't hold these ideals?[2]

Fortunately, this question can be easily answered by also asking people how they ideally want to feel. By measuring respondents' ideals, researchers can examine whether people in different regions of the world want to feel the same way about their lives, and if not, how they differ. Measuring people's ideals can also help GWP researchers interpret the meaning of people's actuals. Knowing whether people learned or did something interesting during the previous day matters a lot if people value learning or doing something interesting, and it matters very little if they do not. In other words, researchers can calibrate people's actuals to their ideals. Finally, by measuring ideals and actuals, researchers can statistically account for social desirability biases. People are more likely to report feeling interest when they think it is desirable (or ideal) to do so and are less likely to report feeling anger when they think it is undesirable to do so. Thus, researchers can achieve a more accurate measure of people's actuals by taking out the degree to which they overlap with their ideals. Last but not least, because ideals are powerful influences on people's behavior in their own right, by measuring people's ideals, the GWP would have a more complete view of what people care about.[3]

We know this because my colleagues, students, and I have been measuring people's "actual affect" (the affective states they actually feel) and their "ideal affect" (the affective states they value and ideally want to feel) since 2000. Based on this work, we find that across the cultures studied, most people do indeed want to feel more positive than negative, and they want to feel more positive and less negative than they actually feel. Moreover, among the positive states, people want to feel happier, more content, and more satisfied than other positive states. But against this backdrop of cultural similarities, we have also observed consistent cultural differences in the degree to which people value or ideally want to feel high arousal positive states like excitement, enthusiasm, and elation. European Americans valued these high-arousal positive states more than various East Asian groups, including Hong Kong Chinese, Taiwanese, Japanese, and South Koreans.[4] Early on, we also found cultural differences in the degree to which people value or ideally want to feel low-arousal positive states like calm, relaxation, and serenity, with East Asians valuing these states more than European Americans.[5] Most recently, these cultural differences in the valuation of these states have been less pronounced, perhaps because of recent world events.[6] Cultures also differ in the degree to which they want to maximize positive and minimize negative states, with European Americans wanting to maximize the positive and minimize the negative more than Beijing and Hong Kong Chinese samples.[7] These cultural differences are related to specific aspects of individualism and collectivism, respectively.[8]

Moreover, because in our studies we assessed actual and ideal affect in similar ways, we were able to examine the relative impact of each on a variety of behaviors. Our studies reveal that differences in ideal affect—above and beyond actual affect—are related to a whole host of behaviors, ranging from what consumer products people choose to what exercise they participate in, what physicians they prefer, what they post on social media, whom they view as friendly and whom they befriend, whom they hire and choose to lead, and even whom they share resources with.[9]

There are other ways in which assessing ideals can matter for well-being. Asking people to reflect on their ideals may remind people what matters to them and ultimately help them to achieve those ideals. Learning about different ideals can broaden people's own views of a happy and meaningful life. Finally, recognizing that people differ in their ideals can be critical to understanding them better and minimizing unintended biases that may stem from different ideals.

INCLUDE FEELINGS THAT MATTER MORE IN COLLECTIVISTIC CULTURES AND OTHER RELIGIOUS TRADITIONS

People create products that reflect their cultural ideals. For instance, U.S. children storybooks, women's magazines, and even leaders' official website photos contain more open toothy "excited" smiles and fewer closed "calm" smiles than East Asian storybooks, magazines, and leaders' official website photos.[10] The 2022 WHR is no different: photos in the report contained three times more excited than calm smiles!

Similarly, we have observed that Western well-being inventories contain more high-arousal positive than low-arousal positive content, presumably because they were developed by Western clinicians and scientists who value high arousal positive states more.[11] But what about the content of the GWP? As mentioned earlier, to assess positive emotions, the GWP typically asks respondents if they smiled, laughed, or did something interesting the day before, which assumes that when people feel good, they feel these emotions and express them in these specific ways. There are cultural differences in the emotions that people associate with well-being as well as cultural differences in whether people savor and express their positive emotions by smiling and laughing (vs. dampen and suppress their positive emotions).[12] Therefore, it is possible that the GWP does not adequately capture the well-being of individuals from cultures that have different ideals or views of emotion, especially more collectivistic ones.

In response to this concern, the most recent GWP broadened its measures of positive emotion to include measures of balance, peace, and calm states not only valued in many East Asian contexts but many Buddhist traditions more specifically.[13] This is a step in the right direction. Unfortunately, the GWP primarily focused on the degree to which respondents actually felt these states and included only one measure of ideals ("Would you prefer an exciting or calm life?"). As argued before, in order to evaluate people's reports of actual balance and peace, we need to know how much they value those states. Moreover, in order to be comparable, actuals and ideals have to be measured in the same way. Despite this, consistent with our early findings, the authors still observed that more respondents in East Asian countries preferred a calm vs. exciting life compared to respondents in the United States and Canada.[14] Moreover, they observed that during a world pandemic, most people across the world preferred a calm over an exciting life. Whether these findings will generalize to nonpandemic times remains to be seen, but the findings illustrate another reason to include other feelings that matter to other parts of the world and other traditions: we may discover that other states matter to us more than we realize.

Similar arguments can be made for negative emotion. The GWP focuses on three negative states—worry, sadness, and anger—and assumes that people want to avoid feeling these specific states. Once again, we know from our work that people and cultures vary in the degree to which people want to avoid feeling negative overall as well as the degree to which they want to feel and avoid specific negative emotions.[15] European Americans, for example, want to avoid feeling negative more than Germans, and this is linked to their expressions of sympathy.[16] Taiwanese participants value shame, guilt, and fear more than Canadians do.[17] Moreover, views of negative emotion have implications for the links between the actual experience of these negative states and health.[18]

Future GWP might include other states that have been associated with collectivism, given the prevalence of collectivistic values across the world. For instance, Shinobu Kitayama, Batja Mesquita, and Mayumi Karasawa have demonstrated that people in cultures that are more collectivistic like Japan experience more socially engaging positive (e.g., feelings of friendliness and respect) and negative (e.g., feelings of pity and shame) emotions; therefore, these would be good states to include in future polls.[19]

VALIDATE SELF-REPORTS WITH REAL-WORLD BEHAVIORS

The WHR primarily relies on self-report data from the GWP to assess how people are doing across the world. Although self-report is one of the best ways of assessing people's subjective experiences, there are a host of problems with it, including social desirability biases, response style biases, and lack of awareness or insight. One of the most important concerns is whether people's self-reports of how they are doing reflect anything about people's everyday lives. For instance, are people's assessments of their lives truly a reflection of what their lives are like? Does a measure of whether people smiled, laughed, or did something interesting the day before say anything about people's lives overall? To answer these questions, it is critical to validate these self-reports with other behavioral and biological measures of how people are doing.

The 2022 WHR has already moved in this direction by examining whether the affective content of Twitter posts during the COVID-19 pandemic reflects the same patterns as the GWP data. The question is what the affective content in the posts reflects. In our own work comparing the affective content of U.S. and Japanese Twitter posts, we observe patterns that suggest that people are posting content that reflects their ideal affect more than their actual affect.[20] By measuring ideals and actuals, GWP might be able to determine whether this is true for its respondents as well.

As described earlier, we have employed a variety of behavioral and biological measures to examine the behavioral expressions of cultural differences in ideal affect, as well as the neural mechanisms that support these behaviors. For instance, in one study, based on their self-reports of ideal affect, European Americans valued excited (high-arousal positive) states vs. calm (low-arousal positive) states less than Chinese. Within cultures, European Americans valued excited and calm states similarly, whereas Chinese value calm more than excited states. To examine how these cultural differences influence people's immediate responses to excited vs. calm facial expressions, we combined a facial rating task with functional magnetic resonance imaging.[21] During scanning, European American and Chinese females viewed and rated excited and calm faces that varied by race (white, Asian) and sex (male, female). As predicted, European Americans showed greater activity in brain circuits associated with affect and reward (bilateral ventral striatum, left caudate) while viewing excited vs calm faces than did Chinese. Within cultures, European Americans responded to excited vs. calm faces similarly, whereas Chinese showed greater activity in these circuits in response to calm vs. excited expressions regardless of targets' race or sex. Across cultures, greater ventral striatal activity while viewing excited vs. calm faces predicted greater preference for excited vs. calm faces several months later. These findings not only provide neural evidence that people find viewing the specific positive facial expressions that match their culture's ideal affect to be rewarding and relevant but also validate the cultural differences that have emerged in self-reports.

DEMONSTRATE MEASUREMENT EQUIVALENCE

As the authors of *Against Happiness* argue, the questions included in the WHR may have different meanings in different cultures, especially if the translations are not accurate. As a result, comparing ratings of these happiness metrics across cultures may ultimately be meaningless.

Indeed, this is a fundamental issue that cross-cultural psychologists have confronted for decades, which is why standard practice is to demonstrate measurement equivalence *before* comparing group responses.[22] Demonstrating measurement equivalence requires showing that responses to questions on a survey relate to each other in similar ways across the cultures sampled. For instance, in the GWP, are smiling, laughing, and doing something interesting related to each other for each of the nations sampled? They should be if they are truly assessing positive emotion in each culture. If so, then comparisons of positive emotion across nations are warranted. But if they aren't, then they should be compared separately across nations and not referred to as "positive emotion." Similarly, do "balance" and "harmony" have the same associations in the 150 nations sampled?

Because we have established measurement equivalence for our measures of actual and ideal affect for the cultural samples we have studied, we are confident that we can compare actual and ideal affect between these cultures. Thus, we know that for our participants, how people want to feel differs from how they actually feel, and there are cultural differences in how people ideally want to feel.

ACCOUNT FOR CULTURAL DIFFERENCES IN RESPONSE STYLES

A central aspect of the GWP and WHR is the ranking of nations by average level of life satisfaction on a 10-point scale. Rating scales like this one allow nuance and variability more than simple yes or no questions, but they have issues, too. For instance, decades of research in cross-cultural psychology have revealed cultural differences in how people respond to rating scales.[23] While East Asians tend to use the middle of the scales, Americans tend to use the extreme ends of the scales. This is not a problem when comparing ratings within cultures, but across cultures it means that one cannot know whether the observed national differences in life satisfaction reflect real differences in life satisfaction or more general differences in how much people use the middle vs. top and bottom ends of the scale. Yes and no questions, which the GWP uses to assess positive and negative emotions, are similarly sensitive to cultural differences in "acquiescence bias," or their willingness to provide affirmative answers.[24]

In our own work, we ask participants to use a 5-point rating scale to indicate how much they actually feel thirty-eight different states that vary in terms of valence and arousal on average and then how much they ideally want to feel the same thirty-eight states on average. Although we sometimes reduce the number of items depending on our purposes, these thirty-eight states include filler items or items that are not central to our hypotheses so that we can assess and then account for differences in response styles. One popular way of doing this is "ipsatizing," or calculating standardized scores for each individual. We then compare the ipsatized scores across cultural groups. Although this method has its limitations, it addresses response style biases and allows us to infer more confidently that the observed cultural differences reflect specific differences in ideal affect and not more general differences in response styles.[25]

PROVIDE MORE CULTURAL DEPTH (EVEN AT THE COST OF NATIONAL BREADTH)

The GWP samples 1,000 respondents from 150 nations ranging from Finland to Afghanistan. This is not an easy task, especially assuming that the GWP employs translators and researchers in each of these nations to collect these data. If you have the resources, why wouldn't you collect data from as many nations as possible?

From a scientific perspective, one reason is that this approach almost always comes at the cost of understanding of any particular nation or collection of nations well. For instance, at least in the most recent WHR, almost no information is provided about the specific cultural ideas and practices represented in this collection of 150 nations that might be related to different conceptions of happiness or well-being. This is not specific to the GWP; it is almost always the case that in studies that include more than a handful of nations, the more nations the researchers include in their studies, the less cultural the study becomes. Although empirical studies are by definition reductive, with respect to culture, the GWP takes this to an extreme.

This is exactly why when I began studying culture influences on emotion, I focused on two ethnic groups: European Americans and Chinese Americans.[26] I chose these groups because they were differentially influenced by and oriented to "American" and "Chinese" cultures, cultures that differed in individualism and collectivism, which scholars had predicted would shape a variety of psychological processes, including emotion.[27] By focusing on these two groups, my team and I could also consider and quantify the variation within each cultural group in terms not only of individuals' cultural orientation but also in their endorsement of individualistic and collectivistic values. We also used specific recruitment criteria to ensure that we were recruiting individuals who were oriented to the cultures of interest (e.g., typically first- and second-generation Chinese Americans and third- or higher generation European Americans).

In subsequent studies for various theoretically and empirical driven reasons, we broadened our samples to include other East Asian Americans, then participants living in Taiwan and Hong Kong, then mainland China, and then other East Asian cultures (Japan, Korea) as well as other Western cultures (England, France, Germany) and other collectivistic cultures (Mexico).[28] By choosing nations for cultural reasons, we believe that we have been able to increase our national breadth without completely compromising cultural depth (although some anthropologists might disagree).

This focused approach has also allowed us to study cultural differences in ideal affect more deeply. Specifically, we have been able to test our predictions about the sources of cultural differences in ideal affect, examine how cultural differences in ideal affect are reflected in popular media, look into age differences in ideal affect, explore the interpersonal consequences of cultural differences in ideal affect, reveal the neural mechanisms underlying cultural differences in ideal affect, study the effects of differences in ideal affect in employment and health settings, and most recently to chart changes in ideal affect over time.[29] We would not have been able to do any of this if we did not have a solid understanding of what ideal affect looked like in the specific cultural samples we have studied.

By starting out with U.S.–East Asian comparisons, we did not mean to imply that they were the only cultures that vary in the valuation of high and low arousal positive states, and I certainly believe that we need to know more about the ideal affect of other parts of the world, which other scholars have fortunately initiated.[30] In my own lab, we have started studying ideal affect in Turkey and India, with collaborators who know these cultures well, in part because these cultures (and the subcultures within them) have different expressions and combinations of individualism and collectivism that should show different patterns from those we have observed in our samples.

WHY IMPLEMENT THESE CHANGES?

Implementing these six changes would require additional time and resources, but they are necessary if the authors of the WHR really want to understand the meaning of happiness and well-being in different cultures. Armed with better data, the WHR would have more to say to government policymakers about how their constituents feel compared to how they ideally want to feel. As I read the WHR, I was heartened to learn that the WHR and GWP have evolved over time, and that at least some of its authors share the points raised here and by the authors of *Against Happiness*. Perhaps by implementing the six changes described here, the GWP will begin to define and measure happiness in ways that help get us all closer to understanding happiness and well-being across the world.

NOTES

INTRODUCTION

1. Mariano Rojas, "Happiness, Public Policy and the Notion of Development," *Behavioural Public Policy* 4, no. 2 (July 2020): 166–76, https://doi.org/10.1017/bpp.2019.40. Rojas thinks that the "Happiness Movement" is at a third stage of development where it is mature enough to be used as a guide to public policy. See also Action for Happiness, "Happier and Kinder, Together," https://actionforhappiness.org/; Simon Burnett, *The Happiness Agenda: A Modern Obsession* (New York: Palgrave Macmillan, 2012); Ashley Frawley, "Happiness Research: A Review of Critiques," *Sociology Compass* 9, no. 1 (2015): 62–77, https://doi.org/10.1111/soc4.12236.
2. Matthew Adler, "Happiness Surveys and Public Policy: What's the Use?" *Duke Law Journal* 62 (January 2013): 1509, https://scholarship.law.upenn.edu/faculty_scholarship/414.
3. United Nations, Happiness: Towards a Holistic Approach to Development (Resolution 65/309), August 25, 2011, https://digitallibrary.un.org/record/715187.
4. Joseph Henrich, Steven J. Heine, and Ara Norenzayan, "The Weirdest People in the World?" *Behavioral and Brain Sciences* 33, nos. 2–3 (June 2010): 61–83, https://doi.org/10.1017/S0140525X0999152X.
5. Amartya Sen, "Well-Being, Agency and Freedom: The Dewey Lectures 1984," *The Journal of Philosophy* 82, no. 4 (1985): 188–89, https://doi.org/10.2307/2026184.

6. David B. Yaden and Daniel M. Haybron, "The Emotional State Assessment Tool: A Brief, Philosophically Informed, and Cross-Culturally Sensitive Measure," *Journal of Positive Psychology* 17, no. 2 (March 4, 2022): 151–65, https://doi.org/10.1080/17439760.2021.2016910.
7. Barbara L. Fredrickson, *Positivity* (New York: Crown Publishers, 2009).
8. Sonja Lyubomirsky and Heidi S. Lepper, "A Measure of Subjective Happiness: Preliminary Reliability and Construct Validation," *Social Indicators Research* 46, no. 2 (February 1, 1999): 137–55, https://doi.org/10.1023/A:1006824100041. Positive vs. negative in the psychology of the emotions is a measure of hedonic tone, feeling good or bad, so sadness is negative hedonically. From the point of view of the psychology of mental or moral health, hedonically positive or negative emotions can switch values, so laughing at a joke is hedonically positive. If it is a racist joke it is evaluatively negative. Sadness at a death is negative hedonically, but it is the right way to feel for a mentally healthy and decent human being.
9. Antonella Delle Fave et al., "Lay Definitions of Happiness Across Nations: The Primacy of Inner Harmony and Relational Connectedness," *Frontiers in Psychology* 7 (2016): 30, https://doi.org/10.3389/fpsyg.2016.00030.
10. An exception is Yaden and Haybron, "The Emotional State."
11. Richard E. Nisbett and Timothy D. Wilson, "Telling More Than We Can Know: Verbal Reports on Mental Processes," *Psychological Review* 84, no. 3 (1977): 231–59, https://doi.org/10.1037/0033-295X.84.3.231; Daniel Gilbert, *Stumbling on Happiness* (New York: Knopf, 2006); Eric Schwitzgebel, *Perplexities of Consciousness* (Cambridge, MA: MIT Press, 2011); Peter Carruthers, *The Opacity of Mind: An Integrative Theory of Self-Knowledge* (New York: Oxford University Press, 2011).
12. Phillip J. Ivanhoe, *Oneness: East Asian Conceptions of Virtue, Happiness, and How We Are All Connected* (New York: Oxford University Press, 2017).
13. Owen Flanagan, *The Bodhisattva's Brain: Buddhism Naturalized* (Cambridge, MA: MIT Press, 2011).

14. WHR 2022, figure 6.1.
15. Throughout, we resist allowing definitions inside some research tradition to resolve a substantive matter. For example, inside the subfield of well-being studies in philosophy, well-being is defined as the study of a certain kind of value dubbed "prudential value," which is often deemed distinct from moral or aesthetic value, and it pertains to what is *good for* an individual. However, many well-being theorists resist excluding moral value from what is "good for" a person.
16. Yew-Kwang Ng and Lok Sang Ho, *Happiness and Public Policy: Theory, Case Studies and Implications* (London: Palgrave Macmillan UK, 2006).
17. Paul Frijters et al., "A Happy Choice: Wellbeing as the Goal of Government," *Behavioural Public Policy* 4, no. 2 (July 2020): 126–65, at 152, https://doi.org/10.1017/bpp.2019.39.
18. United Nations, "Universal Declaration of Human Rights," 1948, https://www.un.org/en/about-us/universal-declaration-of-human-rights; United Nations, "Transforming Our World: The 2030 Agenda for Sustainable Development," 2015, https://sdgs.un.org/2030agenda.
19. See, for example, Burnett, *The Happiness Agenda*; Frawley, "Happiness Research."
20. Carol D. Ryff, Jennifer Morozink Boylan, and Julie A. Kirsch, "Advancing the Science of Well-Being: A Dissenting View on Measurement Recommendations," in *Measuring Well-Being: Interdisciplinary Perspectives from the Social Sciences and the Humanities*, ed. Matthew T. Lee, Laura D. Kubzansky, and Tyler J. VanderWeele (New York: Oxford University Press, 2021) 521–35.
21. Yukiko Uchida, Vinai Norasakkunkit, and Shinobu Kitayama, "Cultural Constructions of Happiness: Theory and Empirical Evidence," *Journal of Happiness Studies* 5, no. 3 (September 1, 2004): 223–39, https://doi.org/10.1007/s10902-004-8785-9; Hazel Rose Markus and Shinobu Kitayama, "Culture and the Self: Implications for Cognition, Emotion, and Motivation," *Psychological Review* 98, no. 2 (1991): 224–53, https://doi.org/10.1037/0033-295X.98.2.224.
22. John Helliwell et al., "World Happiness, Trust and Deaths Under COVID-19," in *World Happiness Report 2021*, ed. John Helliwell et al. (New York: Sustainable Development Solutions Network, 2021), 34,

https://worldhappiness.report/ed/2021/happiness-trust-and-deaths-under-covid-19/.

1. THE HAPPINESS AGENDA

1. Elizabeth Arias et al., "Provisional Life Expectancy Estimates for 2020," National Center for Health Statistics (U.S.), https://www.cdc.gov/nchs/data/vsrr/vsrr015-508.pdf.
2. Sherry Everett Jones et al., "Mental Health, Suicidality, and Connectedness Among High School Students During the COVID-19 Pandemic—Adolescent Behaviors and Experiences Survey, United States, January–June 2021," *MMWR Supplements* 71, no. 3 (April 1, 2022): 16–21, https://doi.org/10.15585/mmwr.su7103a3.
3. Gallup, "Life Satisfaction," https://news.gallup.com/topic/category_life_satisfaction.aspx.
4. John Helliwell et al., "World Happiness, Trust and Deaths Under COVID-19," and "Happiness, Benevolence, and Trust During COVID-19 and Beyond," in *World Happiness Report 2022*, ed. John Helliwell et al. (New York: Sustainable Development Solutions Network, 2022), https://worldhappiness.report/ed/2022/happiness-benevolence-and-trust-during-covid-19-and-beyond/.
5. Richard A. Easterlin, "Does Economic Growth Improve the Human Lot? Some Empirical Evidence," in *Nations and Households in Economic Growth*, ed. Paul A. David and Melvin W. Reder (San Diego, CA: Academic Press, 1974), 89–125.
6. Betsey Stevenson and Justin Wolfers, "Economic Growth and Subjective Well-Being: Reassessing the Easterlin Paradox," National Bureau of Economic Research, Working Paper 14282 (August 2008), https://doi.org/10.3386/w14282.
7. Simon Burnett, *The Happiness Agenda: A Modern Obsession* (New York: Palgrave Macmillan, 2012); Ashley Frawley, "Happiness Research: A Review of Critiques," *Sociology Compass* 9, no. 1 (2015): 62–77, https://doi.org/10.1111/soc4.12236.
8. Martin E. P. Seligman, *Authentic Happiness: Using the New Positive Psychology to Realize Your Potential for Lasting Fulfillment* (New York: Simon & Schuster, 2002).

I. THE HAPPINESS AGENDA ⊗ 253

9. Shigehiro Oishi and Ed Diener, "Can and Should Happiness Be a Policy Goal?" *Policy Insights from the Behavioral and Brain Sciences* 1, no. 1 (October 1, 2014): 195–203, https://doi.org/10.1177/2372732214548427.
10. "Plan to Measure Happiness 'Not Woolly'—Cameron," *BBC News*, November 25, 2010, https://www.bbc.com/news/uk-11833241.
11. Anthony M. Annett, *Cathonomics: How Catholic Tradition Can Create a More Just Economy* (Washington, DC: Georgetown University Press, 2022).
12. William Davies, *The Happiness Industry: How the Government and Big Business Sold Us Well-Being* (New York: Verso Books, 2015).
13. Christopher Barrington-Leigh, "Trends in Conceptions of Progress and Well-Being," in Helliwell et al., *World Happiness Report 2022*, 71, https://worldhappiness.report/ed/2022/trends-in-conceptions-of-progress-and-well-being/.
14. Karma Ura et al., *A Short Guide to Gross National Happiness Index* (Thimphu: Centre for Bhutan Studies, 2012).
15. Edward W. Said, *Orientalism* (New York: Pantheon Books, 1978).
16. "Ardern to Her Ministers: Want More Money? Deliver on Wellbeing," *NZ Herald*, https://www.nzherald.co.nz/nz/pm-jacinda-ardern-if-a-minister-wants-more-money-they-need-to-prove-how-it-will-better-wellbeing/YIRFYIPHY3VLIGLVQZEYQEV2RM/.
17. Nicola Sturgeon, "Why Governments Should Prioritize Well-Being," TED Talk, 1564411787 (July 2019), https://www.ted.com/talks/nicola_sturgeon_why_governments_should_prioritize_well_being.
18. Chatham House—International Affairs Think Tank, "Iceland and the Wellbeing Economy," https://www.chathamhouse.org/events/all/members-event/iceland-and-wellbeing-economy.
19. Organisation for Economic Co-operation and Development (OECD), "OECD Better Life Index," https://www.oecdbetterlifeindex.org/#/11111111111.
20. United Nations, Transforming Our World: The 2030 Agenda for Sustainable Development (Resolution 70/1), September 25, 2015, https://sdgs.un.org/2030agenda.
21. Jan-Emmanuel De Neve and Jeffrey D. Sachs, "The SDGs and Human Well-Being: A Global Analysis of Synergies, Trade-Offs, and Regional

Differences," *Scientific Reports* 10, no. 1 (September 15, 2020): 15113, https://doi.org/10.1038/s41598-020-71916-9.
22. Helliwell et al., "Happiness, Benevolence, and Trust During COVID-19 and Beyond."
23. OECD, "OECD Better Life Index."

2. VARIETIES OF THEORIES AND MEASURES OF WELL-BEING AND HAPPINESS

1. Jan-Emmanuel De Neve and Jeffrey D. Sachs, "The SDGs and Human Well-Being: A Global Analysis of Synergies, Trade-Offs, and Regional Differences," *Scientific Reports* 10, no. 1 (September 15, 2020): 15113, https://doi.org/10.1038/s41598-020-71916-9.
2. Jeremy Bentham, *An Introduction to the Principles of Morals and Legislation* (London: W. Pickering, 1823); Richard Layard, "Happiness: Has Social Science a Clue? Lecture 1: What Is Happiness? Are We Getting Happier?" GBR, 2003, http://cep.lse.ac.uk/_new/events/robbins.asp; Daniel Kahneman, "Experienced Utility and Objective Happiness: A Moment-Based Approach," in *Choices, Values, and Frames*, ed. Daniel Kahneman and Amos Tversky (New York: Cambridge University Press, 2000), 673–92.
3. Richard B. Brandt, "The Concept of Welfare," in *The Structure of Economic Science*, ed. S. R. Krupp (Englewood Cliffs, NJ: Prentice-Hall, 1966), 257–76; Richard Mervyn Hare, *Moral Thinking: Its Levels, Method, and Point* (New York: Oxford University Press, 1981); Valerie Tiberius, *The Reflective Life: Living Wisely with Our Limits* (New York: Oxford University Press, 2008), and *Well-Being as Value Fulfillment: How We Can Help Each Other to Live Well* (New York: Oxford University Press, 2018).
4. Daniel M. Haybron, "An Emotional State Account of Happiness," in *Theories of Happiness: An Anthology*, ed. Jennifer Wilson Mulnix and M. J. Mulnix (Peterborough, ON: Broadview Press, 2015), 96–114.
5. Theodore M. Benditt, "Happiness," *Philosophical Studies: An International Journal for Philosophy in the Analytic Tradition* 25, no. 1 (1974): 1–20; Jussi Suikkanen, "An Improved Whole Life Satisfaction Theory

of Happiness," *International Journal of Well-Being* 1, no. 1 (January 30, 2011): 1–18.

6. International Health Conference, "Summary Report on Proceedings, Minutes and Final Acts of the International Health Conference Held in New York from 19 June to 22 July 1946" (United Nations, World Health Organization, Interim Commission, 1948), https://apps.who.int/iris/handle/10665/85573.
7. Matthew T. Lee, Laura D. Kubzansky, and Tyler J. VanderWeele, *Measuring Well-Being: Interdisciplinary Perspectives from the Social Sciences and the Humanities* (New York: Oxford University Press, 2021).
8. Seth Margolis et al., "Empirical Relationships Among Five Types of Well-Being," in Lee, Kubzansky, and VanderWeele, *Measuring Well-Being* (New York: Oxford University Press, 2021), 339–76.
9. Martha C. Nussbaum, *Women and Human Development: The Capabilities Approach* (New York: Cambridge University Press, 2001).
10. John Helliwell, Haifang Huang, and Shun Wang, "Changing World Happiness," in *World Happiness Report 2019*, ed. John Helliwell et al. (New York: Sustainable Development Solutions Network, 2019), https://worldhappiness.report/ed/2019/changing-world-happiness/
11. "FAQ," *World Happiness Report* (WHR), https://worldhappiness.report/faq/.
12. Center for Compassion and Altruism Research and Education, "Good Social Relationships Are the Most Consistent Predictor of a Happy Life," http://ccare.stanford.edu/press_posts/good-social-relationships-are-the-most-consistent-predictor-of-a-happy-life/.
13. Thomas Hurka, *Perfectionism* (Oxford: Clarendon Press, 1993).
14. John Rawls, *A Theory of Justice* (Cambridge, MA: Harvard University Press, 1971), 427.
15. PYMNTS.com, "New Reality Check: The Paycheck-to-Paycheck Report," https://www.pymnts.com/study/reality-check-paycheck-to-paycheck-credit-scores-consumer-card-debt-inflation/.
16. Centers for Disease Control and Prevention (CDC), "ABES Table: Summary | DASH | CDC," March 25, 2022, https://www.cdc.gov/healthyyouth/data/abes/tables/summary.htm.
17. Roy F. Baumeister et al., "Some Key Differences Between a Happy Life and a Meaningful Life," *Journal of Positive Psychology* 8, no. 6

(November 1, 2013): 505–16, https://doi.org/10.1080/17439760.2013 .830764.

18. Friedrich Nietzsche, *The Anti-Christ, Ecce Homo, Twilight of the Idols* (New York: Cambridge University Press, 2005), 157.

19. Anna Wierzbicka, "'Happiness' in Cross-Linguistic and Cross-Cultural Perspective," *Daedalus* 133, no. 2 (April 1, 2004): 34–43, https://doi.org/10.1162/001152604323049370; Daniel M. Haybron, "Mental State Approaches to Well-Being," in *The Oxford Handbook of Well-Being and Public Policy*, ed. Matthew D. Alder and Marc Fleurbaey (New York: Oxford University Press, 2016), 347–78.

20. David B. Yaden and Daniel M. Haybron, "The Emotional State Assessment Tool: A Brief, Philosophically Informed, and Cross-Culturally Sensitive Measure," *Journal of Positive Psychology* 17, no. 2 (March 4, 2022): 151–65, https://doi.org/10.1080/17439760.2021.2016910; Daniel M. Haybron, *Happiness: A Very Short Introduction* (New York: Oxford University Press, 2013); Haybron, "An Emotional State Account of Happiness"; Sonja Lyubomirsky and Heidi S. Lepper, "A Measure of Subjective Happiness: Preliminary Reliability and Construct Validation," *Social Indicators Research* 46, no. 2 (February 1, 1999): 137–55, https://doi.org/10.1023/A:1006824100041; Lomas et al., "Insights from the First Global Survey of Balance and Harmony," in Helliwell et al., *World Happiness Report 2022*, https://worldhappiness.report/ed /2022/insights-from-the-first-global-survey-of-balance-and-harmony/.

21. John Helliwell et al., "Happiness, Benevolence, and Trust During COVID-19 and Beyond," in Helliwell et al., *World Happiness Report 2022*, 13–52. Some happiness researchers understand how Aristotle's views differ from Jeremy Bentham's hedonic conception. Bentham thought happiness was a matter of maximizing the quantity of pleasure. The happiness economist Richard Layard sees things clearly when he says explicitly that he is a Benthamite, not an Aristotelian. The reason: Layard thinks the concept of flourishing is a matter of the quantity of pleasant experiences or the ratio of pleasant to unpleasant experiences. Human flourishing does not require qualitative or ethical assessment of the bases of or reasons for the happiness or flourishing, as J. S. Mill and Aristotle, respectively, thought. That said, in conversation, Layard says that the two kinds of views converge since virtue normally increases happiness overall.

22. Aristotle, *Nicomachean Ethics*, trans. Terence Irwin (Indianapolis, IN: Hackett, 1999), 1174b30.
23. Aristotle, *Nicomachean Ethics*.
24. John F. Helliwell, "Three Questions About Happiness," *Behavioural Public Policy* 4, no. 2 (July 2020): 177–87, https://doi.org/10.1017/bpp.2019.41.
25. "Insights from the First Global Survey of Balance and Harmony."
26. Owen Flanagan, *The Geography of Morals: Varieties of Moral Possibility* (New York: Oxford University Press, 2017).
27. Wole Soyinka, *Chronicles from the Land of the Happiest People on Earth* (New York: Knopf, 2021).

3. HOW SHOULD WE THINK ABOUT THE EMOTION OF HAPPINESS SCIENTIFICALLY?

1. Charles Darwin, *The Expression of the Emotions in Man and Animals* (London: Fontana Press, 1872).
2. Silvan Tomkins, *Affect, Imagery, Consciousness* (New York: Springer, 1962); Paul Ekman, "Biological and Cultural Contributions to Body and Facial Movement in the Expression of Emotions," in *Explaining Emotions*, ed. Amélie Oskenberg Rorty (Berkeley: University of California Press, 1980), 73–102; Carroll E. Izard, "Basic Emotions, Relations Among Emotions, and Emotion-Cognition Relations," *Psychological Review* 99, no. 3 (1992): 561–65, https://doi.org/10.1037/0033-295X.99.3.561.
3. Paul Ekman, "Are There Basic Emotions?" *Psychological Review* 99, no. 3 (1992): 550–53, https://doi.org/10.1037/0033-295X.99.3.550; Izard, "Basic Emotions"; Andrea Scarantino, "Are LeDoux's Survival Circuits Basic Emotions Under a Different Name?" *Current Opinion in Behavioral Sciences* 24 (December 1, 2018): 75–82, https://doi.org/10.1016/j.cobeha.2018.06.001.
4. Stanley Schachter and Jerome Singer, "Cognitive, Social, and Physiological Determinants of Emotional State," *Psychological Review* 69, no. 5 (1962): 379–99, https://doi.org/10.1037/h0046234.
5. James A. Russell, "A Circumplex Model of Affect," *Journal of Personality and Social Psychology* 39, no. 6 (1980): 1161–78, https://doi.org/10.1037/h0077714; Klaus R. Scherer, "On the Nature and Function of

Emotion: A Component Process Approach," in *Approaches to Emotion*, ed. Klaus R. Scherer and Paul Ekman (Mahwah, NJ: Lawrence Erlbaum Associates, 1984), 293–317; Nico H. Frijda, *The Emotions* (New York: Cambridge University Press, 1986); Andrew Ortony, Gerald L. Clore, and Allan Collins, *The Cognitive Structure of Emotions* (New York: Cambridge University Press, 1988); Batja Mesquita and Nico H. Frijda, "Cultural Variations in Emotions: A Review," *Psychological Bulletin* 112, no. 2 (1992): 179–204, https://doi.org/10.1037/0033-2909.112.2.179; Gerald L. Clore and Andrew Ortony, "Psychological Construction in the OCC Model of Emotion," *Emotion Review* 5, no. 4 (2013): 335–43, https://doi.org/10.1177/1754073913489751; Batja Mesquita, Michael Boiger, and Jozefien De Leersnyder, "The Cultural Construction of Emotions," *Current Opinion in Psychology* 8 (April 2016): 31–36, https://doi.org/10.1016/j.copsyc.2015.09.015; Lisa Feldman Barrett, *How Emotions Are Made: The Secret Life of the Brain* (New York: Houghton Mifflin Harcourt, 2017); Joseph E. LeDoux, *The Emotional Brain: The Mysterious Underpinnings of Emotional Life* (New York: Simon & Schuster, 1996); Joseph E. LeDoux, "Thoughtful Feelings," *Current Biology* 30, no. 11 (June 1, 2020): R619–23, https://doi.org/10.1016/j.cub.2020.04.012; Owen Flanagan, *How to Do Things with Emotions: The Morality of Anger and Shame Across Cultures* (Princeton, NJ: Princeton University Press, 2021); Batja Mesquita, *Between Us: How Cultures Create Emotions* (New York: Norton, 2022).

6. LeDoux, *The Emotional Brain*.

7. Jaak Panksepp, *Affective Neuroscience: The Foundations of Human and Animal Emotions* (New York: Oxford University Press, 1998); Jaak Panksepp and Lucy Biven, *The Archaeology of Mind: Neuroevolutionary Origins of Human Emotions* (New York: Norton, 2012).

8. Barrett, *How Emotions Are Made*; Joseph E. LeDoux and Richard Brown, "A Higher-Order Theory of Emotional Consciousness," *Proceedings of the National Academy of Sciences* 114, no. 10 (March 7, 2017): E2016–25, https://doi.org/10.1073/pnas.1619316114; LeDoux, "Thoughtful Feelings"; Joseph E. LeDoux, "What Emotions Might Be Like in Other Animals," *Current Biology* 31, no. 13 (July 12, 2021): R824–29, https://doi.org/10.1016/j.cub.2021.05.005; Joseph E. LeDoux, "As Soon as There Was Life, There Was Danger: The Deep History of Survival

Behaviours and the Shallower History of Consciousness," *Philosophical Transactions of the Royal Society B: Biological Sciences* 377, no. 1844 (February 14, 2022): 20210292, https://doi.org/10.1098/rstb.2021.0292; Vincent Taschereau-Dumouchel et al., "Towards an Unconscious Neural Reinforcement Intervention for Common Fears," *Proceedings of the National Academy of Sciences* 115, no. 13 (March 27, 2018): 3470–75, https://doi.org/10.1073/pnas.1721572115; Vincent Taschereau-Dumouchel, Ka-Yuet Liu, and Hakwan Lau, "Unconscious Psychological Treatments for Physiological Survival Circuits," *Current Opinion in Behavioral Sciences* 24 (December 1, 2018): 62–68, https://doi.org/10.1016/j.cobeha.2018.04.010; Vincent Taschereau-Dumouchel, Mitsuo Kawato, and Hakwan Lau, "Multivoxel Pattern Analysis Reveals Dissociations between Subjective Fear and Its Physiological Correlates," *Molecular Psychiatry* 25, no. 10 (October 2020): 2342–54, https://doi.org/10.1038/s41380-019-0520-3.

9. LeDoux, *The Emotional Brain*; LeDoux and Brown, "A Higher-Order Theory of Emotional Consciousness"; Joseph E. LeDoux and Daniel S. Pine, "Using Neuroscience to Help Understand Fear and Anxiety: A Two-System Framework," *American Journal of Psychiatry* 173, no. 11 (November 2016): 1083–93, https://doi.org/10.1176/appi.ajp.2016.16030353; LeDoux, *The Emotional Brain*; Joseph E. LeDoux, "How Does the Non-Conscious Become Conscious?," *Current Biology* 30, no. 5 (March 9, 2020): R196–99, https://doi.org/10.1016/j.cub.2020.01.033.

10. LeDoux, "Thoughtful Feelings."

11. Joshua Conrad Jackson et al., "Emotion Semantics Show Both Cultural Variation and Universal Structure," *Science* 366, no. 6472 (December 20, 2019): 1517–22, https://doi.org/10.1126/science.aaw8160; Alan Page Fiske, "The Lexical Fallacy in Emotion Research: Mistaking Vernacular Words for Psychological Entities," *Psychological Review* 127, no. 1 (2020): 95–113, https://doi.org/10.1037/rev0000174; Flanagan, *How to Do Things with Emotions*; Mesquita, *Between Us*.

12. Lisa Feldman Barrett and James A. Russell, eds., *The Psychological Construction of Emotion* (New York: Guilford Publications, 2014); Clore and Ortony, "Psychological Construction in the OCC Model of Emotion"; LeDoux, "Thoughtful Feelings"; Jackson et al., "Emotion Semantics."

13. Meike Bartels et al., "Exploring the Biological Basis for Happiness," In John Helliwell et al., *World Happiness Report 2022* (Paris: Sustainable Development Solutions Network, 2022), 2, https://worldhappiness.report/ed/2022/exploring-the-biological-basis-for-happiness/.
14. Jeanne L. Tsai, Brian Knutson, and Helene H. Fung, "Cultural Variation in Affect Valuation," *Journal of Personality and Social Psychology* 90, no. 2 (2006): 288–307, https://doi.org/10.1037/0022-3514.90.2.288. /
15. Tim Lomas et al., "Insights from the First Global Survey of Balance and Harmony," in Helliwell et al., *World Happiness Report 2022*, 137, https://worldhappiness.report/ed/2022/insights-from-the-first-global-survey-of-balance-and-harmony/.
16. Sonja Lyubomirsky and Heidi S. Lepper, "A Measure of Subjective Happiness: Preliminary Reliability and Construct Validation," *Social Indicators Research* 46, no. 2 (February 1, 1999): 137–55. https://doi.org/10.1023/A:1006824100041
17. Barbara L. Fredrickson, *Positivity* (New York: Crown Publishers, 2009).
18. Daniel M. Haybron, "What Do We Want from a Theory of Happiness?" *Metaphilosophy* 34, no. 3 (2003): 305–29, https://doi.org/10.1111/1467-9973.00275.
19. Gallup, "Gallup 2020 Global Emotions Report." Gallup.com, https://www.gallup.com/analytics/324191/gallup-global-emotions-report-2020.aspx.
20. John Stuart Mill, *Utilitarianism, and the 1868 Speech on Capital Punishment* (Indianapolis, IN: Hackett, 2001).
21. Mesquita, *Between Us*; Anna Sun, "The Confucian Common Good," in *Ethics in Action for Sustainable Development* (New York: Columbia University Press, 2022).
22. Hazel R. Markus and Shinobu Kitayama, "Culture and the Self: Implications for Cognition, Emotion, and Motivation," *Psychological Review* 98, no. 2 (1991): 224–53, https://doi.org/10.1037/0033-295X.98.2.224; Owen Flanagan, *The Geography of Morals: Varieties of Moral Possibility* (New York: Oxford University Press, 2017); Shinobu Kitayama, Hazel Rose Markus, and Masaru Kurokawa, "Culture, Emotion, and Well-Being: Good Feelings in Japan and the United States,"

Cognition and Emotion 14, no. 1 (January 1, 2000): 93–124, https://doi.org/10.1080/026999300379003; Jeanne L. Tsai, Brian Knutson, and Helene H. Fung, "Cultural Variation in Affect Valuation," *Journal of Personality and Social Psychology* 90, no. 2 (2006): 288–307, https://doi.org/10.1037/0022-3514.90.2.288; Mesquita, *Between Us.*

23. Jeanne L. Tsai, Jennifer Y. Louie, Eva E. Chen, and Yukiko Uchida, "Learning What Feelings to Desire: Socialization of Ideal Affect Through Children's Storybooks," *Personality and Social Psychology Bulletin* 33, no. 1 (January 1, 2007): 17–30, https://doi.org/10.1177/0146167206292749.

24. Mesquita, *Between Us.*

25. Christopher Lasch, *The Culture of Narcissism: American Life in An Age of Diminishing Expectations* (New York: Norton, 2018); Mark R. Leary et al., "Blowhards, Snobs, and Narcissists: Interpersonal Reactions to Excessive Egotism," in *Aversive Interpersonal Behaviors*, edited by Robin M. Kowalski (New York: Plenum Press, 1997), 111–31, https://doi.org/10.1007/978-1-4757-9354-3_6.

26. Markus Kneer and Daniel M. Haybron, "Happiness and Well-Being: Is It All in Your Head? Evidence from the Folk," 2019, https://doi.org/10.13140/RG.2.2.12958.69448.

27. Anna Wierzbicka, "'Happiness' in Cross-Linguistic and Cross-Cultural Perspective," *Daedalus* 133, no. 2 (April 1, 2004): 34–43. https://doi.org/10.1162/001152604323049370.

28. Darrin M. McMahon, *Happiness: A History* (New York: Grove Press, 2006).

29. Markus and Kitayama, "Culture and the Self"; Yukiko Uchida, Vinai Norasakkunkit, and Shinobu Kitayama, "Cultural Constructions of Happiness: Theory and Empirical Evidence," *Journal of Happiness Studies* 5, no. 3 (September 1, 2004): 223–39, https://doi.org/10.1007/s10902-004-8785-9; Flanagan, *The Geography of Morals.*

30. Jaak Panksepp, *Affective Neuroscience: The Foundations of Human and Animal Emotions* (New York: Oxford University Press, 1998).

31. Mill, *Utilitarianism.*

32. LeDoux, "What Emotions Might Be Like in Other Animals."

33. Joseph E. LeDoux, *The Deep History of Ourselves: The Four-Billion-Year Story of How We Got Conscious Brains* (New York: Penguin Books,

2019); Joseph E. LeDoux, "As Soon as There Was Life"; LeDoux, "What Emotions Might Be Like in Other Animals"; Michael Corballis, "The Uniqueness of Human Recursive Thinking," *American Scientist* 95 (May 1, 2007), https://doi.org/10.1511/2007.65.1025; Thomas Suddendorf, *The Gap: The Science of What Separates Us from Other Animals* (New York: Basic Books, 2013); Derek C. Penn, Keith J. Holyoak, and Daniel J. Povinelli, "Darwin's Mistake: Explaining the Discontinuity between Human and Nonhuman Minds," *Behavioral and Brain Sciences* 31, no. 2 (April 2008): 109–30, https://doi.org/10.1017/S0140525X08003543; Michael Tomasello and Hannes Rakoczy, "What Makes Human Cognition Unique? From Individual to Shared to Collective Intentionality," *Mind & Language* 18, no. 2 (2003): 121–47, https://doi.org/10.1111/1468-0017.00217; Etienne Koechlin and Alexandre Hyafil, "Anterior Prefrontal Function and the Limits of Human Decision-Making," *Science* 318, no. 5850 (October 26, 2007): 594–98, https://doi.org/10.1126/science.1142995.

34. Barrett, *How Emotions Are Made*; Barrett and Russell, *The Psychological Construction of Emotion*.
35. Flanagan, *How to Do Things with Emotions*.
36. Lyubomirsky and Lepper, "A Measure of Subjective Happiness"; Daniel M. Haybron, *The Pursuit of Unhappiness: The Elusive Psychology of Well-Being* (New York: Oxford University Press, 2008); Daniel Haybron, "An Emotional State Account of Happiness," in *Theories of Happiness: An Anthology*, edited by Jennifer Wilson Mulnix and M. J. Mulnix (Peterborough, ON: Broadview Press, 2015), 96–114.
37. Bartels et al., "Exploring the Biological Basis for Happiness."
38. Bartels et al., "Exploring the Biological Basis for Happiness."
39. Bartels et al., "Exploring the Biological Basis for Happiness."

4. WHY AVERAGING HAPPINESS SCORES AND COMPARING THEM IS A TERRIBLE IDEA

1. Erik Angner, "The Politics of Happiness: Subjective Vs. Economic Measures as Measures of Social Well-Being," In *Philosophy and Happiness*, ed. Lisa Bortolotti (London: Palgrave Macmillan, 2009),

149–66; Daniel M. Hausman and Michael S. McPherson, *Economic Analysis, Moral Philosophy and Public Policy*, 2nd ed. (Cambridge: Cambridge University Press, 2006).

2. Grant Duncan, "Should Happiness-Maximization Be the Goal of Government?," *Journal of Happiness Studies: An Interdisciplinary Forum on Subjective Well-Being* 11, no. 2 (2010): 163–78, https://doi.org/10.1007/s10902-008-9129-y.

5. POSITIVE AND NEGATIVE EMOTIONS

1. Barbara L. Fredrickson and Michael A. Cohn, "Positive Emotions," in *Handbook of Emotions*, 3rd ed., ed. Michael Lewis, Jeannette M. Haviland-Jones, and Lisa Feldman Barrett (New York: Guilford Press, 2010), 777–96.
2. Ed Diener, Ronald Inglehart, and Louis Tay, "Theory and Validity of Life Satisfaction Scales," *Social Indicators Research* 112, no. 3 (July 1, 2013): 497–527, https://doi.org/10.1007/s11205-012-0076-y; Marcial Losada and Emily Heaphy, "The Role of Positivity and Connectivity in the Performance of Business Teams: A Nonlinear Dynamics Model," *American Behavioral Scientist* 47, no. 6 (February 1, 2004): 740–65, https://doi.org/10.1177/0002764203260208; Jan-Emmanuel De Neve et al., "The Objective Benefits of Subjective Well-Being," SSRN Scholarly Paper 2306651, August 6, 2013, https://papers.ssrn.com/abstract=2306651; Sheldon Cohen et al., "Sociability and Susceptibility to the Common Cold," *Psychological Science* 14, no. 5 (September 1, 2003): 389–95, https://doi.org/10.1111/1467-9280.01452; Deborah D. Danner, David A. Snowdon, and Wallace V. Friesen, "Positive Emotions in Early Life and Longevity: Findings from the Nun Study," *Journal of Personality and Social Psychology* 80, no. 5 (2001): 804–13, https://doi.org/10.1037/0022-3514.80.5.804.
3. Fredrickson and Cohn, "Positive Emotions"; James R. Averill, "On the Paucity of Positive Emotions," in *Assessment and Modification of Emotional Behavior*, ed. Kirk R. Blankstein, Patricia Pliner, and Janet Polivy (Boston: Springer, 1980), 7–45; Janice K. Kiecolt-Glaser et al., "Psychoneuroimmunology: Psychological Influences on Immune Function and Health," *Journal of Consulting and Clinical Psychology* 70, no. 3

(2002): 537–47, https://doi.org/10.1037/0022-006X.70.3.537; Megan L. Rogers et al., "Negative Emotions in Veterans Relate to Suicide Risk Through Feelings of Perceived Burdensomeness and Thwarted Belongingness," *Journal of Affective Disorders* 208 (January 15, 2017): 15–21, https://doi.org/10.1016/j.jad.2016.09.038; Andrea R. Kaniuka et al., "Gratitude and Suicide Risk Among College Students: Substantiating the Protective Benefits of Being Thankful," *Journal of American College Health* 69, no. 6 (August 18, 2021): 660–67, https://doi.org/10.1080/07448481.2019.1705838; Matthew Feinberg, Brett Q. Ford, and Francis J. Flynn, "Rethinking Reappraisal: The Double-Edged Sword of Regulating Negative Emotions in the Workplace," *Organizational Behavior and Human Decision Processes* 161 (November 1, 2020): 1–19, https://doi.org/10.1016/j.obhdp.2020.03.005.

4. Robert C. Solomon, "Against Valence ('Positive' and 'Negative' Emotions) (2001)," in *Not Passion's Slave* (New York: Oxford University Press, 2003), 162–77; Kristján Kristjánsson, "On the Very Idea of 'Negative Emotions,'" *Journal for the Theory of Social Behaviour* 33, no. 4 (2003): 351–64, https://doi.org/10.1046/j.1468-5914.2003.00222.x.
5. Fredrickson and Cohn, "Positive Emotions"; Barbara L. Fredrickson and L. E. Kurtz, "Cultivating Positive Emotions to Enhance Human Flourishing," in *Applied Positive Psychology: Improving Everyday Life, Health, Schools, Work, and Society*, ed. Jeanne Nakamura, Mihaly Csikszentmihalyi, and Stewart I. Donaldson (New York: Routledge/Taylor & Francis, 2011), 35–47.
6. Solomon, "Against Valence."
7. Fredrickson and Kurtz, "Cultivating Positive Emotions," 35.
8. PositivePsychology.com. "Positive Emotions: A List of 26 Examples + Definition in Psychology," March 12, 2018, https://positivepsychology.com/positive-emotions-list-examples-definition-psychology/.
9. Ed Diener et al., *Well-Being for Public Policy* (New York: Oxford University Press, 2009).
10. Andrea Scarantino and Ronald de Sousa, "Emotion," in *The Stanford Encyclopedia of Philosophy*, ed. Edward N. Zalta, Stanford University, 2021, https://plato.stanford.edu/archives/sum2021/entries/emotion/.
11. John Stuart Mill, *Utilitarianism, and the 1868 Speech on Capital Punishment* (Indianapolis, IN: Hackett, 2001), 10.

5. POSITIVE AND NEGATIVE EMOTIONS ☙ 265

12. M. J. Good and B. J. Good, "Ritual, the State, and the Transformation of Emotional Discourse in Iranian Society," *Culture, Medicine and Psychiatry* 12, no. 1 (1988): 43–63; Usha Menon, "Hinduism, Happiness and Wellbeing: A Case Study of Adulthood in an Oriya Hindu Temple Town," in *Happiness Across Cultures: Views of Happiness and Quality of Life in Non-Western Cultures*, ed. Helaine Selin and Gareth Davey (Dordrecht: Springer Netherlands, 2012), 417–34.
13. Mohsen Joshanloo and Dan Weijers, "Aversion to Happiness Across Cultures: A Review of Where and Why People Are Averse to Happiness," *Journal of Happiness Studies* 15, no. 3 (June 1, 2014): 717–35, https://doi.org/10.1007/s10902-013-9489-9.
14. Olga Khazan, "Should Governments Try to Make Us Happy?" *The Atlantic*, September 13, 2013, https://www.theatlantic.com/international/archive/2013/09/should-governments-try-to-make-us-happy/279665/.
15. Karma Ura et al., *A Short Guide to Gross National Happiness Index* (Thimphu: Centre for Bhutan Studies, 2012).
16. Owen Flanagan, *The Geography of Morals: Varieties of Moral Possibility* (New York: Oxford University Press, 2017).
17. Jeanne L. Tsai, Brian Knutson, and Helene H. Fung, "Cultural Variation in Affect Valuation," *Journal of Personality and Social Psychology* 90, no. 2 (2006): 288–307, https://doi.org/10.1037/0022-3514.90.2.288.
18. Yukiko Uchida and Shinobu Kitayama, "Happiness and Unhappiness in East and West: Themes and Variations," *Emotion* 9, no. 4 (2009): 441–56, https://doi.org/10.1037/a0015634.
19. Jeanne L. Tsai et al., "Learning What Feelings to Desire: Socialization of Ideal Affect Through Children's Storybooks," *Personality and Social Psychology Bulletin* 33, no. 1 (January 1, 2007): 17–30, https://doi.org/10.1177/0146167206292749.
20. Hazel Rose Markus and Shinobu Kitayama, "Culture and the Self: Implications for Cognition, Emotion, and Motivation," *Psychological Review* 98, no. 2 (1991): 224–53, https://doi.org/10.1037/0033-295X.98.2.224; Shinobu Kitayama, Hazel Rose Markus, and Masaru Kurokawa, "Culture, Emotion, and Well-Being: Good Feelings in Japan and the United States," *Cognition and Emotion* 14, no. 1 (January 1, 2000): 93–124, https://doi.org/10.1080/026999300379003.

21. Markus and Kitayama, "Culture and the Self."
22. Markus and Kitayama, "Culture and the Self."
23. Shinobu Kitayama, Batja Mesquita, and Mayumi Karasawa, "Cultural Affordances and Emotional Experience: Socially Engaging and Disengaging Emotions in Japan and the United States," *Journal of Personality and Social Psychology* 91, no. 5 (2006): 890–903, https://doi.org/10.1037/0022-3514.91.5.890.
24. Kaiping Peng, Julie Spencer-Rodgers, and Zhong Nian, "Naïve Dialecticism and the Tao of Chinese Thought," in *Indigenous and Cultural Psychology: Understanding People in Context*, ed. Uichol Kim, Kuo-Shu Yang, and Kwang-Kuo Hwang (Boston: Springer, 2006), 247–62, https://doi.org/10.1007/0-387-28662-4_11.
25. Peng, Spencer-Rodgers, and Nian, "Naïve Dialecticism and the Tao of Chinese Thought"; Janxin Leu, Jennifer Wang, and Kelly Koo, "Are Positive Emotions Just as 'Positive' Across Cultures?" *Emotion* 11, no. 4 (2011): 994–99, https://doi.org/10.1037/a0021332; Yuri Miyamoto, Xiaoming Ma, and Amelia G. Petermann, "Cultural Differences in Hedonic Emotion Regulation After a Negative Event," *Emotion* 14, no. 4 (2014): 804–15, https://doi.org/10.1037/a0036257.
26. Miyamoto, Ma, and Petermann, "Cultural Differences in Hedonic Emotion Regulation."
27. Joshanloo and Weijers, "Aversion to Happiness Across Cultures."
28. J. Koo and Eunkook Mark Suh, "Is Happiness a Zero-Sum Game? Belief in Fixed Amount of Happiness (BIFAH) and Subjective Well-Being," *Korean Journal of Social and Personality Psychology* 21, no. 4 (2007): 1–19.
29. Yukiko Uchida and Shinobu Kitayama, "Happiness and Unhappiness in East and West: Themes and Variations," *Emotion* 9, no. 4 (2009): 441–56, https://doi.org/10.1037/a0015634.
30. Hiroshi Minami, *Psychology of the Japanese People* (Tokyo: University of Tokyo Press, 1971); Joshanloo and Weijers. "Aversion to Happiness"; Fred B. Bryant and Joseph Veroff, *Savoring: A New Model of Positive Experience* (New York: Psychology Press, 2007).
31. Owen Flanagan, *How to Do Things with Emotions: The Morality of Anger and Shame Across Cultures* (Princeton, NJ: Princeton University Press, 2021); Batja Mesquita, *Between Us: How Cultures Create Emotions*

(New York: Norton, 2022); Catherine Lutz, *Unnatural Emotions* (Chicago: University of Chicago Press, 1988); Andrew Beatty, "Current Emotion Research in Anthropology: Reporting the Field," *Emotion Review* 5, no. 4 (October 1, 2013): 414–22, https://doi.org/10.1177/1754073913490045.

6. HAPPINESS AND WELL-BEING AS CULTURAL PROJECTS

1. Shalom H. Schwartz, "Cultural Value Orientations: Nature and Implications of National Differences," *Journal of the Higher School of Economics* 5, no. 2 (2008): 37–67.
2. Schwartz, "Cultural Value Orientations."
3. Jozefien De Leersnyder et al., "Emotions and Concerns: Situational Evidence for Their Systematic Co-Occurrence," *Emotion* 18, no. 4 (2018): 597–614, https://doi.org/10.1037/emo0000314.
4. Eunkook Mark Suh et al., "The Shifting Basis of Life Satisfaction Judgments Across Cultures: Emotions Versus Norms," *Journal of Personality and Social Psychology* 74, no. 2 (1998): 482–93, https://doi.org/10.1037/0022-3514.74.2.482.
5. Shigehiro Oishi and Ed Diener, "Goals, Culture, and Subjective Well-Being," *Personality and Social Psychology Bulletin* 27, no. 12 (December 1, 2001): 1674–82, https://doi.org/10.1177/01461672012712010.
6. Brock Bastian et al., "Is Valuing Positive Emotion Associated with Life Satisfaction?" *Emotion* 14, no. 4 (2014): 639–45, https://doi.org/10.1037/a0036466.
7. Richard P. Bagozzi, Nancy Wong, and Youjae Yi, "The Role of Culture and Gender in the Relationship Between Positive and Negative Affect," *Cognition and Emotion* 13, no. 6 (October 1, 1999): 641–72, https://doi.org/10.1080/026999399379023; Janxin Leu et al., "Situational Differences in Dialectical Emotions: Boundary Conditions in a Cultural Comparison of North Americans and East Asians," *Cognition and Emotion* 24, no. 3 (April 1, 2010): 419–35, https://doi.org/10.1080/02699930802650911; Batja Mesquita and Mayumi Karasawa, "Different Emotional Lives," *Cognition and Emotion* 16, no. 1 (2002): 127–41, https://doi.org/10.1080/0269993014000176; Alexander

Kirchner-Häusler et al., "Relatively Happy: The Role of the Positive-to-Negative Affect Ratio in Japanese and Belgian Couples," *Journal of Cross-Cultural Psychology* 53, no. 1 (January 1, 2022): 66–86, https://doi.org/10.1177/00220221211051016; Ulrich Schimmack, Shigehiro Oishi, and Ed Diener, "Cultural Influences on the Relation Between Pleasant Emotions and Unpleasant Emotions: Asian Dialectic Philosophies or Individualism-Collectivism?" *Cognition and Emotion* 16, no. 6 (November 1, 2002): 705–19, https://doi.org/10.1080/02699930143000590; Xiaoming Ma, Maya Tamir, and Yuri Miyamoto, "A Socio-Cultural Instrumental Approach to Emotion Regulation: Culture and the Regulation of Positive Emotions," *Emotion* 18, no. 1 (2018): 138–52, https://doi.org/10.1037/emo0000315; Yuri Miyamoto and Xiaoming Ma, "Dampening or Savoring Positive Emotions: A Dialectical Cultural Script Guides Emotion Regulation," *Emotion* 11, no. 6 (2011): 1346–57, https://doi.org/10.1037/a0025135; Yuri Miyamoto, Xiaoming Ma, and Amelia G. Petermann, "Cultural Differences in Hedonic Emotion Regulation After a Negative Event," *Emotion* 14, no. 4 (2014): 804–15, https://doi.org/10.1037/a0036257.
8. Suh et al., "Shifting Basis of Life Satisfaction Judgments."
9. Bastian et al., "Is Valuing Positive Emotion Associated with Life Satisfaction?"
10. Brock Bastian et al., "Feeling Bad about Being Sad: The Role of Social Expectancies in Amplifying Negative Mood," *Emotion* 12, no. 1 (2012): 69–80, https://doi.org/10.1037/a0024755; Bastian et al., "Is Valuing Positive Emotion Associated with Life Satisfaction?"
11. Barbara Ehrenreich, *Bright-Sided: How Positive Thinking Is Undermining America* (London: Picador, 2009).
12. Anna Sun. "The Confucian Conception of the Common Good in Contemporary China," In *Ethics in Action for Sustainable Development*, ed. Jeffrey Sachs et al. (New York: Columbia University Press, 2022), 83–91.
13. Brett Q. Ford et al., "Culture Shapes Whether the Pursuit of Happiness Predicts Higher or Lower Well-Being," *Journal of Experimental Psychology: General* 144, no. 6 (2015): 1053–62, https://doi.org/10.1037/xge0000108.
14. Maya Tamir and Tony Gutentag, "Desired Emotional States: Their Nature, Causes, and Implications for Emotion Regulation," *Current*

6. HAPPINESS AND WELL-BEING AS CULTURAL PROJECTS ⊗ 269

Opinion in Psychology, Emotion 17 (October 1, 2017): 84–88, https://doi.org/10.1016/j.copsyc.2017.06.014.

15. Maya Tamir and Brett Q. Ford, "Choosing to Be Afraid: Preferences for Fear as a Function of Goal Pursuit," *Emotion* 9, no. 4 (2009): 488–97. https://doi.org/10.1037/a0015882; Maya Tamir, Christopher Mitchell, and James J. Gross, "Hedonic and Instrumental Motives in Anger Regulation," *Psychological Science* 19, no. 4 (April 1, 2008): 324–28, https://doi.org/10.1111/j.1467-9280.2008.02088.x; Jeanne L. Tsai et al., "Learning What Feelings to Desire: Socialization of Ideal Affect Through Children's Storybooks," *Personality and Social Psychology Bulletin* 33, no. 1 (2007): 17–30, https://doi.org/10.1177/0146167206292749.

16. Batja Mesquita, Michael Boiger, and Jozefien De Leersnyder, "The Cultural Construction of Emotions," *Current Opinion in Psychology* 8 (April 2016): 31–36, https://doi.org/10.1016/j.copsyc.2015.09.015; Batja Mesquita, Michael Boiger, and Jozefien De Leersnyder, "Doing Emotions: The Role of Culture in Everyday Emotions." *European Review of Social Psychology* 28, no. 1 (January 1, 2017): 95–133, https://doi.org/10.1080/10463283.2017.1329107.

17. Michael Boiger et al., "Condoned or Condemned: The Situational Affordance of Anger and Shame in the United States and Japan," *Personality and Social Psychology Bulletin* 39, no. 4 (April 1, 2013): 540–53, https://doi.org/10.1177/0146167213478201; Owen Flanagan, *The Geography of Morals: Varieties of Moral Possibility* (New York: Oxford University Press, 2017); Owen Flanagan, *How to Do Things with Emotions: The Morality of Anger and Shame Across Cultures* (Princeton, NJ: Princeton University Press, 2021).

18. Maya Tamir et al., "Desired Emotions Across Cultures: A Value-Based Account," *Journal of Personality and Social Psychology* 111, no. 1 (2016): 67–82, https://doi.org/10.1037/pspp0000007; Shinobu Kitayama, Batja Mesquita, and Mayumi Karasawa, "Cultural Affordances and Emotional Experience: Socially Engaging and Disengaging Emotions in Japan and the United States," *Journal of Personality and Social Psychology* 91, no. 5 (2006): 890–903, https://doi.org/10.1037/0022-3514.91.5.890; Boiger et al., "Condoned or Condemned"; Tsai et al., "Learning What Feelings to Desire."

19. Kitayama, Mesquita, and Karasawa, "Cultural Affordances and Emotional Experience"; Batja Mesquita, "Emotions as Dynamic Cultural

Phenomena," in *Handbook of Affective Sciences*, ed. R. J. Davidson, K. R. Scherer, and H. H. Goldsmith (New York: Oxford University Press, 2003), 871–90; Batja Mesquita, Michael Boiger, and Jozefien De Leersnyder, "The Cultural Construction of Emotions," *Current Opinion in Psychology* 8 (April 2016): 31–36, https://doi.org/10.1016/j.copsyc.2015.09.015; Jeanne L. Tsai, Brian Knutson, and Helene H. Fung, "Cultural Variation in Affect Valuation," *Journal of Personality and Social Psychology* 90, no. 2 (February 2006): 288–307, https://doi.org/10.1037/0022-3514.90.2.288.

20. Yuri Miyamoto, Jiah Yoo, and Brooke Wilken, "Well-Being and Health: A Cultural Psychology of Optimal Human Functioning," in *Handbook of Cultural Psychology*, 2nd ed., ed. Dov Cohen and Shinobu Kitayama (New York: Guilford Press, 2019), 319–42.

21. Tsai et al., "Learning What Feelings to Desire."

22. Tsai, Knutson, and Fung, "Cultural Variation in Affect Valuation."

23. Jozefien De Leersnyder, Heejung Kim, and Batja Mesquita, "Feeling Right Is Feeling Good: Psychological Well-Being and Emotional Fit with Culture in Autonomy- Versus Relatedness-Promoting Situations," *Frontiers in Psychology* 6 (2015): 1–12, https://www.frontiersin.org/article/10.3389/fpsyg.2015.00630; Jozefien De Leersnyder et al., "Emotional Fit with Culture: A Predictor of Individual Differences in Relational Well-Being," *Emotion* 14, no. 2 (2014): 241–45, https://doi.org/10.1037/a0035296; Kitayama, Mesquita, and Karasawa, "Cultural Affordances and Emotional Experience"; Tsai, Knutson, and Fung, "Cultural Variation in Affect Valuation."

24. Magali Clobert et al., "Feeling Excited or Taking a Bath: Do Distinct Pathways Underlie the Positive Affect–Health Link in the U.S. and Japan?" *Emotion* 20, no. 2 (2020): 164–78, https://doi.org/10.1037/emo0000531; Bastian et al., "Is Valuing Positive Emotion Associated with Life Satisfaction?"; Katherine B. Curhan et al., "Subjective and Objective Hierarchies and Their Relations to Psychological Well-Being: A U.S./Japan Comparison," *Social Psychological and Personality Science* 5, no. 8 (November 1, 2014): 855–64, https://doi.org/10.1177/1948550614538461; Yuri Miyamoto et al., "Negative Emotions Predict Elevated Interleukin-6 in the United States but Not in Japan," *Brain, Behavior, and Immunity* 34 (November 1, 2013): 79–85, https://doi.org/10.1016/j.bbi.2013.07.173.

25. Miyamoto, Yoo, and Wilken, "Well-Being and Health."
26. J. W. Berry et al., *Immigrant Youth in Cultural Transition: Acculturation, Identity, and Adaptation Across National Contexts* (Mahwah, NJ: Lawrence Erlbaum Associates, 2006); C. Ward and A. Rana-Deuba, "Home and Host Culture Influences on Sojourner Adjustment," *International Journal of Intercultural Relations* 24, no. 3 (2000): 291–306, https://doi.org/10.1016/S0147-1767(00)00002-X; Alejandro Portes and Julia Sensenbrenner, "Embeddedness and Immigration: Notes on the Social Determinants of Economic Action," *American Journal of Sociology* 98, no. 6 (May 1993): 1320–50, https://doi.org/10.1086/230191.
27. Ronald S. Burt, "The Network Structure of Social Capital," *Research in Organizational Behavior* 22 (January 1, 2000): 345–423, https://doi.org/10.1016/S0191-3085(00)22009-1.
28. Gülseli Baysu and Karen Phalet, "Staying on or Dropping Out? The Role of Intergroup Friendship and Perceived Teacher Support in Minority and Nonminority School Careers," *Teachers College Record* 114, no. 5 (May 1, 2012): 1–25, https://doi.org/10.1177/016146811211400507; Bram Lancee, "The Economic Returns of Immigrants' Bonding and Bridging Social Capital: The Case of the Netherlands," *International Migration Review* 44, no. 1 (2010): 202–26, https://doi.org/10.1111/j.1747-7379.2009.00803.x.
29. Burt, "The Network Structure of Social Capital."
30. The reported research on acculturation made use of a newly developed a novel measure of emotional fit between minority and majority members, the Emotional Patterns Questionnaire (EPQ). This measure captures the *objective* emotional fit between minority and majority members (and thus goes beyond the fit *as perceived* by the immigrant minority individuals). The best predictor of minorities' emotional acculturation was actual contact with the majority; the desire to adopt the majority culture, which has been the focus of much previous acculturation research, was unrelated to emotional acculturation.
31. Alba Jasini et al., "Tuning in Emotionally: Associations of Cultural Exposure with Distal and Proximal Emotional Fit in Acculturating Youth," *European Journal of Social Psychology* 49, no. 2 (2019): 352–65, https://doi.org/10.1002/ejsp.2516; Jozefien De Leersnyder, Batja Mesquita, and Heejung S. Kim, "Where Do My Emotions Belong? A Study of Immigrants' Emotional Acculturation," *Personality and Social*

Psychology Bulletin 37, no. 4 (April 1, 2011): 451–63, https://doi.org/10.1177/0146167211399103.

32. Nathan S. Consedine, Yulia E. Chentsova-Dutton, and Yulia S. Krivoshekova, "Emotional Acculturation Predicts Better Somatic Health: Experiential and Expressive Acculturation Among Immigrant Women from Four Ethnic Groups," *Journal of Social and Clinical Psychology* 33, no. 10 (December 2014): 867–89, https://doi.org/10.1521/jscp.2014.33.10.867.

33. Alba Jasini et al., "Tuning in Emotionally: Associations of Cultural Exposure with Distal and Proximal Fit in Acculturating Youth," *European Journal of Social Psychology* 49, no. 2 (20190301): 352–65, https://doi.org/10.1002/ejsp.2516.

34. Jennifer Crocker and Brenda Major, "Social Stigma and Self-Esteem: The Self-Protective Properties of Stigma," *Psychological Review* 96, no. 4 (1989): 608–30, https://doi.org/10.1037/0033-295X.96.4.608.

35. Batja Mesquita, Jozefien De Leersnyder, and Alba Jasini, "The Cultural Psychology of Acculturation," in *Handbook of Cultural Psychology, Second Edition*, ed. Shinobu Kitayama and Dov Cohen (New York: Guilford Press, 2019), 502–35.

36. Jozefien De Leersnyder, Heejung S. Kim, and Batja Mesquita, "My Emotions Belong Here and There: Extending the Phenomenon of Emotional Acculturation to Heritage Culture Fit," *Cognition and Emotion* 34, no. 8 (November 16, 2020): 1573–90, https://doi.org/10.1080/02699931.2020.1781063.

37. De Leersnyder, Kim, and Mesquita, "My Emotions Belong Here and There"; Wei Qi Elaine Perunovic, Daniel Heller, and Eshkol Rafaeli, "Within-Person Changes in the Structure of Emotion: The Role of Cultural Identification and Language," *Psychological Science* 18, no. 7 (July 2007): 607–13, https://doi.org/10.1111/j.1467-9280.2007.01947.x.

38. Marina Doucerain, Jessica Dere, and Andrew G. Ryder, "Travels in Hyper-Diversity: Multiculturalism and the Contextual Assessment of Acculturation," *International Journal of Intercultural Relations* 37, no. 6 (November 1, 2013): 686–99, https://doi.org/10.1016/j.ijintrel.2013.09.007; Laurence J. Kirmayer, Jaswant Guzder, and Cécile Rousseau, *Cultural Consultation: Encountering the Other in Mental Health Care* (New York: Springer, 2014).

7. HAPPINESS AND WELL-BEING IN CONTEMPORARY CHINA

1. Lydia Davis, *The Thirteenth Woman and Other Stories* (New York: Living Hand, 1976), 50.
2. Joseph E. LeDoux, *The Deep History of Ourselves: The Four-Billion-Year Story of How We Got Conscious Brains* (New York: Penguin Books, 2019), 351, 354–57.
3. Hazel Rose Markus and Shinobu Kitayama, "Culture and the Self: Implications for Cognition, Emotion, and Motivation," *Psychological Review* 98, no. 2 (1991): 224–53, https://doi.org/10.1037/0033-295X.98.2.224; Shinobu Kitayama, Hazel Rose Markus, and Masaru Kurokawa, "Culture, Emotion, and Well-Being: Good Feelings in Japan and the United States," *Cognition and Emotion* 14, no. 1 (January 1, 2000): 93–124, https://doi.org/10.1080/026999300379003.
4. Owen Flanagan, *The Geography of Morals: Varieties of Moral Possibility* (New York: Oxford University Press, 2017), 21.
5. Julia Annas, *The Morality of Happiness* (New York: Oxford University Press, 1993).
6. Annas, *The Morality of Happiness*, 15.
7. Sébastien Billioud, ed., *The Varieties of Confucian Experience: Documenting a Grassroots Revival of Tradition* (Leiden: Brill, 2018); Sébastien Billioud and Joël Thoraval, *The Sage and the People: The Confucian Revival in China* (New York: Oxford University Press, 2015); Kenneth J. Hammond and Jeffrey L. Richey, eds., *The Sage Returns: Confucian Revival in Contemporary China* (Albany: State University of New York Press, 2014); Anna Sun, *Confucianism as a World Religion: Contested Histories and Contemporary Realities* (Princeton, NJ: Princeton University Press, 2013); Stephen C. Angle, *Contemporary Confucian Political Philosophy* (New York: Polity, 2012); Daniel A. Bell, *China's New Confucianism: Politics and Everyday Life in a Changing Society* (Princeton, NJ: Princeton University Press, 2008).
8. Sebastien Billioud and Joël Thoraval, *The Sage and the People: The Confucian Revival in China* (Leiden: Brill, 2018); Anna Sun, *Confucianism as a World Religion: Contested Histories and Contemporary Realities* (Princeton, NJ: Princeton University Press, 2013); Bell, *China's New Confucianism*.

9. Robert N. Bellah et al., *Habits of the Heart: Individualism and Commitment in American Life* (Berkeley: University of California Press, 1985).
10. Kwong-Loi Shun and David B. Wong, *Confucian Ethics: A Comparative Study of Self, Autonomy, and Community* (New York: Cambridge University Press, 2004).
11. Max Weber, *The Theory of Social and Economic Organization* (New York: Simon & Schuster, 2009).
12. John Osburg, *Anxious Wealth: Money and Morality Among China's New Rich* (Stanford, CA: Stanford University Press, 2013); Hai Ren, *The Middle Class in Neoliberal China: Governing Risk, Life-Building, and Themed Spaces* (London: Routledge, 2012); Hai Ren, *Neoliberalism and Culture in China and Hong Kong: The Countdown of Time* (London: Routledge, 2010).
13. Lisa Rofel, *Desiring China: Experiments in Neoliberalism, Sexuality, and Public Culture* (Durham, NC: Duke University Press, 2007), 3.
14. Russell M. Jeung, Seanan S. Fong, and Helen Jin Kim, *Family Sacrifices: The Worldviews and Ethics of Chinese Americans* (New York: Oxford University Press, 2019); Philip J. Ivanhoe, *Three Streams: Confucian Reflections on Learning and the Moral Heart-Mind in China, Korea, and Japan* (New York: Oxford University Press, 2016); Fenggang Yang and Joseph Tamney, eds., *Confucianism and Spiritual Traditions in Modern China and Beyond* (Leiden: Brill, 2011); Weiming Tu, *Confucian Traditions in East Asian Modernity: Moral Education and Economic Culture in Japan and the Four Mini-Dragons* (Cambridge, MA: Harvard University Press, 1996); Phillip J. Ivanhoe, *Confucian Moral Self Cultivation* (New York: Peter Lang, 1993).
15. R. Inglehart et al., eds., World Values Survey: Round Four—Country-Pooled Datafile Version, 2014, www.worldvaluessurvey.org/WVSDocumentationWV4.jsp.
16. Horizon, "Chinese Spiritual Life Survey," Association of Religious Data Archives, 2007, https://www.thearda.com/data-archive?fid=SPRTCHNA.
17. Horizon, "The Meaning of a Good Life Survey," 2016.
18. Anna Sun, "To Be or Not to Be a Confucian: Explicit and Implicit Religious Identities in the Global Twenty-First Century," *Chinese*

Religions Going Global 11 (December 7, 2020): 210–35, https://doi.org
/10.1163/9789004443327_013; Anna Sun, "Thinking with Weber's Religion of China in the Twenty-First Century," *Review of Religion and Chinese Society* 7, no. 2 (December 4, 2020): 250–70, https://doi.org/10
.1163/22143955-00702006; Sun, *Confucianism as a World Religion*; Horizon, "The Meaning of a Good Life Survey."

19. Horizon, "The Meaning of a Good Life Survey"; Horizon, "Chinese Spiritual Life Survey."
20. Sun, "To Be or Not to Be a Confucian."
21. Kelly James Clark and Justin T. Winslett, "The Evolutionary Psychology of Chinese Religion: Pre-Qin High Gods as Punishers and Rewarders," *Journal of the American Academy of Religion* 79, no. 4 (December 1, 2011): 928–60, https://doi.org/10.1093/jaarel/lfr018.
22. Edward Slingerland, "Big Gods, Historical Explanation, and the Value of Integrating the History of Religion into the Broader Academy," *Religion* 45, no. 4 (October 2, 2015): 585–602, https://doi.org/10.1080/0048721X.2015.1073487.
23. Ara Norenzayan, *Big Gods: How Religion Transformed Cooperation and Conflict* (Princeton, NJ: Princeton University Press, 2015).
24. Yingtao Li and Di Wang, "China's 'State Feminism' in Context," in *Women of Asia: Globalization, Development, and Gender Equity*, ed. Mehrangiz Najafizadeh and Linda Lindsey (Routledge, 2019), 74.
25. CPPCC (Chinese People's Political Consultative Conference). "Modern History Sourcebook: The Common Program of the Chinese People's Political Consultative Conference, 1949," https://sourcebooks.fordham.edu/mod/1949-ccp-program.asp
26. Some contend that the socialist feminist movement fell short of achieving gender equality. Mayfair Mei-hui Yang, for example, argues that although women were "catapulted into the public sphere of labor and politics," this was simply a means to projects of nation building. Rather than being liberated from the shackles of patriarchy, women were in fact transformed into "state subjects in a new masculine state order" (63). Yang further suggests that the fragility of socialist feminism reveals itself "in the rapidity and ease with which a more overt patriarchal culture has reasserted itself with the return to a privatized economy and transnational capital in the post-Mao era" (39). Mayfair

Mei-hui Yang, "From Gender Erasure to Gender Difference: State Feminism, Consumer Sexuality, and Women's Public Sphere in China," in *Spaces of Their Own: Women's Public Sphere in Transnational China*, ed. Mayfair Mei-hui Yang (University of Minnesota Press, 1999), 35–67.

27. Zheng Wang, "Gender, Employment and Women's Resistance," in *Chinese Society: Change, Conflict and Resistance*, ed. Elizabeth J. Perry and Mark Selden (Routledge, 2003), 162–86; Yige Dong, "The Crisis of Social Reproduction and 'Made-in-China' Feminism," *Soundings: A Journal of Politics and Culture* 79, (November 1, 2021): 10–23, https://doi.org/10.3898/SOUN.79.01.2021.

28. World Economic Forum. "Global Gender Gap Report 2021," https://www.weforum.org/reports/global-gender-gap-report-2021/; World Economic Forum. "Global Gender Gap Report 2008," https://www.weforum.org/reports/global-gender-gap-report-2008/.

29. Mariya Brussevich, Era Dabla-Norris, and Bin Grace Li, "China's Rebalancing and Gender Inequality," SSRN Scholarly Paper, https://papers.ssrn.com/abstract=4026314, 1.

30. Brussevich, Dabla-Norris, and Li, "China's Rebalancing," 20.

31. Titan Alon, Matthias Doepke, Jane Olmstead-Rumsey, and Michèle Tertilt, "The Impact of COVID-19 on Gender Equality," Working Paper 26947, National Bureau of Economic Research, April 2020, https://doi.org/10.3386/w26947; John Bluedorn et al., "Gender and Employment in the COVID-19 Recession: Evidence on 'She-cessions,'" *IMF Working Papers* 95 (March 31, 2021); Hai-Anh H. Dang and Cuong Viet Nguyen, "Gender Inequality During the COVID-19 Pandemic: Income, Expenditure, Savings, and Job Loss," *World Development* 140 (April 1, 2021): 105296, https://doi.org/10.1016/j.worlddev.2020.105296.

32. World Economic Forum, "Global Gender Gap Report 2021," 36.

33. Leta Hong Fincher, *Leftover Women: The Resurgence of Gender Inequality in China* (London: Zed Books, 2014), 187.

34. World Economic Forum, "Global Gender Gap Report 2021," 36.

35. Fincher, *Leftover Women*.

36. Fincher, *Leftover Women*, 44.

37. Leta Hong Fincher, *Betraying Big Brother: The Feminist Awakening in China* (New York: Verso Books, 2021).
38. Fincher, *Betraying Big Brother*.
39. Fincher, *Betraying Big Brother*.
40. Fincher, *Betraying Big Brother*.
41. China's first feminist awakening can be traced to the end of nineteenth century, a period when the nation was in the throes of internal crises as well as invasions from Japan and the Western imperial powers. Jin Tianhe, a male liberal educator and political activist, wrote the first feminist manifesto entitled *The Women's Bell* in 1903. This was challenged by He-Yin Zhen, a preeminent female theorist who published works in the anarcho-feminist journal that she founded in 1907. Lydia He Liu, Rebecca E. Karl, and Dorothy Ko, eds., *The Birth of Chinese Feminism: Essential Texts in Transnational Theory* (New York: Columbia University Press, 2013).
42. Woo adds that from the classical period to the Song, not only Confucianism, but also Daoism, Buddhism, and "their syncreticized folk religious relatives" contained concepts that were unfriendly and antagonistic to women. Tak-Ling Terry Woo, "Two Discourses on Women from the Classical Period to the Song: An Integrated Approach," in *The Bloomsbury Research Handbook of Chinese Philosophy and Gender*, ed. Ann A. Pang-White (New York: Bloomsbury, 2016), 37.
43. Zhongshu Dong, *Chunqiu Fanlu* (Beijing: Zhonghua Shuju, 1996).
44. Recently, there have been theoretical attempts to reformulate and revitalize Confucianism in ways that are amenable to feminism. For example, Li argues that a key concept in Confucianism, *ren* (benevolence) has a lot in common with the feminist notion of care, which makes it possible for the two to "learn from and support each other." Chenyang Li, "The Confucian Concept of Jen and the Feminist Ethics of Care: A Comparative Study," in *The Sage and the Second Sex*, ed. Chenyang Li (LaSalle, IL: Open Court, 2000), 23. Zheng Wang, "Research on Women in Contemporary China," in *Guide to Women's Studies in China*, ed. Gail Hershatter, Emily Honig, Susan Mann, and Lisa Rofel (Berkeley: Institute of East Asian Studies, University of California, Berkeley, 1998), 1-43.

45. Wang, "Research on Women in Contemporary China."
46. Wang, "Research on Women in Contemporary China."
47. Yang, "From Gender Erasure to Gender Difference."
48. Emily Honig, "Maoist Mappings of Gender: Reassessing the Red Guards," in *Chinese Femininities, Chinese Masculinities: A Reader*, ed. Susan Brownell (Berkeley: University of California Press, 2002), 255--66.
49. Zheng Wang, "Feminist Struggles in a Changing China," in *Feminisms with Chinese Characteristics*, ed. Ping Zhu and Hui Faye Xiao (Syracuse University Press, 2021), 135.
50. Nicola Spakowski, "'Gender' Trouble: Feminism in China Under the Impact of Western Theory and the Spatialization of Identity," *Positions: Asia Critique* 19, no. 1 (February 1, 2011): 31–54, https://doi.org/10.1215/10679847-2010-023, 34.

8. HAPPINESS, RACE, AND HERMENEUTICAL JUSTICE

1. Ed Diener et al., *Well-Being for Public Policy* (New York: Oxford University Press, 2009).
2. Carol Graham, *Happiness for All? Unequal Hopes and Lives in Pursuit of the American Dream* (Princeton, NJ: Princeton University Press, 2017), 98.
3. Ta-Nehisi Coates, *Between the World and Me* (New York: Random House, 2015).
4. Miranda Fricker, *Epistemic Injustice: Power and the Ethics of Knowing* (New York: Oxford University Press, 2007).
5. Fricker, *Epistemic Injustice*, 148.
6. Ian James Kidd, José Medina, and Gaile Pohlhaus Jr., *The Routledge Handbook of Epistemic Injustice* (New York: Routledge, 2017).
7. Arlie Russell Hochschild, "Emotion Work, Feeling Rules, and Social Structure," *American Journal of Sociology* 85, no. 3 (1979): 551–75.
8. Amia Srinivasan, "The Aptness of Anger," *Journal of Political Philosophy* 26, no. 2 (2018): 123–44, https://doi.org/10.1111/jopp.12130.
9. James Baldwin et al., "The Negro in American Culture," *Crosscurrents* 11, no. 3 (1961): 205–24.

10. American Psychiatric Association, "APA's Apology to Black, Indigenous and People of Color for Its Support of Structural Racism in Psychiatry," 2021, https://www.psychiatry.org/newsroom/apa-apology-for-its-support-of-structural-racism-in-psychiatry.
11. Benjamin Rush, *Medical Inquiries and Observations, Upon the Diseases of the Mind* (London: Kimber & Richardson, 1812).
12. Benjamin Rush, "Observations Intended to Favour a Supposition That the Black Color (As It Is Called) of the Negroes Is Derived from the Leprosy," *Transactions of the American Philosophical Society* 4 (1799): 289–97, https://doi.org/10.2307/1005108.
13. Samuel A. Cartwright, "Report on Diseases and Peculiarities of the Negro race," reprinted in *Health, Disease, and Illness: Concepts in Medicine*, ed. Arthur L. Caplan, James J. McCartney, and Dominic A. Sisti (Washington, DC: Georgetown University Press, 2004), 28–39.
14. Jonathan M. Metzl, *The Protest Psychosis: How Schizophrenia Became a Black Disease* (Boston: Beacon Press, 2010).
15. Shankar Vendantam, "Racial Disparities Found in Pinpointing Mental Illness," *Washington Post*, June 28, 2005.
16. Carl C. Bell, Willie Mae Jackson, and Briatta H. Bell, "Misdiagnosis of African-Americans with Psychiatric Issues—Part I," *Journal of the National Medical Association* 107, no. 3 (June 1, 2015): 25–34, https://doi.org/10.1016/S0027-9684(15)30048-1; "Misdiagnosis of African-Americans with Psychiatric Issues—Part II," *Journal of the National Medical Association* 107, no. 3 (June 1, 2015): 35–41, https://doi.org/10.1016/S0027-9684(15)30049-3.
17. Bell, Jackson, and Bell, "Misdiagnosis of African-Americans with Psychiatric Issues—Part I," 25.
18. American Psychiatric Association (APA), *Diagnostic and Statistical Manual of Mental Disorders*, 5th ed. (New York: American Psychiatric Publishing, 2013).
19. Nassir Ghaemi, *A First-Rate Madness: Uncovering the Links Between Leadership and Mental Illness* (New York: Penguin Books, 2012), 101–6.
20. Rahn Kennedy Bailey, Holly L. Blackmon, and Francis L. Stevens, "Major Depressive Disorder in the African American Population: Meeting the Challenges of Stigma, Misdiagnosis, and Treatment

Disparities," *Journal of the National Medical Association* 101, no. 11 (November 1, 2009): 1084–89, https://doi.org/10.1016/S0027-9684(15)31102-0.
21. F. M. Baker, "Diagnosing Depression in African Americans," *Community Mental Health Journal* 37, no. 1 (February 1, 2001): 31–38, https://doi.org/10.1023/A:1026540321366.
22. Baker, "Diagnosing Depression in African Americans," 34.
23. Baker, "Diagnosing Depression in African Americans."
24. Baker, "Diagnosing Depression in African Americans"; Derek H. Suite, Robert La Bril, Annelle Primm, and Phyllis Harrison-Ross, "Beyond Misdiagnosis, Misunderstanding and Mistrust: Relevance of the Historical Perspective in the Medical and Mental Health Treatment of People of Color," *Journal of the National Medical Association* 99, no. 8 (August 2007): 879–85; Bell, Jackson, and Bell, "Misdiagnosis of African Americans with Psychiatric Issues—Part II," 35–41.
25. Baker, "Diagnosing Depression in African Americans."
26. Johns Hopkins Medicine, "Study Suggests Overdiagnosis of Schizophrenia: Reported Symptoms of Anxiety and Hearing Voices Most Common Reasons for Misdiagnosis by Non-Specialty Physicians," *Science Daily*, April 22, 2019, https://www.sciencedaily.com/releases/2019/04/190422090842.htm.
27. Congressional Black Caucus, "Emergency Task Force on Black Youth Suicide and Mental Health," https://watsoncoleman.house.gov/suicidetaskforce.
28. Roslyn Holliday-Moore, "Alarming Suicide Trends in African American Children: An Urgent Issue," 2019, https://www.samhsa.gov/blog/alarming-suicide-trends-african-american-children-urgent-issue.
29. Denise Mann, "Pandemic Tied to Higher Suicide Rate in Blacks, Lowered Rate in Whites: Study," *USA Today*, December 17, 2020.
30. Diener et al., *Well-Being for Public Policy*, 3.
31. Jason Cherkis, "What Happens to Your Mental Health When You Can't Pay Your Rent?" *New York Times*, March 10, 2021, https://www.nytimes.com/2021/03/10/opinion/minimum-wage-mental-health.html.
32. Daniel M. Haybron and Valerie Tiberius, "Normative Foundations for Well-Being Policy," *Papers on Economics and Evolution* (2012): 1202, https://www.econstor.eu/handle/10419/57571.

9. INTERPRETING SELF-REPORTS OF WELL-BEING

1. Carol D. Ryff, "Happiness Is Everything, or Is It? Explorations on the Meaning of Psychological Well-Being," *Journal of Personality and Social Psychology* 57, no. 6 (1989): 1069–81, https://doi.org/10.1037/0022-3514.57 .6.1069.; Julie Butler and Margaret L. Kern, "The PERMA Profiler: A Brief Multidimensional Measure of Flourishing," 2015, available from http://www.peggykern.org/questionnaries.html.
2. Ed Diener, Richard E. Lucas, and Shigehiro Oishi, "Advances and Open Questions in the Science of Subjective Well-Being," *Collabra: Psychology* 4, no. 1 (2018): 15, https://doi.org/10.1525/collabra.115; Ed Diener, Shigehiro Oishi, and Louis Tay, eds., *Handbook of Well-Being* (Salt Lake City, UT: DEF Publishers, 2018); Michael Eid and Randy J. Larsen, eds., *The Science of Subjective Well-Being* (New York: Guilford Press, 2008).
3. Anna Alexandrova, *A Philosophy for the Science of Well-Being* (New York: Oxford University Press, 2017); Anna Alexandrova and Daniel M. Haybron, "Is Construct Validation Valid?" *Philosophy of Science* 83, no. 5 (December 2016): 1098–1109, https://doi.org/10.1086 /687941.
4. Betsey Stevenson and Justin Wolfers, "Economic Growth and Subjective Well-Being: Reassessing the Easterlin Paradox," National Bureau of Economic Research, Working Paper 14282 (August 2008), https://doi.org/10.3386/w14282.
5. Diener, Lucas, and Oishi, "Advances and Open Questions."
6. Alexandrova and Haybron, "Is Construct Validation Valid?"
7. John Helliwell et al., "World Happiness, Trust and Deaths Under COVID-19," in Helliwell et al., *World Happiness Report 2021* (New York: Sustainable Development Solutions Network, 2021), https://worldhap piness.report/ed/2021/happiness-trust-and-deaths-under-covid-19/; John Helliwell et al., "Happiness, Benevolence, and Trust During COVID-19 and Beyond," in John Helliwell et al., *World Happiness Report 2022* (New York: Sustainable Development Solutions Network, 2022), https://worldhappiness.report/ed/2022/happiness-benevolence -and-trust-during-covid-19-and-beyond/.
8. Michael Wex, *Born to Kvetch* (New York: St. Martin's Press, 2015), 114.

9. Steven J. Heine et al., "What's Wrong with Cross-Cultural Comparisons of Subjective Likert Scales?: The Reference-Group Effect," *Journal of Personality and Social Psychology* 82, no. 6 (2002): 903–18, https://doi.org/10.1037/0022-3514.82.6.903; Daniel M. Haybron, "Philosophy and the Science of Subjective Well-Being," in *The Science of Subjective Well-Being* (New York: Guilford Press, 2008), 17–43; Barbara M. Byrne and Fons J. R. van De Vijver, "Testing for Measurement and Structural Equivalence in Large-Scale Cross-Cultural Studies: Addressing the Issue of Nonequivalence," *International Journal of Testing* 10, no. 2 (2010): 107–32, https://doi.org/10.1080/15305051003637306.
10. Haybron, "Philosophy and the Science of Subjective Well-Being."
11. Solava Ibrahim, "Poverty, Aspirations and Well-Being: Afraid to Aspire and Unable to Reach a Better Life—Voices from Egypt," Brooks World Poverty Institute Working Paper 141 (January 25, 2011), https://doi.org/10.2139/ssrn.1747798.
12. For a clever example of a method for quantifying difference in positivity, see Ed Diener et al., "Positivity and the Construction of Life Satisfaction Judgments: Global Happiness Is Not the Sum of Its Parts," *Journal of Happiness Studies* 1, no. 2 (June 1, 2000): 159–76, https://doi.org/10.1023/A:1010031813405.
13. Nirmita Panchal et al., "The Implications of COVID-19 for Mental Health and Substance Use," KFF, February 10, 2021, https://www.kff.org/coronavirus-covid-19/issue-brief/the-implications-of-covid-19-for-mental-health-and-substance-use/.
14. Yolonda Y. Wilson, "Race, COVID-19, and the Public 'We' (Symposium) [2020 C4eJ 86]," *University of Toronto Centre for Ethics Journal* 86 (November 30, 2020), https://c4ejournal.net/2020/11/30/yolonda-wilson-race-covid-19-and-the-public-we-symposium/.
15. Owen Flanagan, *How to Do Things with Emotions: The Morality of Anger and Shame Across Cultures* (Princeton, NJ: Princeton University Press, 2021); Veljko Jovanović et al., "Measurement Invariance of the Scale of Positive and Negative Experience Across 13 Countries," PubMed, June 9, 2021, https://doi.org/10.1177/10731911211021494; Batja Mesquita, *Between Us: How Cultures Create Emotions* (New York: Norton, 2022).
16. Arlie Russell Hochschild, "Emotion Work, Feeling Rules, and Social Structure." *American Journal of Sociology* 85, no. 3 (1979): 551–75.

17. Flanagan, *How to Do Things with Emotions*.
18. Ruth Tennant et al., "The Warwick-Edinburgh Mental Well-Being Scale (WEMWBS): Development and UK Validation," *Health and Quality of Life Outcomes* 5, no. 1 (November 27, 2007): 63, https://doi.org/10.1186/1477-7525-5-63; Christian Winther Topp et al., "The WHO-5 Well-Being Index: A Systematic Review of the Literature," *Psychotherapy and Psychosomatics* 84, no. 3 (2015): 167–76, https://doi.org/10.1159/000376585.
19. Daniel M. Haybron, "Happiness and the Metaphysics of Affect," *Les Ateliers de l'Éthique/The Ethics Forum* (2022).
20. Ed Diener et al., "Wealth and Happiness Across the World: Material Prosperity Predicts Life Evaluation, Whereas Psychosocial Prosperity Predicts Positive Feeling," *Journal of Personality and Social Psychology* 99, no. 1 (2010): 52–61, https://doi.org/10.1037/a0018066; Weiting Ng and Ed Diener, "What Matters to the Rich and the Poor? Subjective Well-Being, Financial Satisfaction, and Postmaterialist Needs Across the World," *Journal of Personality and Social Psychology* 107, no. 2 (2014): 326–38, https://doi.org/10.1037/a0036856; Louis Tay and Ed Diener, "Needs and Subjective Well-Being Around the World," *Journal of Personality and Social Psychology* 101, no. 2 (2011): 354–65, https://doi.org/10.1037/a0023779. The life evaluation correlations were not included in the Yaden and Haybron paper but are available on request.
21. Ibrahim, "Poverty, Aspirations and Well-Being"; I. Ponocny et al., "Are Most People Happy? Exploring the Meaning of Subjective Well-Being Ratings," *Journal of Happiness Studies* 17, no. 6 (December 1, 2016): 2635–53, https://doi.org/10.1007/s10902-015-9710-; Hazel Rose Markus et al., "In Their Own Words: Well-Being at Midlife Among High School-Educated and College-Educated Adults," in *How Healthy Are We?: A National Study of Well-Being at Midlife*, ed. Orville G. Brim, Carol D. Ryff, and Ronald C. Kessler (Chicago: University of Chicago Press, 2004), 273–319.
22. P. Brent Ferrell and Howard L. McLeod, "Carbamazepine, HLA-B*1502 and Risk of Stevens–Johnson Syndrome and Toxic Epidermal Necrolysis: US FDA Recommendations," *Pharmacogenomics* 9, no. 10 (October 2008): 1543–46, https://doi.org/10.2217/14622416.9.10.1543.

23. Carol Graham, *Happiness for All?: Unequal Hopes and Lives in Pursuit of the American Dream* (Princeton, NJ: Princeton University Press, 2017); Carol Graham and Sergio Pinto, "Unequal Hopes and Lives in the USA: Optimism, Race, Place, and Premature Mortality," *Journal of Population Economics* 32, no. 2 (April 1, 2019): 665–733, https://doi.org/10.1007/s00148-018-0687-y.
24. Graham and Pinto, "Unequal Hopes and Lives."
25. Tanjala S. Purnell et al., "Achieving Health Equity: Closing the Gaps in Health Care Disparities, Interventions, and Research," *Health Affairs* 35, no. 8 (August 2016): 1410–15, https://doi.org/10.1377/hlthaff.2016.0158.
26. S. Le Roux et al., "Cultural Coping as a Risk for Depression and Hypertension: The SABPA Prospective Study," *Cardiovascular Journal of Africa* 29, no. 6; Yolonda Y. Wilson et al., "Intersectionality in Clinical Medicine: The Need for a Conceptual Framework," *American Journal of Bioethics* 19, no. 2 (February 1, 2019): 8–19, https://doi.org/10.1080/15265161.2018.1557275; Purnell et al. "Achieving Health Equity."

10. RECOMMENDATIONS FOR POLICY USE OF HAPPINESS METRICS

1. Markus Kneer and Daniel M. Haybron, "Happiness and Well-Being: Is It All in Your Head? Evidence from the Folk," 2019, https://doi.org/10.13140/RG.2.2.12958.69448; Daniel M. Haybron, "Happiness," in *The Stanford Encyclopedia of Philosophy*, ed. Edward N. Zalta, Summer 2020, https://plato.stanford.edu/archives/sum2020/entries/happiness/.
2. Willard Van Orman Quine, "Speaking of Objects," in *Ontological Relativity and Other Essays* (New York: Columbia University Press, 1969); Willard Van Orman Quine, *Word and Object* (Eastford, CT: Martino Fine Books, 2013); Lisa Feldman Barrett, *How Emotions Are Made: The Secret Life of the Brain* (New York: Houghton Mifflin Harcourt, 2017); Joshua Conrad Jackson et al., "Emotion Semantics Show Both Cultural Variation and Universal Structure," *Science* 366, no. 6472 (December 20, 2019): 1517–22, https://doi.org/10.1126/science.aaw8160; Anna

Wierzbicka, *Understanding Cultures Through Their Key Words: English, Russian, Polish, German, and Japanese* (New York: Oxford University Press, 1997).
3. Peter Winch, "Understanding a Primitive Society," *American Philosophical Quarterly* 1, no. 4 (1964): 307–24; Andrew Beatty, "Current Emotion Research in Anthropology: Reporting the Field," *Emotion Review* 5, no. 4 (October 1, 2013): 414–22, https://doi.org/10.1177/17540 73913490045; Jonathan Lear, *Happiness, Death, and the Remainder of Life* (Cambridge, MA: Harvard University Press, 2000); Owen Flanagan, *How to Do Things with Emotions: The Morality of Anger and Shame Across Cultures* (Princeton, NJ: Princeton University Press, 2021).

11. UNIVERSAL RIGHTS, SUSTAINABLE DEVELOPMENT, AND HAPPINESS

1. United Nations (UN), "Universal Declaration of Human Rights," 1948, https://www.un.org/en/about-us/universal-declaration-of-human-rights; United Nations (UN), Transforming Our World: The 2030 Agenda for Sustainable Development (Resolution 70/1), September 25, 2015, https://sdgs.un.org/2030agenda.
2. UN, "Universal Declaration of Human Rights."
3. UN, "Universal Declaration of Human Rights."
4. UN, "Universal Declaration of Human Rights."
5. UN, "Transforming Our World."
6. UN, "Transforming Our World."
7. UN, "Happiness: Towards a Holistic Approach to Development (Resolution 65/309)."
8. UN General Assembly, "Happiness."
9. UN General Assembly, "Happiness."
10. UN General Assembly, "Happiness."
11. UN General Assembly, "Happiness."
12. UN General Assembly, "Happiness."
13. Martin Luther King Jr., "Remaining Awake Through a Great Revolution," address at Morehouse College Commencement (June 2, 1959), https://kinginstitute.stanford.edu/king-papers/documents/remaining-awake-through-great-revolution-address-morehouse-college.

12. ON ERSATZ HAPPINESS

1. Terry Eagleton, *The Meaning of Life: A Very Short Introduction* (New York: Oxford University Press, 2008), 81.

13. WHY THE ANALYSIS AND ASSESSMENT OF HAPPINESS MATTERS

1. Hazel Rose Markus, "What Moves People to Action? Culture and Motivation," *Current Opinion in Psychology* 8 (2016): 161–66, https://doi.org/10.1016/j.copsyc.2015.10.028.
2. John F. Helliwell et al., *World Happiness Report 2022* (New York: Sustainable Development Solutions Network, 2022), https://worldhappiness.report/ed/2022/.
3. Richard A. Shweder, *Thinking Through Cultures: Expeditions in Cultural Psychology* (Cambridge, MA: Harvard University Press, 1991); Hazel R. Markus and Shinobu Kitayama, "Culture and the Self: Implications for Cognition, Emotion, and Motivation," *Psychological Review* 98, no. 2 (1991): 224–53, https://doi.org/10.1037/0033-295X.98.2.224.
4. Shinobu Kitayama, Hazel Rose Markus, and Masaru Kurokawa, "Culture, Emotion, and Well-Being: Good Feelings in Japan and the United States," *Cognition and Emotion* 14, no. 1 (2000): 93–124, https://doi.org/10.1080/026999300379003.
5. Dov Cohen and Shinobu Kitayama, eds., *Handbook of Cultural Psychology* (New York: Guilford Press, 2010).
6. Shweder, *Thinking Through Cultures*; Markus and Kitayama, "Culture and the Self"; Shinobu Kitayama, Sean Duffy, and Yukiko Uchida, "Self as Cultural Mode of Being," in Cohen and Kitayama, *Handbook of Cultural Psychology*, 136–74; Alan Page Fiske et al., "The Cultural Matrix of Social Psychology," in *The Handbook of Social Psychology*, 4th ed., vols. 1–2 (New York: McGraw-Hill, 1998), 915–81; Yoshihisa Kashima, "Maintaining Cultural Stereotypes in the Serial Reproduction of Narratives," *Personality and Social Psychology Bulletin* 26, no. 5 (2000): 594–604, https://doi.org/10.1177/0146167200267007; Cohen and Kitayama, *Handbook of Cultural Psychology*; Takie Sugiyama Lebra, *The*

Japanese Self in Cultural Logic (Honolulu: University of Hawai'i Press, 2004); Hazel Rose Markus and Shinobu Kitayama, "Cultures and Selves: A Cycle of Mutual Constitution," *Perspectives on Psychological Science: A Journal of the Association for Psychological Science* 5, no. 4 (July 2010): 420–30, https://doi.org/10.1177/1745691610375557; Hazel Rose Markus and Alana Conner, *Clash!: How to Thrive in a Multicultural World* (New York: Penguin Books, 2013); Batja Mesquita and Nico H. Frijda, "Cultural Variations in Emotions: A Review," *Psychological Bulletin* 112, no. 2 (September 1992): 179–204, https://doi.org/10.1037/0033-2909.112.2.179; Batja Mesquita, *Between Us: How Cultures Create Emotions* (New York: Norton, 2022); Harry C. Triandis, "The Self and Social Behavior in Differing Cultural Contexts," *Psychological Review* 96, no. 3 (1989): 506–20, https://doi.org/10.1037/0033-295X.96.3.506; Jeanne L. Tsai and Magali Clobert, "Cultural Influences on Emotion: Established Patterns and Emerging Trends," in *Handbook of Cultural Psychology*, 2nd ed. (New York: Guilford Press, 2019), 292–318; Kuba Krys et al., "Outside the 'Cultural Binary': Understanding Why Latin American Collectivist Societies Foster Independent Selves," *Perspectives on Psychological Science: A Journal of the Association for Psychological Science* 17, no. 4 (July 2022): 1166–87, https://doi.org/10.1177/17456916211029632.

7. Markus and Kitayama, "Culture and the Self."
8. Shinobu Kitayama et al., "Independence and Interdependence Predict Health and Wellbeing: Divergent Patterns in the United States and Japan," *Frontiers in Psychology* 1 (2010), https://doi.org/10.3389/fpsyg.2010.001; Cynthia S. Levine et al., "Culture and Healthy Eating: The Role of Independence and Interdependence in the United States and Japan," *Personality & Social Psychology Bulletin* 42, no. 10 (October 2016): 1335–48, https://doi.org/10.1177/0146167216658645.
9. Yuri Miyamoto and Carol D. Ryff, "Culture and Health: Recent Developments and Future Directions," *Japanese Journal of Psychological Research* 64, no. 2 (April 2022): 90–108, https://doi.org/10.1111/jpr.12378; Emily C. Willroth et al., "Being Happy and Becoming Happier as Independent Predictors of Physical Health and Mortality," *Psychosomatic Medicine* 82, no. 7 (September 2020): 650–57, https://doi.org/10.1097/PSY.0000000000000832.

10. Katherine B. Curhan et al., "Just How Bad Negative Affect Is for Your Health Depends on Culture," *Psychological Science* 25, no. 12 (December 2014): 2277–80, https://doi.org/10.1177/0956797614543802.
11. Yulia E. Chentsova-Dutton and Jeanne L. Tsai, "Self-Focused Attention and Emotional Reactivity: The Role of Culture," *Journal of Personality and Social Psychology* 98, no. 3 (March 2010): 507–19, https://doi.org/10.1037/a0018534; Mesquita, *Between Us*; Yuri Miyamoto and Xiaoming Ma, "Dampening or Savoring Positive Emotions: A Dialectical Cultural Script Guides Emotion Regulation," *Emotion* 11, no. 6 (2011): 1346–57, https://doi.org/10.1037/a0025135; Yukiko Uchida et al., "Emotions as Within or Between People? Cultural Variation in Lay Theories of Emotion Expression and Inference," *Personality and Social Psychology Bulletin* 35, no. 11 (November 1, 2009): 1427–39, https://doi.org/10.1177/0146167209347322.
12. Miyamoto and Ryff, "Culture and Health"; Carol D. Ryff et al., "Culture and the Promotion of Well-Being in East and West: Understanding Varieties of Attunement to the Surrounding Context," in *Increasing Psychological Well-Being in Clinical and Educational Settings: Interventions and Cultural Contexts*, ed. Giovanni Andrea Fava and Chiara Ruini (Dordrecht: Springer Netherlands, 2014), 1–19; Carol Ryff et al., "Adult Development in Japan and the United States: Comparing Theories and Findings about Growth, Maturity, and Well-Being," in *The Oxford Handbook of Human Development and Culture: An Interdisciplinary Perspective* (New York: Oxford University Press, 2015), 666–79.
13. Nicole M. Stephens et al., "Unseen Disadvantage: How American Universities' Focus on Independence Undermines the Academic Performance of First-Generation College Students," *Journal of Personality and Social Psychology* 102, no. 6 (2012): 1178–97, https://doi.org/10.1037/a0027143; Jiah Yoo and Yuri Miyamoto, "Cultural Fit of Emotions and Health Implications: A Psychosocial Resources Model," *Social and Personality Psychology Compass* 12, no. 2 (2018): e12372, https://doi.org/10.1111/spc3.12372.
14. Jeremy Rappleye et al., "'Better Policies for Better Lives?': Constructive Critique of the OECD's (Mis)Measure of Student Well-Being," *Journal of Education Policy* 35, no. 2 (March 3, 2020): 258–82, https://doi.org/10.1080/02680939.2019.1576923.

15. Rappleye et al., "Better Policies."
16. Rappleye et al., "Better Policies."
17. Xingyu Li et al., "Passion Matters but Not Equally Everywhere: Predicting Achievement from Interest, Enjoyment, and Efficacy in 59 Societies," *Proceedings of the National Academy of Sciences* 118, no. 11 (March 16, 2021): e2016964118, https://doi.org/10.1073/pnas.2016964118.
18. Helliwell et al., *World Happiness Report 2022*.

14. THREE OUT OF THREE IS BETTER

1. United Nations, Happiness: Towards a Holistic Approach to Development (Resolution 65/309), August 25, 2011, https://digitallibrary.un.org/record/715187.
2. John F. Helliwell et al., *World Happiness Report 2022* (New York: Sustainable Development Solutions Network, 2022), https://worldhappiness.report/ed/2022/.
3. Aristotle, *Nicomachean Ethics*, trans. Terence Irwin (Indianapolis, IN: Hackett, 1999), 1098a18.
4. Aristotle, *Politics: A New Translation*, trans. C. D. C. Reeve (Indianapolis, IN: Hackett, 2017).
5. Helliwell et al., *World Happiness Report 2022*.
6. Aristotle, *Politics*.
7. Immanuel Kant, *Groundwork of the Metaphysics of Morals* (New York: Cambridge University Press, 2012).
8. John Rawls, *A Theory of Justice* (Cambridge, MA: Harvard University Press, 2009).

15. WHAT THE GALLUP WORLD POLL (GWP) COULD DO TO DEEPEN OUR UNDERSTANDING OF HAPPINESS IN DIFFERENT CULTURES

1. John F. Helliwell et al., *World Happiness Report 2022* (New York: Sustainable Development Solutions Network, 2022), https://worldhappiness.report/ed/2022/.

2. Although the Cantril Ladder asks respondents to rate their current lives in the context of their best and worst possible lives, it still measures people's feelings about their current life.
3. While the most recent GWP included one question related to ideals (i.e., preference for calm vs. exciting life), the rest of the questions focused on actuals.
4. Jeanne L. Tsai, Brian Knutson, and Helene H. Fung, "Cultural Variation in Affect Valuation," *Journal of Personality and Social Psychology* 90, no. 2 (2006): 288–307, https://doi.org/10.1037/0022-3514.90.2.288; Jeanne L. Tsai et al., "Leaders' Smiles Reflect Cultural Differences in Ideal Affect," *Emotion* 16, no. 2 (2016): 183–95, https://doi.org/10.1037/emo0000133.
5. Tsai, Knutson, and Fung, "Cultural Variation in Affect Valuation."
6. Lucy Zhang Bencharit et al., "Should Job Applicants Be Excited or Calm? The Role of Culture and Ideal Affect in Employment Settings," *Emotion* 19, no. 3 (2019): 377–401, https://doi.org/10.1037/emo0000444.
7. Tamara Sims et al., "Wanting to Maximize the Positive and Minimize the Negative: Implications for Mixed Affective Experience in American and Chinese Contexts," *Journal of Personality and Social Psychology* 109, no. 2 (August 2015): 292–315, https://doi.org/10.1037/a0039276.
8. Jeanne L. Tsai et al., "Influence and Adjustment Goals: Sources of Cultural Differences in Ideal Affect," *Journal of Personality and Social Psychology* 92, no. 6 (June 2007): 1102–17, https://doi.org/10.1037/0022-3514.92.6.1102.
9. Jeanne L. Tsai, Louise Chim, and Tamara Sims, "Consumer Behavior, Culture, and Emotion," in *Handbook of Culture and Consumer Behavior* (New York: Oxford University Press, 2015), 68–98; Jeanne Tsai, "Ideal Affect: Cultural Causes and Behavioral Consequences," *Perspectives on Psychological Science* 2 (September 1, 2007), https://doi.org/10.1111/j.1745-6916.2007.00043.x; Tamara Sims et al., "Choosing a Physician Depends on How You Want to Feel: The Role of Ideal Affect in Health-Related Decision Making," *Emotion* 14, no. 1 (February 2014): 187–92, https://doi.org/10.1037/a0034372; Tiffany W. Hsu et al., "Social Media Users Produce More Affect That Supports Cultural Values, but Are More Influenced by Affect That Violates Cultural Values," *Journal of Personality and Social Psychology* 121, no. 5 (2021): 969–83, https://doi.org/10.1037/pspa0000282; Jeanne L. Tsai et al.,

"Cultural Variation in Social Judgments of Smiles: The Role of Ideal Affect," *Journal of Personality and Social Psychology* 116, no. 6 (2019): 966–88, https://doi.org/10.1037/pspp0000192; L. Z. Bencharit et al., "Should Job Applicants Be Excited or Calm? The Role of Culture and Ideal Affect in Employment Settings," *Emotion* 19, no. 3 (2019): 377–401. https://doi.org/10.1037/emo0000444; BoKyung Park et al., "Neurocultural Evidence That Ideal Affect Match Promotes Giving," *Social Cognitive and Affective Neuroscience* 12, no. 7 (2017): 1083–96, https://doi.org/10.1093/scan/nsx047; BoKyung Park et al., "Culturally Valued Facial Expressions Enhance Loan Request Success," *Emotion* 20, no. 7 (October 2020): 1137–53, https://doi.org/10.1037/emo0000642.

10. Tsai, "Ideal Affect"; Jeanne L. Tsai et al., "Learning What Feelings to Desire: Socialization of Ideal Affect Through Children's Storybooks," *Personality & Social Psychology Bulletin* 33, no. 1 (January 2007): 17–30, https://doi.org/10.1177/0146167206292749; Tsai et al., "Leaders' Smiles."

12. Yuri Miyamoto and Xiaoming Ma, "Dampening or Savoring Positive Emotions: A Dialectical Cultural Script Guides Emotion Regulation," *Emotion* 11, no. 6 (2011): 1346–57, https://doi.org/10.1037/a0025135.

13. Birgit Koopmann-Holm et al., "Buddhist-Inspired Meditation Increases the Value of Calm," *Emotion* 13, no. 3 (2013): 497–505, https://doi.org/10.1037/a0031070; Jeanne L. Tsai, Felicity F. Miao, and Emma Seppala, "Good Feelings in Christianity and Buddhism: Religious Differences in Ideal Affect," *Personality & Social Psychology Bulletin* 33, no. 3 (March 2007): 409–21, https://doi.org/10.1177/0146167206296107.

14. Magali Clobert et al., "Valuing High Arousal Negative States Increases Negative Responses Toward Outgroups Across Cultures," *Emotion* 22, no. 7 (2022): 1450–72, https://doi.org/10.1037/emo0001101.

15. Birgit Koopmann-Holm and Jeanne L. Tsai, "Focusing on the Negative: Cultural Differences in Expressions of Sympathy," *Journal of Personality and Social Psychology* 107, no. 6 (December 2014): 1092–1115, https://doi.org/10.1037/a0037684.

16. Clobert et al., "Valuing High Arousal Negative States."

17. Katherine B. Curhan et al., "Just How Bad Negative Affect Is for Your Health Depends on Culture," *Psychological Science* 25, no. 12 (December 2014): 2277–80, https://doi.org/10.1177/0956797614543802; Gloria Luong et al., "When Bad Moods May Not Be So Bad: Valuing

Negative Affect Is Associated with Weakened Affect-Health Links," *Emotion* 16, no. 3 (April 2016): 387–401, https://doi.org/10.1037/emo 0000132.

18. Shinobu Kitayama, Hazel Rose Markus, and Masaru Kurokawa, "Culture, Emotion, and Well-Being: Good Feelings in Japan and the United States," *Cognition and Emotion* 14, no. 1 (2000): 93–124, https://doi.org/10.1080/026999300379003; Shinobu Kitayama, Batja Mesquita, and Mayumi Karasawa, "Cultural Affordances and Emotional Experience: Socially Engaging and Disengaging Emotions in Japan and the United States," *Journal of Personality and Social Psychology* 91, no. 5 (November 2006): 890–903, https://doi.org/10.1037/0022-3514.91 .5.890. Similar arguments could be made for "prosocial" and "altruistic" behaviors, which are often defined as actions toward strangers in individualistic cultures. However, in more collectivistic cultures, sharing resources with complete strangers is not viewed as particularly prosocial or altruistic, and therefore the GWP would need to include behaviors that better signal prosociality and altruism in those cultures.
19. Hsu et al., "Social Media Users."
20. BoKyung Park et al., "Neural Evidence for Cultural Differences in the Valuation of Positive Facial Expressions," *Social Cognitive and Affective Neuroscience* 11, no. 2 (February 2016): 243–52, https://doi.org/10.1093 /scan/nsv113.
21. Gordon W. Cheung and Roger B. Rensvold, "Testing Factorial Invariance Across Groups: A Reconceptualization and Proposed New Method," *Journal of Management* 25, no. 1 (1999): 1–27, https://doi.org /10.1177/014920639902500101.
22. Chuansheng Chen, Shin-ying Lee, and Harold W. Stevenson, "Response Style and Cross-Cultural Comparisons of Rating Scales Among East Asian and North American Students," *Psychological Science* 6, no. 3 (1995): 170–75, https://doi.org/10.1111/j.1467-9280.1995 .tb00327.x.
23. Peter B. Smith, "Acquiescent Response Bias as an Aspect of Cultural Communication Style," *Journal of Cross-Cultural Psychology* 35, no. 1 (January 1, 2004): 50–61, https://doi.org/10.1177/0022022103260380.
24. Jeanne L. Tsai, Brian Knutson, and Helene H. Fung, "Cultural Variation in Affect Valuation," *Journal of Personality and Social*

Psychology 90, no. 2 (2006): 288–307, https://doi.org/10.1037/0022-3514 .90.2.288. /
25. J. L. Tsai, R. W. Levenson, and L. L. Carstensen, "Autonomic, Subjective, and Expressive Responses to Emotional Films in Older and Younger Chinese Americans and European Americans," *Psychology and Aging* 15, no. 4 (December 2000): 684–93, https://doi.org/10.1037//0882-7974.15.4.684; Jeanne L. Tsai, Robert W. Levenson, and Kimberly McCoy, "Cultural and Temperamental Variation in Emotional Response," *Emotion* 6, no. 3 (August 2006): 484–97, https://doi.org/10.1037/1528-3542.6.3.484; Jeanne L. Tsai and Robert W. Levenson, "Cultural Influences on Emotional Responding: Chinese American and European American Dating Couples During Interpersonal Conflict," *Journal of Cross-Cultural Psychology* 28, no. 5 (September 1, 1997): 600–625, https://doi.org/10.1177/0022022197285006.
26. Hazel R. Markus and Shinobu Kitayama, "Culture and the Self: Implications for Cognition, Emotion, and Motivation," *Psychological Review* 98, no. 2 (1991): 224–53, https://doi.org/10.1037/0033-295X.98.2.224.
27. Tsai et al., "Leaders' Smiles."
28. Tsai et al., "Influence and Adjustment Goals"; Tsai et al., "Learning What Feelings to Desire"; Jeanne L. Tsai et al., "Valuing Excitement Makes People Look Forward to Old Age Less and Dread It More," *Psychology and Aging* 33, no. 7 (November 2018): 975–92, https://doi.org/10.1037/pag0000295; Tsai et al., "Cultural Variation in Social Judgments of Smiles"; Park et al., "Neurocultural Evidence"; Park et al., "Neural Evidence for Cultural Differences"; BoKyung Park et al., "Ventral Striatal Activity Mediates Cultural Differences in Affiliative Judgments of Smiles," *Culture and Brain* 6, no. 2 (October 1, 2018): 102–17, https://doi.org/10.1007/s40167-018-0061-7; Tamara Sims et al., "Asian Americans Respond Less Favorably to Excitement (vs. Calm)-Focused Physicians Compared to European Americans," *Cultural Diversity & Ethnic Minority Psychology* 24, no. 1 (January 2018): 1–14, https://doi.org/10.1037/cdp0000171; Bencharit et al., "Should Job Applicants Be Excited or Calm?"
29. Matthew B. Ruby et al., "Not All Collectivisms Are Equal: Opposing Preferences for Ideal Affect Between East Asians and Mexicans," *Emotion* 12, no. 6 (2012): 1206–9, https://doi.org/10.1037/a0029118.

REFERENCES

Action for Happiness. "Happier and Kinder, Together." https://actionfor happiness.org/.
Adler, Matthew. "Happiness Surveys and Public Policy: What's the Use?" *Duke Law Journal* 62 (January 2013): 1509. https://scholarship.law.upenn.edu/faculty_scholarship/414.
Alexandrova, Anna. *A Philosophy for the Science of Well-Being*. New York: Oxford University Press, 2017.
Alexandrova, Anna, and Daniel M. Haybron. "Is Construct Validation Valid?" *Philosophy of Science* 83, no. 5 (December 2016): 1098–1109. https://doi.org/10.1086/687941.
Alon, Titan, Matthias Doepke, Jane Olmstead-Rumsey, and Michèle Tertilt. "The Impact of COVID-19 on Gender Equality." Working Paper 26947. National Bureau of Economic Research, April 2020. https://doi.org/10.3386/w26947.
American Psychiatric Association (APA). "APA's Apology to Black, Indigenous and People of Color for Its Support of Structural Racism in Psychiatry." 2021. https://www.psychiatry.org/newsroom/apa-apology-for-its-support-of-structural-racism-in-psychiatry.
———. *Diagnostic and Statistical Manual of Mental Disorders*, 5th ed. New York: American Psychiatric Publishing, 2013.
American Association of Suicidology (ASA). African American Suicide Fact Sheet Based on 2016 Data. 2018. http://riversidetraumacenter.org/wp-content/uploads/2018/08/AfricanAmericanSuicideFactSheet2016.pdf.

Angle, Stephen C. *Contemporary Confucian Political Philosophy*. New York: Polity, 2012.

Angner, Erik. "The Politics of Happiness: Subjective vs. Economic Measures as Measures of Social Well-Being." In *Philosophy and Happiness*, ed. Lisa Bortolotti, 149–66. London: Palgrave Macmillan, 2009.

Annas, Julia. *The Morality of Happiness*. New York: Oxford University Press, 1993.

Annett, Anthony M. *Cathonomics: How Catholic Tradition Can Create a More Just Economy*. Washington, DC: Georgetown University Press, 2022.

"Ardern to Her Ministers: Want More Money? Deliver on Wellbeing." *NZ Herald*. https://www.nzherald.co.nz/nz/pm-jacinda-ardern-if-a-minister-wants-more-money-they-need-to-prove-how-it-will-better-wellbeing/YIRFYIPHY3VLIGLVQZEYQEV2RM/.

Arias, Elizabeth, Betzaida Tejada-Vera, Farida Ahmad, and Kenneth D. Kochanek. "Provisional Life Expectancy Estimates for 2020." National Center for Health Statistics (U.S.). https://www.cdc.gov/nchs/data/vsrr/vsrr015-508.pdf.

Aristotle. *Nicomachean Ethics*. Trans. Terence Irwin. Indianapolis, IN: Hackett, 1999.

———. *Politics: A New Translation*. Trans. C. D. C. Reeve. Indianapolis, IN: Hackett, 2017.

Averill, James R. "On the Paucity of Positive Emotions." In *Assessment and Modification of Emotional Behavior*, edited by Kirk R. Blankstein, Patricia Pliner, and Janet Polivy, 7–45. Boston: Springer, 1980.

Bagozzi, Richard P., Nancy Wong, and Youjae Yi. "The Role of Culture and Gender in the Relationship Between Positive and Negative Affect." *Cognition and Emotion* 13, no. 6 (October 1, 1999): 641–72. https://doi.org/10.1080/026999399379023.

Bailey, Rahn Kennedy, Holly L. Blackmon, and Francis L. Stevens. "Major Depressive Disorder in the African American Population: Meeting the Challenges of Stigma, Misdiagnosis, and Treatment Disparities." *Journal of the National Medical Association* 101, no. 11 (November 1, 2009): 1084–89. https://doi.org/10.1016/S0027-9684(15)31102-0.

Baker, F. M. "Diagnosing Depression in African Americans." *Community Mental Health Journal* 37, no. 1 (February 1, 2001): 31–38. https://doi.org/10.1023/A:1026540321366.

Baldwin, James, Emile Capouya, Lorraine Hansberry, Nat Hentoff, Langston Hughes, and Alfred Kazin. "The Negro in American Culture." *Crosscurrents* 11, no. 3 (1961): 205–24.

Barrett, Lisa Feldman. *How Emotions Are Made: The Secret Life of the Brain.* New York: Houghton Mifflin Harcourt, 2017.

Barrett, Lisa Feldman, and James A. Russell, eds. *The Psychological Construction of Emotion.* New York: Guilford Press, 2014.

Barrington-Leigh, Christopher. "Trends in Conceptions of Progress and Well-Being." In Helliwell et al., *World Happiness Report 2022.* https://worldhappiness.report/ed/2022/trends-in-conceptions-of-progress-and-well-being/.

Bartels, Meike, Ragnhild Bang Nes, Jessica M. Armitage, Margot P. van de Weijer, Lianne P. de Vries, and Claire M. A. Haworth. "Exploring the Biological Basis for Happiness." In Helliwell et al., *World Happiness Report 2022.* https://worldhappiness.report/ed/2022/exploring-the-biological-basis-for-happiness/.

Bastian, Brock, Peter Kuppens, Kim De Roover, and Ed Diener. "Is Valuing Positive Emotion Associated with Life Satisfaction?" *Emotion* 14, no. 4 (2014): 639–45. https://doi.org/10.1037/a0036466.

Bastian, Brock, Peter Kuppens, Matthew J. Hornsey, Joonha Park, Peter Koval, and Yukiko Uchida. "Feeling Bad About Being Sad: The Role of Social Expectancies in Amplifying Negative Mood." *Emotion* 12, no. 1 (2012): 69–80. https://doi.org/10.1037/a0024755.

Baumeister, Roy F., Kathleen D. Vohs, Jennifer L. Aaker, and Emily N. Garbinsky. "Some Key Differences Between a Happy Life and a Meaningful Life." *Journal of Positive Psychology* 8, no. 6 (November 1, 2013): 505–16. https://doi.org/10.1080/17439760.2013.830764.

Baysu, Gülseli, and Karen Phalet. "Staying on or Dropping Out? The Role of Intergroup Friendship and Perceived Teacher Support in Minority and Nonminority School Careers." *Teachers College Record* 114, no. 5 (May 1, 2012): 1–25. https://doi.org/10.1177/016146811211400507.

Beatty, Andrew. "Current Emotion Research in Anthropology: Reporting the Field." *Emotion Review* 5, no. 4 (October 1, 2013): 414–22. https://doi.org/10.1177/1754073913490045.

Bell, Carl C., Willie Mae Jackson, and Briatta H. Bell. "Misdiagnosis of African-Americans with Psychiatric Issues—Part I." *Journal of the*

National Medical Association 107, no. 3 (June 1, 2015): 25–34. https://doi.org/10.1016/S0027-9684(15)30048-1.

———. "Misdiagnosis of African-Americans with Psychiatric Issues—Part II." *Journal of the National Medical Association* 107, no. 3 (June 1, 2015): 35–41. https://doi.org/10.1016/S0027-9684(15)30049-3.

Bell, Daniel A. *China's New Confucianism: Politics and Everyday Life in a Changing Society*. Princeton, NJ: Princeton University Press, 2008.

Bellah, Robert N., Richard Madsen, William M. Sullivan, Ann Swidler, and Steven M. Tipton. *Habits of the Heart: Individualism and Commitment in American Life*. Berkeley: University of California Press, 1985.

Bencharit, Lucy Zhang, Yuen Wan Ho, Helene H. Fung, Dannii Y. Yeung, Nicole M. Stephens, Rainer Romero-Canyas, and Jeanne L. Tsai. "Should Job Applicants Be Excited or Calm? The Role of Culture and Ideal Affect in Employment Settings." *Emotion* 19, no. 3 (2019): 377–401. https://doi.org/10.1037/emo0000444.

Benditt, Theodore M. "Happiness." *Philosophical Studies: An International Journal for Philosophy in the Analytic Tradition* 25, no. 1 (1974): 1–20.

Bentham, Jeremy. *An Introduction to the Principles of Morals and Legislation*. London: W. Pickering, 1823.

Berry, John W., Jean S. Phinney, David L. Sam, and Paul Vedder, eds. *Immigrant Youth in Cultural Transition: Acculturation, Identity, and Adaptation Across National Contexts*. Mahwah, NJ: Lawrence Erlbaum Associates, 2006.

Billioud, Sébastien, ed. *The Varieties of Confucian Experience: Documenting a Grassroots Revival of Tradition*. Leiden: Brill, 2018.

Billioud, Sebastien, and Joël Thoraval. *The Sage and the People: The Confucian Revival in China*. New York: Oxford University Press, 2015.

Bluedorn, John, Francesca Caselli, Niels-Jakob Hansen, Ippei Shibata, and Marina M. Tavares. "Gender and Employment in the COVID-19 Recession: Evidence on 'She-cessions.'" *IMF Working Papers* 95 (March 31, 2021).

Boiger, Michael, Batja Mesquita, Yukiko Uchida, and Lisa Feldman Barrett. "Condoned or Condemned: The Situational Affordance of Anger and Shame in the United States and Japan." *Personality and Social Psychology Bulletin* 39, no. 4 (April 1, 2013): 540–53. https://doi.org/10.1177/0146167213478201.

Brandt, Richard B. "The Concept of Welfare." In *The Structure of Economic Science*, edited by S. R. Krupp, 257–76. Englewood Cliffs, NJ: Prentice Hall, 1966.

Brussevich, Mariya, Era Dabla-Norris, and Bin Grace Li. "China's Rebalancing and Gender Inequality." SSRN Scholarly Paper. Rochester, NY: Social Science Research Network, May 1, 2021. https://papers.ssrn.com/abstract=4026314.

Bryant, Fred B., and Joseph Veroff. *Savoring: A New Model of Positive Experience*. New York: Psychology Press, 2007.

Burnett, Simon. *The Happiness Agenda: A Modern Obsession*. New York: Palgrave Macmillan, 2012.

Burt, Ronald S. "The Network Structure of Social Capital." *Research in Organizational Behavior* 22 (January 1, 2000): 345–423. https://doi.org/10.1016/S0191-3085(00)22009-1.

Butler, Julie, and Margaret L. Kern. "The PERMA Profiler: A Brief Multidimensional Measure of Flourishing." 2015. Available from http://www.peggykern.org/questionnaires.html.

Byrne, Barbara M., and Fons J. R. van De Vijver. "Testing for Measurement and Structural Equivalence in Large-Scale Cross-Cultural Studies: Addressing the Issue of Nonequivalence." *International Journal of Testing* 10, no. 2 (2010): 107–32. https://doi.org/10.1080/15305051003637306.

Carruthers, Peter. *The Opacity of Mind: An Integrative Theory of Self-Knowledge*. New York: Oxford University Press, 2011.

Cartwright, Samuel A. "Report on Diseases and Peculiarities of the Negro Race." In *Health, Disease, and Illness: Concepts in Medicine*, edited by Arthur L. Caplan, James J. McCartney, and Dominic A. Sisti, 28–39. Washington, DC: Georgetown University Press, 2004.

Center for Compassion and Altruism Research and Education. "Good Social Relationships Are the Most Consistent Predictor of a Happy Life." http://ccare.stanford.edu/press_posts/good-social-relationships-are-the-most-consistent-predictor-of-a-happy-life/.

Centers for Disease Control and Prevention (CDC), "ABES Table: Summary | DASH | CDC," March 25, 2022. https://www.cdc.gov/healthyyouth/data/abes/tables/summary.htm.

Chatham House International Affairs Think Tank. "Iceland and the Wellbeing Economy." https://www.chathamhouse.org/events/all/members-event/iceland-and-wellbeing-economy.

Chen, Chuansheng, Shin-ying Lee, and Harold W. Stevenson. "Response Style and Cross-Cultural Comparisons of Rating Scales Among East Asian and North American Students." *Psychological Science* 6, no. 3 (1995): 170–75. https://doi.org/10.1111/j.1467-9280.1995.tb00327.x.

Chentsova-Dutton, Yulia E., and Jeanne. L. Tsai. "Self-Focused Attention and Emotional Reactivity: The Role of Culture." *Journal of Personality and Social Psychology* 98 (2010): 507–19. http://dx.doi.org/10.1037/a0018534.

Cherkis, Jason. "What Happens to Your Mental Health When You Can't Pay Your Rent?" *New York Times*, March 10, 2021, https://www.nytimes.com/2021/03/10/opinion/minimum-wage-mental-health.html.

Cheung, Gordon W., and Roger B. Rensvold. "Testing Factorial Invariance Across Groups: A Reconceptualization and Proposed New Method." *Journal of Management* 25 (1999): 1–27. https://doi.org/10.1177/014920639902500101.

Clark, Kelly James, and Justin T. Winslett. "The Evolutionary Psychology of Chinese Religion: Pre-Qin High Gods as Punishers and Rewarders." *Journal of the American Academy of Religion* 79, no. 4 (December 1, 2011): 928–60. https://doi.org/10.1093/jaarel/lfr018.

Clobert, Magali, Joni Sasaki, Kwang-Kuo Hwang, and Jeanne L. Tsai. "Valuing High Arousal Negative States Increases Negative Responses Toward Outgroups Across Cultures," *Emotion* 22, no. 7 (2022): 1450–72, https://doi.org/10.1037/emo0001101.

Clobert, Magali, Tamara L. Sims, Jiah Yoo, Yuri Miyamoto, Hazel R. Markus, Mayumi Karasawa, and Cynthia S. Levine. "Feeling Excited or Taking a Bath: Do Distinct Pathways Underlie the Positive Affect–Health Link in the U.S. and Japan?" *Emotion* 20, no. 2 (2020): 164–78. https://doi.org/10.1037/emo0000531.

Clore, Gerald L., and Andrew Ortony. "Psychological Construction in the OCC Model of Emotion." *Emotion Review* 5, no. 4 (2013): 335–43. https://doi.org/10.1177/1754073913489751.

Coates, Ta-Nehisi. *Between the World and Me*. New York: Random House, 2015.

Cohen, Dov, and Shinobu Kitayama, eds. *Handbook of Cultural Psychology*. New York: Guilford Press, 2019.

Cohen, Sheldon, William J. Doyle, Ronald Turner, Cuneyt M. Alper, and David P. Skoner. "Sociability and Susceptibility to the Common Cold."

Psychological Science 14, no. 5 (September 1, 2003): 389–95. https://doi.org/10.1111/1467-9280.01452.

Congressional Black Caucus. "Emergency Task Force on Black Youth Suicide & Mental Health." https://watsoncoleman.house.gov/suicide taskforce.

———. Ring the Alarm: The Crisis of Black Youth Suicide in America: Emergency Task Force Report on Black Youth suicide and Mental Health. 2019. https://watsoncoleman.house.gov/uploadedfiles/full_taskforce_report.pdf.

Consedine, Nathan S., Yulia E. Chentsova-Dutton, and Yulia S. Krivoshekova. "Emotional Acculturation Predicts Better Somatic Health: Experiential and Expressive Acculturation Among Immigrant Women from Four Ethnic Groups." *Journal of Social and Clinical Psychology* 33, no. 10 (December 2014): 867–89. https://doi.org/10.1521/jscp.2014.33.10.867.

Corballis, Michael C. "The Uniqueness of Human Recursive Thinking." *American Scientist* 95 (2007): 240.

CPPCC (Chinese People's Political Consultative Conference). "Modern History Sourcebook: The Common Program of the Chinese People's Political Consultative Conference, 1949." 1949. https://sourcebooks.fordham.edu/mod/1949-ccp-program.asp.

Crocker, Jennifer, and Brenda Major. "Social Stigma and Self-Esteem: The Self-Protective Properties of Stigma." *Psychological Review* 96, no. 4 (1989): 608–30. https://doi.org/10.1037/0033-295X.96.4.608.

Curhan, Katherine B., Cynthia S. Levine, Hazel Rose Markus, Shinobu Kitayama, Jiyoung Park, Mayumi Karasawa, Norito Kawakami, et al. "Subjective and Objective Hierarchies and Their Relations to Psychological Well-Being: A U.S./Japan Comparison." *Social Psychological and Personality Science* 5, no. 8 (November 1, 2014): 855–64. https://doi.org/10.1177/1948550614538461.

Curhan, Katherine B., Tamara Sims, Hazel Rose Markus, Shinobu Kitayama, Mayumi Karasawa, Norito Kawakami, Gayle D. Love, et al. "Just How Bad Negative Affect Is for Your Health Depends on Culture." *Psychological Science* 25, no. 12 (2014): 2277–80. https://doi.org/10.1177/0956797614543802.

Dang, Hai-Anh H., and Cuong Viet Nguyen. "Gender Inequality During the COVID-19 Pandemic: Income, Expenditure, Savings, and Job Loss."

World Development 140 (April 1, 2021): 105296. https://doi.org/10.1016/j.worlddev.2020.105296.

Danner, Deborah D., David A. Snowdon, and Wallace V. Friesen. "Positive Emotions in Early Life and Longevity: Findings from the Nun Study." *Journal of Personality and Social Psychology* 80, no. 5 (2001): 804–13. https://doi.org/10.1037/0022-3514.80.5.804.

Darwin, Charles. *The Expression of the Emotions in Man and Animals*. London: Fontana Press, 1872.

Davies, William. *The Happiness Industry: How the Government and Big Business Sold Us Well-Being*. New York: Verso Books, 2015.

Davis, Lydia. *The Thirteenth Woman and Other Stories*. New York: Living Hand, 1976.

De Leersnyder, Jozefien, Heejung Kim, and Batja Mesquita. "Feeling Right Is Feeling Good: Psychological Well-Being and Emotional Fit with Culture in Autonomy-Versus Relatedness-Promoting Situations." *Frontiers in Psychology* 6 (2015): 1–12. https://www.frontiersin.org/article/10.3389/fpsyg.2015.00630.

———. "My Emotions Belong Here and There: Extending the Phenomenon of Emotional Acculturation to Heritage Culture Fit." *Cognition and Emotion* 34, no. 8 (November 16, 2020): 1573–90. https://doi.org/10.1080/02699931.2020.1781063.

De Leersnyder, Jozefien, Peter Koval, Peter Kuppens, and Batja Mesquita. "Emotions and Concerns: Situational Evidence for Their Systematic Co-Occurrence." *Emotion* 18, no. 4 (2018): 597–614. https://doi.org/10.1037/emo0000314.

De Leersnyder, Jozefien, Batja Mesquita, and Heejung Kim. "Where Do My Emotions Belong? A Study of Immigrants' Emotional Acculturation." *Personality and Social Psychology Bulletin* 37, no. 4 (April 1, 2011): 451–63. https://doi.org/10.1177/0146167211399103.

De Leersnyder, Jozefien, Batja Mesquita, Heejung Kim, Kimin Eom, and Hyewon Choi. "Emotional Fit with Culture: A Predictor of Individual Differences in Relational Well-Being." *Emotion* 14, no. 2 (2014): 241–45. https://doi.org/10.1037/a0035296.

De Neve, Jan-Emmanuel, Ed Diener, Louis Tay, and Cody Xuereb. "The Objective Benefits of Subjective Well-Being." SSRN Scholarly Paper

2306651. Rochester, NY: Social Science Research Network, August 6, 2013. https://papers.ssrn.com/abstract=2306651.

De Neve, Jan-Emmanuel, and Jeffrey D. Sachs. "The SDGs and Human Well-Being: A Global Analysis of Synergies, Trade-Offs, and Regional Differences." *Scientific Reports* 10, no. 1 (September 15, 2020): 15113. https://doi.org/10.1038/s41598-020-71916-9.

Delle Fave, Antonella, Ingrid Brdar, Marié P. Wissing, Ulisses Araujo, Alejandro Castro Solano, Teresa Freire, María Del Rocío Hernández-Pozo, et al. "Lay Definitions of Happiness Across Nations: The Primacy of Inner Harmony and Relational Connectedness." *Frontiers in Psychology* 7 (2016): 30. https://doi.org/10.3389/fpsyg.2016.00030.

Diener, Ed, Ronald Inglehart, and Louis Tay. "Theory and Validity of Life Satisfaction Scales." *Social Indicators Research* 112, no. 3 (July 1, 2013): 497–527. https://doi.org/10.1007/s11205-012-0076-y.

Diener, Ed, Richard Lucas, John F. Helliwell, and Ulrich Schimmack. *Well-Being for Public Policy*. New York: Oxford University Press, 2009.

Diener, Ed, Richard E. Lucas, and Shigehiro Oishi. "Advances and Open Questions in the Science of Subjective Well-Being." *Collabra: Psychology* 4, no. 1 (2018): 15. https://doi.org/10.1525/collabra.115

Diener, Ed, Christie K. Napa-Scollon, Shigehiro Oishi, Vivian Dzokoto, and Eunkook Mark Suh. "Positivity and the Construction of Life Satisfaction Judgments: Global Happiness Is Not the Sum of Its Parts." *Journal of Happiness Studies* 1, no. 2 (June 1, 2000): 159–76. https://doi.org/10.1023/A:1010031813405.

Diener, Ed, Weiting Ng, James Harter, and Raksha Arora. "Wealth and Happiness Across the World: Material Prosperity Predicts Life Evaluation, Whereas Psychosocial Prosperity Predicts Positive Feeling." *Journal of Personality and Social Psychology* 99, no. 1 (2010): 52–61. https://doi.org/10.1037/a0018066.

Diener, Ed, Shigehiro Oishi, and Louis Tay, eds. *Handbook of Well-Being*. Salt Lake City, UT: DEF Publishers, 2018.

Dong, Yige. "The Crisis of Social Reproduction and 'Made-in-China' Feminism." *Soundings: A Journal of Politics and Culture* 79 (November 1, 2021): 10–23. https://doi.org/10.3898/SOUN.79.01.2021.

Dong, Zhongshu. *Chunqiu Fanlu*. Beijing: Zhonghua Shuju, 1996.

Doucerain, Marina, Jessica Dere, and Andrew G. Ryder. "Travels in Hyper-Diversity: Multiculturalism and the Contextual Assessment of Acculturation." *International Journal of Intercultural Relations* 37, no. 6 (November 1, 2013): 686–99. https://doi.org/10.1016/j.ijintrel.2013.09.007.

Duncan, Grant. "Should Happiness-Maximization Be the Goal of Government?" *Journal of Happiness Studies* 11, no. 2 (April 1, 2010): 163–78. https://doi.org/10.1007/s10902-008-9129-y.

Eagleton, Terry. *The Meaning of Life: A Very Short Introduction*. Oxford: Oxford University Press, 2008.

Easterlin, Richard A. "Does Economic Growth Improve the Human Lot? Some Empirical Evidence." In *Nations and Households in Economic Growth*. edited by Paul A. David and Melvin W. Reder, 89–125. San Diego, CA: Academic Press, 1974.

Ehrenreich, Barbara. *Bright-Sided: How Positive Thinking Is Undermining America*. London: Picador, 2009.

Eid, Michael, and Randy J. Larsen, eds. *The Science of Subjective Well-Being*. New York: Guilford Press, 2008.

Ekman, Paul. "Are There Basic Emotions?" *Psychological Review* 99, no. 3 (1992): 550–53. https://doi.org/10.1037/0033-295X.99.3.550.

———. "Biological and Cultural Contributions to Body and Facial Movement in the Expression of Emotions." In *Explaining Emotions*. edited by Amélie Oskenberg Rorty, 73–102. Berkeley: University of California Press, 1980.

Feinberg, Matthew, Brett Q. Ford, and Francis J. Flynn. "Rethinking Reappraisal: The Double-Edged Sword of Regulating Negative Emotions in the Workplace." *Organizational Behavior and Human Decision Processes* 161 (November 1, 2020): 1–19. https://doi.org/10.1016/j.obhdp.2020.03.005.

Ferrell, P. Brent, and Howard L. McLeod. "Carbamazepine, HLA-B*1502 and Risk of Stevens–Johnson Syndrome and Toxic Epidermal Necrolysis: US FDA Recommendations." *Pharmacogenomics* 9, no. 10 (October 2008): 1543–46. https://doi.org/10.2217/14622416.9.10.1543.

Fincher, Leta Hong. *Betraying Big Brother: The Feminist Awakening in China*. London/New York: Verso Books, 2021.

———. *Leftover Women: The Resurgence of Gender Inequality in China*. London: Zed Books, 2014.

Fiske, Alan Page. "The Lexical Fallacy in Emotion Research: Mistaking Vernacular Words for Psychological Entities." *Psychological Review* 127, no. 1 (2020): 95–113. https://doi.org/10.1037/rev0000174.

Fiske, Alan Page, Shinobu Kitayama, Hazel Rose Markus, and Richard E. Nisbett. "The Cultural Matrix of Social Psychology." In *The Handbook of Social Psychology*, 4th ed., vols. 1–2, 915–81. New York: McGraw-Hill, 1998.

Flanagan, Owen J. *The Bodhisattva's Brain: Buddhism Naturalized*. Cambridge, MA: MIT Press, 2011.

———. *The Geography of Morals: Varieties of Moral Possibility*. New York: Oxford University Press, 2017.

———. *How to Do Things with Emotions: The Morality of Anger and Shame Across Cultures*. Princeton, NJ: Princeton University Press, 2021.

Ford, Brett Q., Julia O. Dmitrieva, Daniel Heller, Yulia Chentsova-Dutton, Igor Grossmann, Maya Tamir, Yukiko Uchida, et al. "Culture Shapes Whether the Pursuit of Happiness Predicts Higher or Lower Well-Being." *Journal of Experimental Psychology: General* 144, no. 6 (2015): 1053–62. https://doi.org/10.1037/xge0000108.

Frawley, Ashley. "Happiness Research: A Review of Critiques." *Sociology Compass* 9, no. 1 (2015): 62–77. https://doi.org/10.1111/soc4.12236.

Fredrickson, Barbara L. *Positivity*. New York: Crown Publishers, 2009.

Fredrickson, Barbara L., and Michael A. Cohn. "Positive Emotions." In *Handbook of Emotions*, 3rd ed., edited by Michael Lewis, Jeannette M. Haviland-Jones, and Lisa Feldman Barrett, 777–96. New York: Guilford Press, 2010.

Fredrickson, Barbara L., and Laura E. Kurtz. "Cultivating Positive Emotions to Enhance Human Flourishing." In *Applied Positive Psychology: Improving Everyday Life, Health, Schools, Work, and Society*. edited by Jeanne Nakamura, Mihaly Csikszentmihalyi, and Stewart I. Donaldson, 35–47. New York: Routledge/Taylor & Francis Group, 2011.

Fricker, Miranda. *Epistemic Injustice: Power and the Ethics of Knowing*. New York: Oxford University Press, 2007.

Frijda, Nico H. *The Emotions*. New York: Cambridge University Press, 1986.

Frijters, Paul, Andrew E. Clark, Christian Krekel, and Richard Layard. "A Happy Choice: Wellbeing as the Goal of Government." *Behavioural Public Policy* 4, no. 2 (July 2020): 126–65. https://doi.org/10.1017/bpp.2019.39.

Gallup. *Gallup 2020 Global Emotions Report.* https://www.gallup.com/analytics/324191/gallup-global-emotions-report-2020.aspx.
———.*Gallup 2021 Global Emotions Report.* https://www.gallup.com/analytics/349280/gallup-global-emotions-report.aspx.
———. *Gallup 2022 Global Emotions Report.* https://www.gallup.com/analytics/349280/gallup-global-emotions-report.aspx.
———. "Life Satisfaction." https://news.gallup.com/topic/category_life_satisfaction.aspx.
Ghaemi, Nassir. *A First-Rate Madness: Uncovering the Links Between Leadership and Mental Illness.* New York: Penguin Books, 2012.
Gilbert, Daniel. *Stumbling on Happiness.* New York: Knopf, 2006.
Global Happiness Council. "What Is the Global Happiness Council?" https://www.happinesscouncil.org/council.html.
Good, Mary-Jo D., and Byron J. Good. "Ritual, the State, and the Transformation of Emotional Discourse in Iranian Society." *Culture, Medicine, and Psychiatry: An International Journal of Cross-Cultural Health Research* 12 (1988): 43–63. https://doi.org/10.1007/BF00047038.
GOV.UK. "Wellbeing Guidance for Appraisal: Supplementary Green Book Guidance." https://www.gov.uk/government/publications/green-book-supplementary-guidance-wellbeing.
Graham, Carol. *Happiness for All? Unequal Hopes and Lives in Pursuit of the American Dream.* Princeton, NJ: Princeton University Press, 2017.
Graham, Carol, and Sergio Pinto. "Unequal Hopes and Lives in the USA: Optimism, Race, Place, and Premature Mortality." *Journal of Population Economics* 32, no. 2 (April 1, 2019): 665–733. https://doi.org/10.1007/s00148-018-0687-y.
Hammond, Kenneth J., and Jeffrey L. Richey, eds. *The Sage Returns: Confucian Revival in Contemporary China.* Albany: State University of New York Press, 2014.
Hare, Richard Mervyn. *Moral Thinking: Its Levels, Method, and Point.* New York: Oxford University Press, 1981.
Hausman, Daniel M., and Michael S. McPherson. *Economic Analysis, Moral Philosophy and Public Policy,* 2nd ed. Cambridge: Cambridge University Press, 2006.
Haybron, Daniel M. "An Emotional State Account of Happiness." In *Theories of Happiness: An Anthology,* edited by Jennifer Wilson Mulnix and M. J. Mulnix, 96–114. Peterborough, ON: Broadview Press, 2015.

———. "Happiness." In *The Stanford Encyclopedia of Philosophy*, ed. Edward N. Zalta, Summer 2020. Metaphysics Research Lab, Stanford University, 2020. https://plato.stanford.edu/archives/sum2020/entries/happiness/.

———. *Happiness: A Very Short Introduction*. New York: Oxford University Press, 2013.

———. "Happiness and the Metaphysics of Affect." *Les Ateliers de l'Éthique/The Ethics Forum* (2022).

———. "Mental State Approaches to Well-Being." In *The Oxford Handbook of Well-Being and Public Policy*, edited by Matthew D. Alder and Marc Fleurbaey, 347–78. New York: Oxford University Press, 2016.

———. "Philosophy and the Science of Subjective Well-Being." In *The Science of Subjective Well-Being*, 17–43. New York: Guilford Press, 2008.

———. "What Do We Want from a Theory of Happiness?" *Metaphilosophy* 34, no. 3 (2003): 305–29. https://doi.org/10.1111/1467-9973.00275.

———. *The Pursuit of Unhappiness: The Elusive Psychology of Well-Being*. New York: Oxford University Press, 2008.

Haybron, Daniel M., and Valerie Tiberius. "Normative Foundations for Well-Being Policy." *Papers on Economics and Evolution* (2012): 1202. https://www.econstor.eu/handle/10419/57571.

Heine, Steven J., Darrin R. Lehman, Kaiping Peng, and Joe Greenholtz. "What's Wrong with Cross-Cultural Comparisons of Subjective Likert Scales?: The Reference-Group Effect." *Journal of Personality and Social Psychology* 82, no. 6 (2002): 903–18. https://doi.org/10.1037/0022-3514.82.6.903.

Helliwell, John F. "Three Questions About Happiness." *Behavioural Public Policy* 4, no. 2 (July 2020): 177–87. https://doi.org/10.1017/bpp.2019.41.

Helliwell, John F., Haifang Huang, and Shun Wang. "Changing World Happiness." In Helliwell, Layard, and Sachs, *World Happiness Report 2019*. https://worldhappiness.report/ed/2019/changing-world-happiness/.

Helliwell, John F., Haifang Huang, Shun Wang, and Max Norton. "Happiness, Trust and Deaths Under COVID-19." In Helliwell et al., *World Happiness Report 2021*. https://worldhappiness.report/ed/2021/happiness-trust-and-deaths-under-covid-19/.

Helliwell, John F., Haifang Huang, Shun Wang, and Max Norton. "Happiness, Benevolence, and Trust During COVID-19 and Beyond." In Helliwell et al., *World Happiness Report 2022*. https://worldhappiness.report/ed/2022/happiness-benevolence-and-trust-during-covid-19-and-beyond/.

Helliwell, John F., Richard Layard, and Jeffrey D. Sachs, eds. *World Happiness Report 2012*. New York: Sustainable Development Solutions Network, 2012. https://worldhappiness.report/ed/2012/.
———. *World Happiness Report 2013*. New York: Sustainable Development Solutions Network, 2013. https://worldhappiness.report/ed/2013/.
———. *World Happiness Report 2019*. New York: Sustainable Development Solutions Network, 2019. https://worldhappiness.report/ed/2019/.
Helliwell, John F., Richard Layard, Jeffrey D. Sachs, Jan-Emmanuel De Neve, Lara B. Aknin, and Shun Wang, eds. *World Happiness Report 2021*. New York: Sustainable Development Solutions Network, 2021. https://worldhappiness.report/ed/2021/.
———. *World Happiness Report 2022*. New York: Sustainable Development Solutions Network, 2022. https://worldhappiness.report/ed/2022/.
Hendrischke, Barbara. *The Scripture on Great Peace: The Taiping Jing and the Beginning of Daoism*. Berkeley: University of California Press, 2006.
Henrich, Joseph, Steven J. Heine, and Ara Norenzayan. "The Weirdest People in the World?" *Behavioral and Brain Sciences* 33, nos. 2–3 (June 2010): 61–83. https://doi.org/10.1017/S0140525X0999152X.
Hitokoto, Hidehumi, and Yukiko Uchida. "Interdependent Happiness: Theoretical Importance and Measurement Validity." *Journal of Happiness Studies: An Interdisciplinary Forum on Subjective Well-Being* 16 (2015): 211–39. https://doi.org/10.1007/s10902-014-9505-8.
Hochschild, Arlie Russell. "Emotion Work, Feeling Rules, and Social Structure." *American Journal of Sociology* 85, no. 3 (1979): 551–75.
———. *The Managed Heart: Commercialization of Human Feeling*. Berkeley: University of California Press, 2003.
Holliday-Moore, Roslyn. "Alarming Suicide Trends in African American Children: An Urgent Issue." 2019. https://www.samhsa.gov/blog/alarming-suicide-trends-african-american-children-urgent-issue.
Honig, Emily. "Maoist Mappings of Gender: Reassessing the Red Guards." In *Chinese Femininities, Chinese Masculinities: A Reader*, edited by Susan Brownell, 255–66. Berkeley: University of California Press, 2002.
Horizon. "Chinese Spiritual Life Survey," Association of Religious Data Archives, 2007, https://www.thearda.com/data-archive?fid=SPRTCHNA.
———. "The Meaning of a Good Life Survey." 2016.
Hsu, Tiffany W., Yu Niiya, Mike Thelwall, Michael Ko, Brian Knutson, and Jeanne L. Tsai. "Social Media Users Produce More Affect That

Supports Cultural Values, but Are More Influenced by Affect That Violates Cultural Values." *Journal of Personality and Social Psychology* 121, no. 5 (2021): 969–83. https://doi.org/10.1037/pspa0000282.

Hurka, Thomas. *Perfectionism.* Oxford: Clarendon Press, 1993.

Ibrahim, Solava. "Poverty, Aspirations and Well-Being: Afraid to Aspire and Unable to Reach a Better Life—Voices from Egypt." Brooks World Poverty Institute Working Paper 141 (January 25, 2011). https://doi.org/10.2139/ssrn.1747798.

Inglehart, R., C. Haerpfer, A. Moreno, C. Welzel, K. Kizilova, J. Diez-Medrano, M. Lagos, P. Norris, E. Ponarin, B. Puranen, et al., eds. World Values Survey: Round Four - Country-Pooled Datafile Version. 2014. www.worldvaluessurvey.org/WVSDocumentationWV4.jsp.

International Health Conference. "Summary Report on Proceedings, Minutes and Final Acts of the International Health Conference Held in New York from 19 June to 22 July 1946." United Nations, World Health Organization, Interim Commission, 1948. https://apps.who.int/iris/handle/10665/85573.

Ivanhoe, Phillip J. *Confucian Moral Self Cultivation.* New York: Peter Lang, 1993.

———. *Oneness: East Asian Conceptions of Virtue, Happiness, and How We Are All Connected.* New York: Oxford University Press, 2017.

———. *Three Streams: Confucian Reflections on Learning and the Moral Heart-Mind in China, Korea, and Japan.* New York: Oxford University Press, 2016.

Izard, Carroll E. "Basic Emotions, Relations Among Emotions, and Emotion-Cognition Relations." *Psychological Review* 99, no. 3 (1992): 561–65. https://doi.org/10.1037/0033-295X.99.3.561.

Jackson, Joshua Conrad, Joseph Watts, Teague R. Henry, Johann-Mattis List, Robert Forkel, Peter J. Mucha, Simon J. Greenhill, Russell D. Gray, and Kristen A. Lindquist. "Emotion Semantics Show Both Cultural Variation and Universal Structure." *Science* 366, no. 6472 (December 20, 2019): 1517–22. https://doi.org/10.1126/science.aaw8160.

Jasini, Alba, Jozefien De Leersnyder, Karen Phalet, and Batja Mesquita. "Tuning in Emotionally: Associations of Cultural Exposure with Distal and Proximal Emotional Fit in Acculturating Youth." *European Journal of Social Psychology* 49, no. 2 (2019): 352–65. https://doi.org/10.1002/ejsp.2516.

Jeung, Russell M., Seanan S. Fong, and Helen Jin Kim. *Family Sacrifices: The Worldviews and Ethics of Chinese Americans*. New York: Oxford University Press, 2019.

Johns Hopkins Medicine. "Study Suggests Overdiagnosis of Schizophrenia: Reported Symptoms of Anxiety and Hearing Voices Most Common Reasons for Misdiagnosis by Non-Specialty Physicians." *Science Daily*, April 22, 2019. https://www.sciencedaily.com/releases/2019/04/190422090842.htm.

Jones, Sherry Everett, Kathleen A. Ethier, Marci Hertz, Sarah DeGue, Vi Donna Le, Jemekia Thornton, Connie Lim, et al. "Mental Health, Suicidality, and Connectedness Among High School Students During the COVID-19 Pandemic—Adolescent Behaviors and Experiences Survey, United States, January–June 2021." *MMWR Supplements* 71, no. 3 (April 1, 2022): 16–21. https://doi.org/10.15585/mmwr.su7103a3.

Joshanloo, Mohsen, and Dan Weijers. "Aversion to Happiness Across Cultures: A Review of Where and Why People Are Averse to Happiness." *Journal of Happiness Studies* 15, no. 3 (June 1, 2014): 717–35. https://doi.org/10.1007/s10902-013-9489-9.

Jovanović, Veljko, Mohsen Joshanloo, Marta Martín-Carbonell, Corrado Caudek, Begoña Espejo, Irene Checa, Julia Krasko, et al. "Measurement Invariance of the Scale of Positive and Negative Experience Across 13 Countries." PubMed, June 9, 2021. https://doi.org/10.1177/10731911211021494.

Kahneman, Daniel. "Experienced Utility and Objective Happiness: A Moment-Based Approach." In *Choices, Values, and Frames*, edited by Daniel Kahneman and Amos Tversky, 673–92. New York: Cambridge University Press, 2000.

Kaniuka, Andrea R., Jessica Kelliher Rabon, Byron D. Brooks, Fuschia Sirois, Evan Kleiman, and Jameson K. Hirsch. "Gratitude and Suicide Risk Among College Students: Substantiating the Protective Benefits of Being Thankful." *Journal of American College Health* 69, no. 6 (August 18, 2021): 660–67. https://doi.org/10.1080/07448481.2019.1705838.

Kant, Immanuel. *Groundwork of the Metaphysics of Morals*. New York: Cambridge University Press, 2012.

Kashima, Yoshihisa. "Maintaining Cultural Stereotypes in the Serial Reproduction of Narratives." *Personality and Social Psychology Bulletin* 26, no. 5 (2000): 594–604. https://doi.org/10.1177/0146167200267007.

Kempshall, M. S. *The Common Good in Late Medieval Political Thought.* Oxford: Clarendon Press, 1999.
Kharofa, A. E. "Islamic View of the Well-Being of Man." *Journal of the Islamic Medical Association of North America* 14, no. 1 (1982): 27–9. https://doi.org/10.5915/14-1-12114
Khazan, Olga. "Should Governments Try to Make Us Happy?" *The Atlantic*, September 13, 2013. https://www.theatlantic.com/international/archive/2013/09/should-governments-try-to-make-us-happy/279665/.
Kidd, Ian James, José Medina, and Gaile Pohlhaus Jr. *The Routledge Handbook of Epistemic Injustice.* New York: Routledge, 2017.
Kiecolt-Glaser, Janice K., Lynanne McGuire, Theodore F. Robles, and Ronald Glaser. "Psychoneuroimmunology: Psychological Influences on Immune Function and Health." *Journal of Consulting and Clinical Psychology* 70, no. 3 (2002): 537–47. https://doi.org/10.1037/0022-006X.70.3.537.
King, L. A., and C. K. Napa. "What Makes a Life Good?" *Journal of Personality and Social Psychology* 75, no. 1 (1998): 156–65. https://doi.org/10.1037/0022-3514.75.1.156.
King, Martin Luther, Jr. "Remaining Awake Through a Great Revolution." Address at Morehouse College Commencement (June 2, 1959). https://kinginstitute.stanford.edu/king-papers/documents/remaining-awake-through-great-revolution-address-morehouse-college.
Kirchner-Häusler, Alexander, Michael Boiger, Yukiko Uchida, Yoko Higuchi, Atsuhiko Uchida, and Batja Mesquita. "Relatively Happy: The Role of the Positive-to-Negative Affect Ratio in Japanese and Belgian Couples." *Journal of Cross-Cultural Psychology* 53, no. 1 (January 1, 2022): 66–86. https://doi.org/10.1177/00220221211051016.
Kirmayer, Laurence J., Jaswant Guzder, and Cécile Rousseau. *Cultural Consultation: Encountering the Other in Mental Health Care.* New York: Springer, 2014.
Kitayama, S., S. Duffy, and Y. Uchida. "Self as Cultural Mode of Being." In *Handbook of Cultural Psychology*, edited by Dov Cohen and Shinobu Kitayama, 136–74. New York: Guilford Press, 2007.
Kitayama, Shinobu, Mayumi Karasawa, Katherine Curhan, Carol Ryff, and Hazel Markus. "Independence and Interdependence Predict Health and Wellbeing: Divergent Patterns in the United States and Japan." *Frontiers in Psychology* 1 (2010). https://doi.org/10.3389/fpsyg.2010.001

Kitayama, Shinobu, Hazel Rose Markus, and Masaru Kurokawa. "Culture, Emotion, and Well-Being: Good Feelings in Japan and the United States." *Cognition and Emotion* 14, no. 1 (January 1, 2000): 93–124. https://doi.org/10.1080/026999300379003.

Kitayama, Shinobu, Batja Mesquita, and Mayumi Karasawa. "Cultural Affordances and Emotional Experience: Socially Engaging and Disengaging Emotions in Japan and the United States." *Journal of Personality and Social Psychology* 91, no. 5 (2006): 890–903. https://doi.org/10.1037/0022-3514.91.5.890.

Kneer, Markus, and Daniel M. Haybron. "Happiness and Well-Being: Is It All in Your Head? Evidence from the Folk." 2019. https://doi.org/10.13140/RG.2.2.12958.69448.

Koechlin, Etienne, and Alexandre Hyafil. "Anterior Prefrontal Function and the Limits of Human Decision-Making." *Science* 318, no. 5850 (October 26, 2007): 594–98. https://doi.org/10.1126/science.1142995.

Koo, J., and Eunkook Mark Suh. "Is Happiness a Zero-Sum Game? Belief in Fixed Amount of Happiness (BIFAH) and Subjective Well-Being." *Korean Journal of Social and Personality Psychology* 21, no. 4 (2007): 1–19. https://doi.org/10.21193/kjspp.2007.21.4.001.

Koopmann-Holm, Birgit, Jocelyn Sze, Camaron Ochs, and Jeanne L. Tsai. "Buddhist-Inspired Meditation Increases the Value of Calm." *Emotion* 13, no. 3 (2013): 497–505. https://doi.org/10.1037/a0031070.

Koopmann-Holm, Birgit, and Jeanne L. Tsai. "Focusing on the Negative: Cultural Differences in Expressions of Sympathy." *Journal of Personality and Social Psychology* 107, no. 6 (December 2014): 1092–1115. https://doi.org/10.1037/a0037684.

Kristjánsson, Kristján. "On the Very Idea of 'Negative Emotions.'" *Journal for the Theory of Social Behaviour* 33, no. 4 (2003): 351–64. https://doi.org/10.1046/j.1468-5914.2003.00222.x.

Krys, Kuba, Vivian L. Vignoles, Igor de Almeida, and Yukiko Uchida. "Outside the 'Cultural Binary': Understanding Why Latin American Collectivist Societies Foster Independent Selves." *Perspectives on Psychological Science: A Journal of the Association for Psychological Science* 17, no. 4 (July 2022): 1166–87. https://doi.org/10.1177/17456916211029632.

Lam, Chi-Ming. *Philosophy for Children in Confucian Societies: In Theory and Practice*. New York: Routledge, 2020.

Lancee, Bram. "The Economic Returns of Immigrants' Bonding and Bridging Social Capital: The Case of the Netherlands." *International Migration Review* 44, no. 1 (2010): 202–26. https://doi.org/10.1111/j.1747-7379.2009.00803.x.

Lasch, Christopher. *The Culture of Narcissism: American Life in an Age of Diminishing Expectations*. New York: Norton, 2018.

Layard, Richard. "Happiness: Has Social Science a Clue? Lecture 1: What Is Happiness? Are We Getting Happier?" GBR, 2003. http://cep.lse.ac.uk/_new/events/robbins.asp.

———. *Happiness: Lessons from a New Science*. 2nd ed. New York: Penguin Books, 2006.

Lear, Jonathan. *Happiness, Death, and the Remainder of Life*. Cambridge, MA: Harvard University Press, 2000.

Leary, Mark R., Richard Bednarski, Dudley Hammon, and Timothy Duncan. "Blowhards, Snobs, and Narcissists: Interpersonal Reactions to Excessive Egotism." In *Aversive Interpersonal Behaviors*, edited by Robin M. Kowalski, 111–31. New York: Plenum Press, 1997.

Le Roux, G. A. Lotter, H. S. Steyn, and L. Malan. "Cultural Coping as a Risk for Depression and Hypertension: The SABPA Prospective Study." *Cardiovascular Journal of Africa* 29, no. 6 (2018).

Lebra, Takie Sugiyama. *The Japanese Self in Cultural Logic*. Honolulu: University of Hawai'i Press, 2004.

Lee, Matthew T., Laura D. Kubzansky, and Tyler J. VanderWeele, eds. *Measuring Well-Being: Interdisciplinary Perspectives from the Social Sciences and the Humanities*. New York: Oxford University Press, 2021.

LeDoux, Joseph E. "As Soon as There Was Life, There Was Danger: The Deep History of Survival Behaviours and the Shallower History of Consciousness." *Philosophical Transactions of the Royal Society B: Biological Sciences* 377, no. 1844 (February 14, 2022): 20210292. https://doi.org/10.1098/rstb.2021.0292.

———. *The Deep History of Ourselves: The Four-Billion-Year Story of How We Got Conscious Brains*. New York: Penguin Books, 2019.

———. *The Emotional Brain: The Mysterious Underpinnings of Emotional Life*. New York: Simon & Schuster, 1996.

———. "How Does the Non-Conscious Become Conscious?" *Current Biology* 30, no. 5 (2020): R196–R199.

———. "Thoughtful Feelings." *Current Biology* 30, no. 11 (June 1, 2020): R619–23. https://doi.org/10.1016/j.cub.2020.04.012.

———. "What Emotions Might Be like in Other Animals." *Current Biology* 31, no. 13 (July 12, 2021): R824–29. https://doi.org/10.1016/j.cub.2021.05.005.

LeDoux, Joseph E., and Richard Brown. "A Higher-Order Theory of Emotional Consciousness." *Proceedings of the National Academy of Sciences* 114, no. 10 (March 7, 2017): E2016–25. https://doi.org/10.1073/pnas.1619316114.

LeDoux, Joseph E., and Daniel S. Pine. "Using Neuroscience to Help Understand Fear and Anxiety: A Two-System Framework." *American Journal of Psychiatry* 173, no. 11 (November 2016): 1083–93. https://doi.org/10.1176/appi.ajp.2016.16030353.

Leu, Janxin, Batja Mesquita, Phoebe C. Ellsworth, Zhang Zhiyong, Yuan Huijuan, Emma Buchtel, Mayumi Karasawa, and Takahiko Masuda. "Situational Differences in Dialectical Emotions: Boundary Conditions in a Cultural Comparison of North Americans and East Asians." *Cognition and Emotion* 24, no. 3 (April 1, 2010): 419–35. https://doi.org/10.1080/02699930802650911.

Leu, Janxin, Jennifer Wang, and Kelly Koo. "Are Positive Emotions Just as 'Positive' Across Cultures?" *Emotion* 11, no. 4 (2011): 994–99. https://doi.org/10.1037/a0021332.

Levine, Cynthia S., Yuri Miyamoto, Hazel Rose Markus, Attilio Rigotti, Jennifer Morozink Boylan, Jiyoung Park, Shinobu Kitayama, et al. "Culture and Healthy Eating: The Role of Independence and Interdependence in the United States and Japan." *Personality & Social Psychology Bulletin* 42, no. 10 (October 2016): 1335–48. https://doi.org/10.1177/0146167216658645.

Li, Chenyang. "The Confucian Concept of Jen and the Feminist Ethics of Care: A Comparative Study." In *The Sage and the Second Sex*, edited by Chenyang Li, 23–42. LaSalle, IL: Open Court, 2000.

Li, Xingyu, Miaozhe Han, Geoffrey L. Cohen, and Hazel Rose Markus. "Passion Matters but Not Equally Everywhere: Predicting Achievement from Interest, Enjoyment, and Efficacy in 59 Societies." *Proceedings of the National Academy of Sciences* 118, no. 11 (March 16, 2021): e2016964118. https://doi.org/10.1073/pnas.2016964118.

Li, Yingtao, and Di Wang. "China's 'State Feminism' in Context." In *Women of Asia: Globalization, Development, and Gender Equity*, edited by

Mehrangiz Najafizadeh and Linda Lindsey, 66–82. New York: Routledge, 2019.

Liu, Lydia He, Rebecca E. Karl, and Dorothy Ko, eds. *The Birth of Chinese Feminism: Essential Texts in Transnational Theory*. New York: Columbia University Press, 2013.

Lomas, Tim, Alden Yuanhong Lai, Koichiro Shiba, Pablo Diego-Rosell, Yukiko Uchida, and Tyler J. VanderWeele. "Insights from the First Global Survey of Balance and Harmony." In Helliwell et al., *World Happiness Report 2022*. https://worldhappiness.report/ed/2022/insights-from-the-first-global-survey-of-balance-and-harmony/.

Losada, Marcial, and Emily Heaphy. "The Role of Positivity and Connectivity in the Performance of Business Teams: A Nonlinear Dynamics Model." *American Behavioral Scientist* 47, no. 6 (February 1, 2004): 740–65. https://doi.org/10.1177/0002764203260208.

Luong, Gloria, Cornelia Wrzus, Gert G. Wagner, and Michaela Riediger. "When Bad Moods May Not Be so Bad: Valuing Negative Affect Is Associated with Weakened Affect-Health Links." *Emotion* 16, no. 3 (April 2016): 387–401. https://doi.org/10.1037/emo0000132.

Lutz, Catherine. *Unnatural Emotions*. Chicago: University of Chicago Press, 1988.

Lyubomirsky, Sonja, and Heidi S. Lepper. "A Measure of Subjective Happiness: Preliminary Reliability and Construct Validation." *Social Indicators Research* 46, no. 2 (February 1, 1999): 137–55. https://doi.org/10.1023/A:1006824100041.

Ma, Xiaoming, Maya Tamir, and Yuri Miyamoto. "A Socio-Cultural Instrumental Approach to Emotion Regulation: Culture and the Regulation of Positive Emotions." *Emotion* 18, no. 1 (2018): 138–52. https://doi.org/10.1037/emo0000315.

MacIntyre, Alasdair. *Ethics in the Conflicts of Modernity: An Essay on Desire, Practical Reasoning, and Narrative*. New York: Cambridge University Press, 2016.

Mann, Denise. "Pandemic Tied to Higher Suicide Rate in Blacks, Lowered Rate in Whites: Study." *USA Today*, December 17, 2020.

Margolis, Seth, Eric Schwitzgebel, Daniel J. Ozer, and Sonja Lyubomirsky. "Empirical Relationships Among Five Types of Well-Being." In Lee,

Kubzansky, and VanderWeele, *Measuring Well-Being*, 339–76. New York: Oxford University Press, 2021.

Markus, Hazel Rose. "What Moves People to Action? Culture and Motivation." *Current Opinion on Psychology* 8 (2016): 161–66.

Markus, Hazel Rose, and Alana Conner. *Clash! How to Thrive in a Multicultural World*. New York: Penguin Books, 2013.

Markus, Hazel Rose, and Shinobu Kitayama. "Culture and the Self: Implications for Cognition, Emotion, and Motivation." *Psychological Review* 98, no. 2 (1991): 224–53. https://doi.org/10.1037/0033-295X.98.2.224.

———. "Cultures and Selves: A Cycle of Mutual Constitution." *Perspectives on Psychological Science* 5, no. 4 (2010): 420–30.

Markus, Hazel Rose, Carol D. Ryff, Katherine B. Curhan, and Karen A. Palmersheim. "In Their Own Words: Well-Being at Midlife Among High School-Educated and College-Educated Adults." In *How Healthy Are We?: A National Study of Well-Being at Midlife*, edited by Orville G. Brim, Carol D. Ryff, and Ronald C. Kessler, 273–319. Chicago: University of Chicago Press, 2004.

McCann, D. P., and P. D. Miller. *In Search of the Common Good*. Edinburgh: T & T Clark, 2005.

McMahon, Darrin M. *Happiness: A History*. Grove Press, 2006.

Menon, Usha. "Hinduism, Happiness and Wellbeing: A Case Study of Adulthood in an Oriya Hindu Temple Town." In *Happiness Across Cultures: Views of Happiness and Quality of Life in Non-Western Cultures*, edited by Helaine Selin and Gareth Davey, 417–34. Dordrecht: Springer Netherlands, 2012.

Mesquita, Batja. *Between Us: How Cultures Create Emotions*. New York: Norton, 2022.

———. "Emotions as Dynamic Cultural Phenomena." In *Handbook of Affective Sciences*, edited by R. J. Davidson, Klaus R. Scherer, and H. H. Goldsmith, 871–90. New York: Oxford University Press, 2003.

Mesquita, Batja, Michael Boiger, and Jozefien De Leersnyder. "The Cultural Construction of Emotions." *Current Opinion in Psychology* 8 (April 1, 2016): 31–36. https://doi.org/10.1016/j.copsyc.2015.09.015.

———. "Doing Emotions: The Role of Culture in Everyday Emotions." *European Review of Social Psychology* 28, no. 1 (January 1, 2017): 95–133. https://doi.org/10.1080/10463283.2017.1329107.

Mesquita, Batja, Jozefien De Leersnyder, and Michael Boiger. "The Cultural Psychology of Emotion." In *Handbook of Emotions*, 4th ed., edited by L. F. Barrett, M. Lewis, and J. Haviland-Jones, 393–411. New York: Guilford Press, 2018.

Mesquita, Batja, Jozefien De Leersnyder, and Alba Jasini. "The Cultural Psychology of Acculturation." In *Handbook of Cultural Psychology*, 2nd ed., edited by Shinobu Kitayama and Dov Cohen, 502–35. New York: Guilford Press, 2019.

Mesquita, Batja, and Nico H. Frijda. "Cultural Variations in Emotions: A Review." *Psychological Bulletin* 112, no. 2 (1992): 179–204. https://doi.org/10.1037/0033-2909.112.2.179.

Mesquita, Batja, and Mayumi Karasawa. "Different Emotional Lives." *Cognition and Emotion* 16, no. 1 (2002): 127–41. https://doi.org/10.1080/02699 93014000176

Metzl, Jonathan M. *The Protest Psychosis: How Schizophrenia Became a Black Disease*. Boston: Beacon Press, 2010.

Mill, John Stuart. *Utilitarianism, and the 1868 Speech on Capital Punishment*. Indianapolis, IN: Hackett, 2001.

Minami, Hiroshi. *Psychology of the Japanese People*. Tokyo: University of Tokyo Press, 1971.

Miyamoto, Y., X. Ma, and B. Wilken. "Cultural Variation in Pro-Positive Versus Balanced Systems of Emotions." *Current Opinion in Behavioral Sciences* 15 (2017): 27–32.

Miyamoto, Y., J. Yoo, and B. Wilken, B. "Well-Being and Health: A Cultural Psychology of Optimal Human Functioning." In *Handbook of Cultural Psychology*, 2nd ed., edited by D. Cohen and S. Kitayama, 319–42. New York: Guilford Press, 2019.

Miyamoto, Yuri, Jennifer Morozink Boylan, Christopher L. Coe, Katherine B. Curhan, Cynthia S. Levine, Hazel Rose Markus, Jiyoung Park, et al. "Negative Emotions Predict Elevated Interleukin-6 in the United States but Not in Japan." *Brain, Behavior, and Immunity* 34 (November 1, 2013): 79–85. https://doi.org/10.1016/j.bbi.2013.07.173.

Miyamoto, Yuri, and Xiaoming Ma. "Dampening or Savoring Positive Emotions: A Dialectical Cultural Script Guides Emotion Regulation." *Emotion* 11, no. 6 (2011): 1346–57. https://doi.org/10.1037/a0 025135.

Miyamoto, Yuri, Xiaoming Ma, and Amelia G. Petermann. "Cultural Differences in Hedonic Emotion Regulation After a Negative Event." *Emotion* 14, no. 4 (2014): 804–15. https://doi.org/10.1037/a0036257.

Miyamoto, Yuri, and Carol D. Ryff. "Cultural Differences in the Dialectical and Non-Dialectical Emotional Styles and Their Implications for Health." *Cognition & Emotion* 25 (2011): 22–39.

———. "Culture and Health: Recent Developments and Future Directions." *The Japanese Psychological Research* 64, no. 2 (April 2022): 90–108. https://doi.org/10.1111/jpr.12378.

Miyamoto, Yuri, Yukiko Uchida, and Phoebe C. Ellsworth. "Culture and Mixed Emotions: Co-Occurrence of Positive and Negative Emotions in Japan and the United States." *Emotion* 10, no. 3 (June 2010): 404–15. https://doi.org/10.1037/a0018430.

Miyamoto, Yuri, Jiah Yoo, and Brooke Wilken. "Well-Being and Health: A Cultural Psychology of Optimal Human Functioning." In *Handbook of Cultural Psychology*, 2nd ed., edited by Dov Cohen and Shinobu Kitayama, 319–42. New York: Guilford Press, 2019.

Ng, Weiting, and Ed Diener. "What Matters to the Rich and the Poor? Subjective Well-Being, Financial Satisfaction, and Postmaterialist Needs Across the World." *Journal of Personality and Social Psychology* 107, no. 2 (2014): 326–38. https://doi.org/10.1037/a0036856.

Ng, Yew-Kwang, and Lok Sang Ho. *Happiness and Public Policy: Theory, Case Studies and Implications*. London: Palgrave Macmillan UK, 2006.

Nietzsche, Friedrich. *The Anti-Christ, Ecce Homo, Twilight of the Idols*. New York: Cambridge University Press, 2005.

Nisbett, Richard E., and Timothy D. Wilson. "Telling More Than We Can Know: Verbal Reports on Mental Processes." *Psychological Review* 84, no. 3 (1977): 231–59. https://doi.org/10.1037/0033-295X.84.3.231.

Norenzayan, Ara. *Big Gods: How Religion Transformed Cooperation and Conflict*. Princeton, NJ: Princeton University Press, 2015.

NPR. "To Be In A Rage, Almost All The Time." *NPR*, June 1, 2020. https://www.npr.org/2020/06/01/867153918/-to-be-in-a-rage-almost-all-the-time.

Nussbaum, Martha C. *Women and Human Development: The Capabilities Approach*. New York: Cambridge University Press, 2001.

Oishi, Shigehiro, Hyewon Choi, Minkyung Koo, Iolanda Galinha, Keiko Ishii, Asuka Komiya, Maike Luhmann, et al. "Happiness, Meaning, and Psychological Richness." *Affective Science* 1, no. 2 (June 1, 2020): 107–15. https://doi.org/10.1007/s42761-020-00011-z.

Oishi, Shigehiro, and Ed Diener. "Can and Should Happiness Be a Policy Goal?" *Policy Insights from the Behavioral and Brain Sciences* 1, no. 1 (October 1, 2014): 195–203. https://doi.org/10.1177/2372732214548427.

———. "Goals, Culture, and Subjective Well-Being." *Personality and Social Psychology Bulletin* 27, no. 12 (December 1, 2001): 1674–82. https://doi.org/10.1177/01461672012712010.

Organisation for Economic Co-operation and Development (OECD). "OECD Better Life Index." https://www.oecdbetterlifeindex.org/#/11111111111.

Ortony, Andrew, Gerald L. Clore, and Allan Collins. *The Cognitive Structure of Emotions*. New York: Cambridge University Press, 1988.

Osburg, John. *Anxious Wealth: Money and Morality Among China's New Rich*. Stanford, CA: Stanford University Press, 2013.

Panchal, Nirmita, Rabah Kamal, Cynthia Cox, and Rachel Garfield. "The Implications of COVID-19 for Mental Health and Substance Use." KFF, February 10, 2021. https://www.kff.org/coronavirus-covid-19/issue-brief/the-implications-of-covid-19-for-mental-health-and-substance-use/.

Panksepp, Jaak. *Affective Neuroscience: The Foundations of Human and Animal Emotions*. New York: Oxford University Press, 1998.

Panksepp, Jaak, and Lucy Biven. *The Archaeology of Mind: Neuroevolutionary Origins of Human Emotions*. New York: Norton, 2012.

Park, BoKyung, Elizabeth Blevins, Brian Knutson, and Jeanne L. Tsai. "Neurocultural Evidence That Ideal Affect Match Promotes Giving." *Social Cognitive and Affective Neuroscience* 12, no. 7 (March 31, 2017): 1083–96. https://doi.org/10.1093/scan/nsx047.

Park, BoKyung, Alexander Genevsky, Brian Knutson, and Jeanne Tsai. "Culturally Valued Facial Expressions Enhance Loan Request Success." *Emotion* 20, no. 7 (October 2020): 1137–53. https://doi.org/10.1037/emo0000642.

Park, BoKyung, Yang Qu, Louise Chim, Elizabeth Blevins, Brian Knutson, and Jeanne L. Tsai. "Ventral Striatal Activity Mediates Cultural

Differences in Affiliative Judgments of Smiles." *Culture and Brain* 6, no. 2 (October 1, 2018): 102–17. https://doi.org/10.1007/s40167-018-0061-7.

Park, BoKyung, Jeanne L. Tsai, Louise Chim, Elizabeth Blevins, and Brian Knutson. "Neural Evidence for Cultural Differences in the Valuation of Positive Facial Expressions." *Social Cognitive and Affective Neuroscience* 11, no. 2 (February 2016): 243–52. https://doi.org/10.1093/scan/nsv113.

Peng, Kaiping, Julie Spencer-Rodgers, and Zhong Nian. "Naïve Dialecticism and the Tao of Chinese Thought." In *Indigenous and Cultural Psychology: Understanding People in Context*. edited by Uichol Kim, Kuo-Shu Yang, and Kwang-Kuo Hwang, 247–62. Boston: Springer, 2006.

Penn, Derek C., Keith J. Holyoak, and Daniel J. Povinelli. "Darwin's Mistake: Explaining the Discontinuity Between Human and Nonhuman Minds." *Behavioral and Brain Sciences* 31, no. 2 (April 2008): 109–30. https://doi.org/10.1017/S0140525X08003543.

Perunovic, Wei Qi Elaine, Daniel Heller, and Eshkol Rafaeli. "Within-Person Changes in the Structure of Emotion: The Role of Cultural Identification and Language." *Psychological Science* 18, no. 7 (July 2007): 607–13. https://doi.org/10.1111/j.1467-9280.2007.01947.x.

Peters, Rosalind M. "Racism and Hypertension Among African Americans." *Western Journal of Nursing Research* 26, no. 6 (October 1, 2004): 612–31. https://doi.org/10.1177/0193945904265816.

"Plan to Measure Happiness 'Not Woolly'—Cameron." *BBC News*, November 25, 2010. https://www.bbc.com/news/uk-11833241.

Ponocny, I., C. Weismayer, B. Stross, and S. G. Dressler. "Are Most People Happy? Exploring the Meaning of Subjective Well-Being Ratings." *Journal of Happiness Studies* 17, no. 6 (December 1, 2016): 2635–53. https://doi.org/10.1007/s10902-015-9710-0.

Portes, Alejandro, and Julia Sensenbrenner. "Embeddedness and Immigration: Notes on the Social Determinants of Economic Action." *American Journal of Sociology* 98, no. 6 (May 1993): 1320–50. https://doi.org/10.1086/230191.

PositivePsychology.com. "Positive Emotions: A List of 26 Examples + Definition in Psychology," March 12, 2018. https://positivepsychology.com/positive-emotions-list-examples-definition-psychology/.

Purnell, Jason Q., Melody Goodman, William F. Tate, Kelly M. Harris, Darrell L. Hudson, Brittni D. Jones, Robert Fields, et al. "For the Sake of All: Civic Education on the Social Determinants of Health and Health Disparities in St. Louis." *Urban Education* 53, no. 6 (2018): 711–43. https://doi.org/10.1177/0042085916682574.

Purnell, Tanjala S., Elizabeth A. Calhoun, Sherita H. Golden, Jacqueline R. Halladay, Jessica L. Krok-Schoen, Bradley M. Appelhans, and Lisa A. Cooper. "Achieving Health Equity: Closing the Gaps in Health Care Disparities, Interventions, and Research." *Health Affairs* 35, no. 8 (August 2016): 1410–15. https://doi.org/10.1377/hlthaff.2016.0158.

PYMNTS.com. "New Reality Check: The Paycheck-to-Paycheck Report." https://www.pymnts.com/study/reality-check-paycheck-to-paycheck-credit-scores-consumer-card-debt-inflation/.

Quine, Willard Van Orman. *Ontological Relativity and Other Essays*. New York: Columbia University Press, 1969.

———. *Word and Object*. Eastford, CT: Martino Fine Books, 2013.

Rappleye, Jeremy, Hikaru Komatsu, Yukiko Uchida, Kuba Krys, and Hazel Markus. "'Better Policies for Better Lives'?: Constructive Critique of the OECD's (Mis)Measure of Student Well-Being." *Journal of Education Policy* 35, no. 2 (March 3, 2020): 258–82. https://doi.org/10.1080/02680939.2019.1576923.

Rawls, John. *A Theory of Justice*. Cambridge, MA: Harvard University Press, 1971.

Ren, Hai. *The Middle Class in Neoliberal China: Governing Risk, Life-Building, and Themed Spaces*. London: Routledge, 2012.

———. *Neoliberalism and Culture in China and Hong Kong: The Countdown of Time*. London: Routledge, 2010.

Rofel, Lisa. *Desiring China: Experiments in Neoliberalism, Sexuality, and Public Culture*. Durham, NC: Duke University Press, 2007.

Rogers, Megan L., Jessica Kelliher-Rabon, Christopher R. Hagan, Jameson K. Hirsch, and Thomas E. Joiner. "Negative Emotions in Veterans Relate to Suicide Risk Through Feelings of Perceived Burdensomeness and Thwarted Belongingness." *Journal of Affective Disorders* 208 (January 15, 2017): 15–21. https://doi.org/10.1016/j.jad.2016.09.038.

Rojas, Mariano. "Happiness, Public Policy and the Notion of Development." *Behavioural Public Policy* 4, no. 2 (July 2020): 166–76. https://doi.org/10.1017/bpp.2019.40.

Ruby, Matthew B., Carl F. Falk, Steven J. Heine, Covadonga Villa, and Orly Silberstein. "Not All Collectivisms Are Equal: Opposing Preferences for Ideal Affect Between East Asians and Mexicans." *Emotion* 12 (2012): 1206–9. https://doi.org/10.1037/a0029118.

Rush, Benjamin. *Medical Inquiries and Observations, Upon the Diseases of the Mind.* London: Kimber & Richardson, 1812.

———. "Observations Intended to Favour a Supposition That the Black Color (As It Is Called) of the Negroes Is Derived from the Leprosy." *Transactions of the American Philosophical Society* 4 (1799): 289–97. https://doi.org/10.2307/1005108.

Russell, James A. "A Circumplex Model of Affect." *Journal of Personality and Social Psychology* 39, no. 6 (1980): 1161–78. https://doi.org/10.1037/h0077714.

Ryff, Carol D. "Happiness Is Everything, or Is It? Explorations on the Meaning of Psychological Well-Being." *Journal of Personality and Social Psychology* 57, no. 6 (1989): 1069–81. https://doi.org/10.1037/0022-3514.57.6.1069.

Ryff, Carol, Jennifer Morozink Boylan, Christopher L. Coe, Mayumi Karasawa, Norito Kawakami, Shinobu Kitayama, Chiemi Kan, et al. "Adult Development in Japan and the United States: Comparing Theories and Findings About Growth, Maturity, and Well-Being." In *The Oxford Handbook of Human Development and Culture: An Interdisciplinary Perspective*, 666–79. New York: Oxford University Press, 2015.

Ryff, Carol D., Jennifer Morozink Boylan, and Julie A. Kirsch. "Advancing the Science of Well-Being: A Dissenting View on Measurement Recommendations." In Lee, Kubzansky, and VanderWeele, *Measuring Well-Being*, 521–35.

Ryff, Carol D., Gayle D. Love, Yuri Miyamoto, Hazel Rose Markus, Katherine B. Curhan, Shinobu Kitayama, Jiyoung Park, et al. "Culture and the Promotion of Well-Being in East and West: Understanding Varieties of Attunement to the Surrounding Context." In *Increasing Psychological Well-Being in Clinical and Educational Settings: Interventions and Cultural Contexts*, edited by Giovanni Andrea Fava and Chiara Ruini, 1–19. Dordrecht: Springer Netherlands, 2014.

Said, Edward W. *Orientalism*. New York: Pantheon Books, 1978.

Scarantino, Andrea. "Are LeDoux's Survival Circuits Basic Emotions Under a Different Name?" *Current Opinion in Behavioral Sciences* 24 (December 1, 2018): 75–82. https://doi.org/10.1016/j.cobeha.2018.06.001.

Scarantino, Andrea, and Ronald de Sousa. "Emotion." In *The Stanford Encyclopedia of Philosophy*, edited by Edward N. Zalta, Summer 2021. Metaphysics Research Lab, Stanford University, 2021. https://plato.stanford.edu/archives/sum2021/entries/emotion/.

Schachter, Stanley, and Jerome Singer. "Cognitive, Social, and Physiological Determinants of Emotional State." *Psychological Review* 69, no. 5 (1962): 379–99. https://doi.org/10.1037/h0046234.

Scherer, Klaus R. "On the Nature and Function of Emotion: A Component Process Approach." In *Approaches to Emotion*, edited by Klaus R. Scherer and Paul Ekman, 293–317. Mahwah, NJ: Lawrence Erlbaum Associates, 1984.

Schimmack, Ulrich, Shigehiro Oishi, and Ed Diener. "Cultural Influences on the Relation Between Pleasant Emotions and Unpleasant Emotions: Asian Dialectic Philosophies or Individualism-Collectivism?" *Cognition and Emotion* 16, no. 6 (November 1, 2002): 705–19. https://doi.org/10.1080/02699930143000590.

Schwartz, Shalom H. "Cultural Value Orientations: Nature and Implications of National Differences." *Journal of the Higher School of Economics* 5, no. 2 (2008): 37–67.

Schwitzgebel, Eric. *Perplexities of Consciousness*. Cambridge, MA: MIT Press, 2011.

Seligman, Martin E. P. *Authentic Happiness: Using the New Positive Psychology to Realize Your Potential for Lasting Fulfillment*. New York: Simon & Schuster, 2002.

Sen, Amartya. "Well-Being, Agency and Freedom: The Dewey Lectures 1984." *The Journal of Philosophy* 82, no. 4 (1985): 169–221. https://doi.org/10.2307/2026184.

Shun, Kwong-Loi, and David B. Wong. *Confucian Ethics: A Comparative Study of Self, Autonomy, and Community*. New York: Cambridge University Press, 2004.

Shweder, Richard A. *Thinking Through Cultures: Expeditions in Cultural Psychology*. Cambridge, MA: Harvard University Press; 1991.

Sims, Tamara, Birgit Koopmann-Holm, Henry Young, Da Jiang, Helene Fung, and Jeanne L. Tsai. "Asian Americans Respond Less Favorably to Excitement (vs. Calm)-Focused Physicians Compared to European Americans." *Cultural Diversity & Ethnic Minority Psychology* 24, no. 1 (January 2018): 1–14. https://doi.org/10.1037/cdp0000171.

Sims, Tamara, Jeanne L. Tsai, Da Jiang, Yaheng Wang, Helene H. Fung, and Xiulan Zhang. "Wanting to Maximize the Positive and Minimize the Negative: Implications for Mixed Affective Experience in American and Chinese Contexts." *Journal of Personality and Social Psychology* 109, no. 2 (August 2015): 292–315. https://doi.org/10.1037/a0039276.

Sims, Tamara, Jeanne L. Tsai, Birgit Koopmann-Holm, Ewart A. C. Thomas, and Mary K. Goldstein. "Choosing a Physician Depends on How You Want to Feel: The Role of Ideal Affect in Health-Related Decision Making." *Emotion* 14, no. 1 (February 2014): 187–92. https://doi.org/10.1037/a0034372.

Slingerland, Edward. "Big Gods, Historical Explanation, and the Value of Integrating the History of Religion into the Broader Academy." *Religion* 45, no. 4 (October 2, 2015): 585–602. https://doi.org/10.1080/0048721X.2015.1073487.

Smith, Peter B. "Acquiescent Response Bias as an Aspect of Cultural Communication Style." *Journal of Cross-Cultural Psychology* 35, no. 1 (January 1, 2004): 50–61. https://doi.org/10.1177/0022022103260380.

Solomon, Robert C. *Not Passion's Slave: Emotions and Choice*. New York: Oxford University Press, 2003.

Soyinka, Wole. *Chronicles from the Land of the Happiest People on Earth*. New York: Knopf, 2021.

Spakowski, Nicola. "'Gender' Trouble: Feminism in China Under the Impact of Western Theory and the Spatialization of Identity." *Positions: Asia Critique* 19, no. 1 (February 1, 2011): 31–54. https://doi.org/10.1215/10679847-2010-023.

Srinivasan, Amia. "The Aptness of Anger." *Journal of Political Philosophy* 26, no. 2 (2018): 123–44. https://doi.org/10.1111/jopp.12130.

Stephens, Nicole M., Stephanie A. Fryberg, Hazel Rose Markus, Camille S. Johnson, and Rebecca Covarrubias. "Unseen Disadvantage: How American Universities' Focus on Independence Undermines the Academic Performance of First-Generation College Students." *Journal of Personality and Social Psychology* 102, no. 6 (2012): 1178–97. https://doi.org/10.1037/a0027143.

Stevenson, Betsey, and Justin Wolfers. "Economic Growth and Subjective Well-Being: Reassessing the Easterlin Paradox." National Bureau of

Economic Research, Working Paper 14282 (August 2008). https://doi.org/10.3386/w14282.

Sturgeon, Nicola. "Why Governments Should Prioritize Well-Being." TED Talk, 1564411787, July 2019. https://www.ted.com/talks/nicola_sturgeon_why_governments_should_prioritize_well_being.

Suddendorf, Thomas. *The Gap: The Science of What Separates Us from Other Animals*. New York: Basic Books, 2013.

Suh, Eunkook Mark, Ed Diener, Shigehiro Oishi, and Harry C. Triandis. "The Shifting Basis of Life Satisfaction Judgments Across Cultures: Emotions Versus Norms." *Journal of Personality and Social Psychology* 74, no. 2 (1998): 482–93. https://doi.org/10.1037/0022-3514.74.2.482.

Suikkanen, Jussi. "An Improved Whole Life Satisfaction Theory of Happiness." *International Journal of Well-being* 1, no. 1 (January 30, 2011), 1–18.

Suite, Derek H., Robert La Bril, Annelle Primm, and Phyllis Harrison-Ross. "Beyond Misdiagnosis, Misunderstanding and Mistrust: Relevance of the Historical Perspective in the Medical and Mental Health Treatment of People of Color." *Journal of the National Medical Association* 99, no. 8 (August 2007): 879–85.

Sun, Anna. "The Confucian Conception of the Common Good in Contemporary China." In *Ethics in Action for Sustainable Development*, edited by Jeffrey Sachs et al., 83–91. New York: Columbia University Press, 2022.

———. *Confucianism as a World Religion: Contested Histories and Contemporary Realities*. Princeton, NJ: Princeton University Press, 2013.

———. "Thinking with Weber's Religion of China in the Twenty-First Century." *Review of Religion and Chinese Society* 7, no. 2 (December 4, 2020): 250–70. https://doi.org/10.1163/22143955-00702006.

———. "To Be or Not to Be a Confucian: Explicit and Implicit Religious Identities in the Global Twenty-First Century." *Chinese Religions Going Global* 11 (December 7, 2020): 210–35. https://doi.org/10.1163/9789004443327_013.

Tamir, Maya, and Brett Q. Ford. "Choosing to Be Afraid: Preferences for Fear as a Function of Goal Pursuit." *Emotion* 9, no. 4 (2009): 488–97. https://doi.org/10.1037/a0015882.

Tamir, Maya, and Tony Gutentag. "Desired Emotional States: Their Nature, Causes, and Implications for Emotion Regulation." *Current Opinion in*

Psychology 17 (October 1, 2017): 84–88. https://doi.org/10.1016/j.copsyc.2017.06.014.

Tamir, Maya, Christopher Mitchell, and James J. Gross. "Hedonic and Instrumental Motives in Anger Regulation." *Psychological Science* 19, no. 4 (April 1, 2008): 324–28. https://doi.org/10.1111/j.1467-9280.2008.02088.x.

Tamir, Maya, Shalom H. Schwartz, Jan Cieciuch, Michaela Riediger, Claudio Torres, Christie Scollon, Vivian Dzokoto, Xiaolu Zhou, and Allon Vishkin. "Desired Emotions Across Cultures: A Value-Based Account." *Journal of Personality and Social Psychology* 111, no. 1 (2016): 67–82. https://doi.org/10.1037/pspp0000072.

Taschereau-Dumouchel, Vincent, Aurelio Cortese, Toshinori Chiba, J. D. Knotts, Mitsuo Kawato, and Hakwan Lau. "Towards an Unconscious Neural Reinforcement Intervention for Common Fears." *Proceedings of the National Academy of Sciences* 115, no. 13 (March 27, 2018): 3470–75. https://doi.org/10.1073/pnas.1721572115.

Taschereau-Dumouchel, Vincent, Mitsuo Kawato, and Hakwan Lau. "Multivoxel Pattern Analysis Reveals Dissociations Between Subjective Fear and Its Physiological Correlates." *Molecular Psychiatry* 25, no. 10 (October 2020): 2342–54. https://doi.org/10.1038/s41380-019-0520-3.

Taschereau-Dumouchel, Vincent, Ka-Yuet Liu, and Hakwan Lau. "Unconscious Psychological Treatments for Physiological Survival Circuits." *Current Opinion in Behavioral Sciences* 24 (December 1, 2018): 62–68. https://doi.org/10.1016/j.cobeha.2018.04.010.

Tay, Louis, and Ed Diener. "Needs and Subjective Well-Being Around the World." *Journal of Personality and Social Psychology* 101, no. 2 (2011): 354–65. https://doi.org/10.1037/a0023779.

Tennant, Ruth, Louise Hiller, Ruth Fishwick, Stephen Platt, Stephen Joseph, Scott Weich, Jane Parkinson, Jenny Secker, and Sarah Stewart-Brown. "The Warwick-Edinburgh Mental Well-Being Scale (WEMWBS): Development and UK Validation." *Health and Quality of Life Outcomes* 5, no. 1 (November 27, 2007): 63. https://doi.org/10.1186/1477-7525-5-63.

Tiberius, Valerie. *The Reflective Life: Living Wisely with Our Limits*. New York: Oxford University Press, 2008.

———. *Well-Being as Value Fulfillment: How We Can Help Each Other to Live Well*. New York: Oxford University Press, 2018.

Tomasello, Michael, and Hannes Rakoczy. "What Makes Human Cognition Unique? From Individual to Shared to Collective Intentionality." *Mind & Language* 18, no. 2 (2003): 121–47. https://doi.org/10.1111/1468-0017.00217.

Tomkins, Silvan. *Affect, Imagery, Consciousness*. New York: Springer, 1962.

Topp, Christian Winther, Søren Dinesen Østergaard, Susan Søndergaard, and Per Bech. "The WHO-5 Well-Being Index: A Systematic Review of the Literature." *Psychotherapy and Psychosomatics* 84, no. 3 (2015): 167–76. https://doi.org/10.1159/000376585.

Triandis, Harry C. "The Self and Social Behavior in Differing Cultural Contexts." *Psychological Review* 96 (1989): 506–20.

Tsai, Jeanne L. "Ideal Affect: Cultural Causes and Behavioral Consequences." *Perspectives on Psychological Science* 2, no. 3 (2007): 242–59. https://doi.org/10.1111/j.1745-6916.2007.00043.x

Tsai, Jeanne L., Jen Ying Zhen Ang, Elizabeth Blevins, Julia Goernandt, Helene H. Fung, Da Jiang, Julian Elliott, et al. "Leaders' Smiles Reflect Cultural Differences in Ideal Affect." *Emotion* 16, no. 2 (March 2016): 183–95. https://doi.org/10.1037/emo0000133.

Tsai, Jeanne L., Elizabeth Blevins, Lucy Zhang Bencharit, Louise Chim, Helene H. Fung, and Dannii Y. Yeung. "Cultural Variation in Social Judgments of Smiles: The Role of Ideal Affect." *Journal of Personality and Social Psychology* 116, no. 6 (2019): 966–88. https://doi.org/10.1037/pspp0000192.

Tsai, Jeanne L., Louise Chim, and Tamara Sims. "Consumer Behavior, Culture, and Emotion." In *Handbook of Culture and Consumer Behavior*, edited by Sharon Ng and Angela Y. Lee, 68–98. New York: Oxford University Press, 2015.

Tsai, Jeanne L., and Magali Clobert. "Cultural Influences on Emotion: Established Patterns and Emerging Trends." In *Handbook of Cultural Psychology*, 2nd ed., edited by Dov Cohen and Shinobu Kitayama, 292–318. New York: Guilford Press, 2019.

Tsai, Jeanne L., Brian Knutson, and Helene H. Fung. "Cultural Variation in Affect Valuation." *Journal of Personality and Social Psychology* 90, no. 2 (2006): 288–307. https://doi.org/10.1037/0022-3514.90.2.288.

Tsai, Jeanne L., and Robert W. Levenson. "Cultural Influences on Emotional Responding: Chinese American and European American Dating

Couples During Interpersonal Conflict." *Journal of Cross-Cultural Psychology* 28, no. 5 (September 1, 1997): 600–625. https://doi.org/10.1177/0022022197285006.

Tsai, J. L., R. W. Levenson, and L. L. Carstensen. "Autonomic, Subjective, and Expressive Responses to Emotional Films in Older and Younger Chinese Americans and European Americans." *Psychology and Aging* 15, no. 4 (2000): 684–93.

Tsai, Jeanne L., Robert W. Levenson, and Kimberly McCoy. "Cultural and Temperamental Variation in Emotional Response." *Emotion* 6, no. 3 (August 2006): 484–97. https://doi.org/10.1037/1528-3542.6.3.484.

Tsai, Jeanne L., Jennifer Y. Louie, Eva E. Chen, and Yukiko Uchida. "Learning What Feelings to Desire: Socialization of Ideal Affect Through Children's Storybooks." *Personality & Social Psychology Bulletin* 33, no. 1 (January 2007): 17–30. https://doi.org/10.1177/0146167206292749.

Tsai, Jeanne L., Felicity F. Miao, and Emma Seppala. "Good Feelings in Christianity and Buddhism: Religious Differences in Ideal Affect." *Personality & Social Psychology Bulletin* 33, no. 3 (March 2007): 409–21. https://doi.org/10.1177/0146167206296107.

Tsai, Jeanne L., Felicity F. Miao, Emma Seppala, Helene H. Fung, and Dannii Y. Yeung. "Influence and Adjustment Goals: Sources of Cultural Differences in Ideal Affect." *Journal of Personality and Social Psychology* 92, no. 6 (June 2007): 1102–17. https://doi.org/10.1037/0022-3514.92.6.1102.

Tsai, Jeanne L., Tamara Sims, Yang Qu, Ewart Thomas, Da Jiang, and Helene H. Fung. "Valuing Excitement Makes People Look Forward to Old Age Less and Dread It More." *Psychology and Aging* 33, no. 7 (November 2018): 975–92. https://doi.org/10.1037/pag0000295.

Tu, Weiming. *Confucian Traditions in East Asian Modernity: Moral Education and Economic Culture in Japan and the Four Mini-Dragons*. Cambridge, MA: Harvard University Press, 1996.

Uchida, Yukiko, Sarah S. M. Townsend, Hazel Rose Markus, and Hilary B. Bergsieker. "Emotions as Within or Between People? Cultural Variation in Lay Theories of Emotion Expression and Inference." *Personality and Social Psychology Bulletin* 35, no. 11 (November 1, 2009): 1427–39. https://doi.org/10.1177/0146167209347322.

Uchida, Yukiko, and Shinobu Kitayama. "Happiness and Unhappiness in East and West: Themes and Variations." *Emotion* 9, no. 4 (2009): 441–56. https://doi.org/10.1037/a0015634.

Uchida, Yukiko, Vinai Norasakkunkit, and Shinobu Kitayama. "Cultural Constructions of Happiness: Theory and Empirical Evidence." *Journal of Happiness Studies* 5, no. 3 (September 1, 2004): 223–39. https://doi.org/10.1007/s10902-004-8785-9.

United Nations. Universal Declaration of Human Rights. 1948. https://www.un.org/en/about-us/universal-declaration-of-human-rights.

United Nations. Transforming Our World: The 2030 Agenda for Sustainable Development (Resolution 70/1). September 25, 2015. https://sdgs.un.org/2030agenda.

United Nations. Happiness: Towards a Holistic Approach to Development (Resolution 65/309). August 25, 2011. https://digitallibrary.un.org/record/715187.

Ura, Karma, Sabina Alkire, Tshoki Zangmo, and Karma Wangdi. *A Short Guide to Gross National Happiness Index*. Thimphu: Centre for Bhutan Studies, 2012.

Utsey, Shawn O. "Advances in the Conceptualization and Measurement of Race-Related Stress," January 18, 2018. https://www.stlmag.com/api/content/f3cad220-fa15-11e7-886a-120a1a3c5526/.

Vendantam, Shankar. "Racial Disparities Found in Pinpointing Mental Illness." *Washington Post*, June 28, 2005.

Wang, Zheng. "Feminist Struggles in a Changing China." In *Feminisms with Chinese Characteristics*, edited by Ping Zhu and Hui Faye Xiao, 117–56. Syracuse, NY: Syracuse University Press, 2021.

———. "Gender, Employment and Women's Resistance." In *Chinese Society: Change, Conflict and Resistance*, edited by Elizabeth J. Perry and Mark Selden, 162–86. New York: Routledge, 2003.

———. "Research on Women in Contemporary China." In *Guide to Women's Studies in China*. edited by Gail Hershatter, Emily Honig, Susan Mann, and Lisa Rofel, 1–43. Institute of East Asian Studies, University of California, Berkeley, 1998.

Ward, C., and A. Rana-Deuba. "Home and Host Culture Influences on Sojourner Adjustment." *International Journal of Intercultural Relations* 24, no. 3 (2000): 291–306. https://doi.org/10.1016/S0147-1767(00)00002-X.

Weber, Max. *The Theory of Social and Economic Organization*. New York: Simon & Schuster, 2009.

Wex, Michael. *Born to Kvetch*. New York: St. Martin's Press, 2015.

Wierzbicka, Anna. *Imprisoned in English: The Hazards of English as a Default Language*. New York: Oxford University Press.

———. "'Happiness' in Cross-Linguistic & Cross-Cultural Perspective." *Daedalus* 133, no. 2 (April 1, 2004): 34–43. https://doi.org/10.1162/001152604323049370.

———. *Understanding Cultures Through Their Key Words: English, Russian, Polish, German, and Japanese*. New York: Oxford University Press, 1997.

Willroth, Emily C., Anthony D. Ong, Eileen K. Graham, and Daniel K. Mroczek. "Being Happy and Becoming Happier as Independent Predictors of Physical Health and Mortality." *Psychosomatic Medicine* 82, no. 7 (September 2020): 650–57. https://doi.org/10.1097/PSY.0000000000000832.

Wilson, Y. Yolonda. "Yolonda Wilson, Race, COVID-19, and the Public 'We' (Symposium) [2020 C4eJ 86]." *University of Toronto Centre for Ethics Journal* 86 (November 30, 2020). https://c4ejournal.net/2020/11/30/yolonda-wilson-race-covid-19-and-the-public-we-symposium/.

Wilson, Yolonda Y., Amina White, Akilah Jefferson, and Marion Danis. "Intersectionality in Clinical Medicine: The Need for a Conceptual Framework." *American Journal of Bioethics* 19, no. 2 (February 1, 2019): 8–19. https://doi.org/10.1080/15265161.2018.1557275.

Winch, Peter. "Understanding a Primitive Society." *American Philosophical Quarterly* 1, no. 4 (1964): 307–24.

Woo, Tak-Ling Terry. "Two Discourses on Women from the Classical Period to the Song: An Integrated Approach." In *The Bloomsbury Research Handbook of Chinese Philosophy and Gender*, edited by Ann A. Pang-White, 37–68. New York: Bloomsbury, 2016.

World Economic Forum. "Global Gender Gap Report 2008." World Economic Forum, June 1, 2009. https://www.weforum.org/reports/global-gender-gap-report-2008/.

———. "Global Gender Gap Report 2021." World Economic Forum, March 30, 2021. https://www.weforum.org/reports/global-gender-gap-report-2021/.

World Health Organization. "Preamble to the Constitution of the World Health Organization as adopted by the International Health Conference, New York, 19–22 June 1946, signed on 22 July 1947 by the representatives of 61 States (Official Records of the World Health Organization, no. 2,

p. 100), and entered into force on 7 April 1948." https://apps.who.int/iris/bitstream/handle/10665/85573/Official_record2_eng.pdf;sequence=1.

Yaden, David B., and Daniel M. Haybron. "The Emotional State Assessment Tool: A Brief, Philosophically Informed, and Cross-Culturally Sensitive Measure." *Journal of Positive Psychology* 17, no. 2 (March 4, 2022): 151–65. https://doi.org/10.1080/17439760.2021.2016910.

Yang, Fenggang, and Joseph Tamney, eds. *Confucianism and Spiritual Traditions in Modern China and Beyond*. Leiden: Brill, 2011.

Yang, Mayfair Mei-hui. "From Gender Erasure to Gender Difference: State Feminism, Consumer Sexuality, and Women's Public Sphere in China." In *Spaces of Their Own: Women's Public Sphere in Transnational China*, edited by Mayfair Mei-hui Yang, 35–67. Minneapolis: University of Minnesota Press, 1999.

Yoo, Jiah, and Yuri Miyamoto. "Cultural Fit of Emotions and Health Implications: A Psychosocial Resources Model." *Social and Personality Psychology Compass* 12, no. 2 (2018): e12372. https://doi.org/10.1111/spc3.12372.

INDEX

acculturation, 126, 271n30
actuals, 236, 237, 240, 242, 290n3
adaptive preferences, 31, 150, 160, 171, 180–82
affect: actual, 237–38, 242; ideal, 237–38, 242, 243, 245, 246–47; positive/negative, 81, 118–20, 220, 224. *See also* injustice, affective
affect balance, 164
affective autonomy, 118
affective injustice, 23
affective states, 50, 237, 237–38; in collectivistic cultures, 239–41; cultural differences in, 242–43; cultural variations of, 246–47. *See also* emotions
affect program, 76, 77, 89
Afghanistan, 169, 245
African Americans: adaptation to hermeneutical injustice, 159–62; happiness of, 23–24, 30; life expectancy of, 30; mental health of, 154–59; resilience of, 151, 153;
self-reports of life satisfaction, 178–80; suicide rate among, 158–59; well-being and life satisfaction of, 150, 152, 153
All-China Women's Federation (ACWF), 139–40, 144
altruistic behavior, 292n18
America. *See* United States
American Psychiatric Association (APA), 154
amygdala, 77–78, 89, 95
anger, 121, 153, 158, 176
Annas, Julia, 129
Annett, Anthony, 35
Anscombe, Elizabeth, 67, 205
anthropological realism, 129
anthropology, 5, 9, 10, 201, 236, 246
anxiety, 15, 29, 30, 165; existential, 58
anxiety disorder, 61, 174
Aquinas. *See* Thomas Aquinas
Arden, Jacinda, 37–38
Aristotelianism, 36, 56, 209, 229, 233
Aristotelian principle, 55

Aristotle: on education, 63; ethics of, 129; on happiness (*eudaimonia*), 2, 10, 11, 33, 36, 55, 59, 61–63, 64, 85, 149, 208–9, 229–30, 231, 232, 256n21; influence on philosophy, 4, 205, 233; on natural slavery, 124
Asians, 178. *See also* East Asians
Augustine of Hippo (saint), 4
authentic living, 56–57
Averroes, 4

Bahrain, 192
Baker, F. M., 157–58
balance: affect, 164; emotional, 108, 113, 119, 185, 214; hedonic, 164; as indicator of happiness, 7, 21, 68–69, **70**, 72, 80, 102, **103**, 240, 243; work/life, 41. *See also* harmony
Baldwin, James, 153
Barrington-Leigh, Christopher, 36
Bartholomew (patriarch), 233
Belgium, 124
Bellah, Robert, 131
Bentham, Jeremy, 13, 256n21
Better Life Index (OECD), 38, 41
Bhutan, 13, 37, 66–67, 113, 170, 198
bipolar disorder, 177. *See also* schizophrenia
Black Americans. *See* African Americans
British Household Panel Survey, **9**
Buddhism: in Bhutan, 13, 37, 113; happiness in 11, 66; and the meaning of life, 132, 133–34; positive emotions in, 240; on women, 277n42

calmness, **71**, 72, 102, **104**, 113
Cameron, David, 33–34
Canada, 41, 240, 241
Cantril Ladder, 169, 228, 229, 230, 231, 290n2
capabilities approach, 34, 39, 55, 195
capitalism, 133
Cartwright, Samuel, 154
Categorical Imperative (Kant), 233
Catholic social gospel, 35
Central America, 68
China: changing moral landscape of, 128–29; contemporary habits of the heart, 130–34; feminist movements in, 22, 141–45, 277n41; gender inequality in, 140–41; happiness and well-being in, 22, 41, 86, 115, 127–45; religion in, 136–39; study of emotion in, 246; transition to market economy, 130–31
Chinese Americans, 246
Christianity, 56, 71, 132, 134, 135, 136, 138
Clark, Kelly, 138
climate crisis, 39–40
climate justice, 44
cognitive theory, 76–77
Cohn, Michael, 107
collectivist cultures, 98, 114, 118, 238–41, 246, 292n18
common good(s), 14, 35, 120, 210; in China, 132
compassion, 6, 11, 15, 31, 66, 113, 114. *See also* empathy
Confucianism: ethical values of, 130, 134; on filial piety, 132, 133,

134; on happiness, 11, 22, 56, 71; on heaven, 137; on the meaning of life, 132; on politics, 132; ritual duties of, 135, 137; on well-being, 130, 138; and women, 22, 139, 143–44, 145, 277n42, 277n44
Confucian Way, 11, 56
Confucius: on doctrine of the mean, 109; on education, 63; on "God," 138; on happiness, 11; on life satisfaction, 46
contentment, 107, 113
Costa Rica, 69
COVID pandemic: life satisfaction during, 49, 60, 150–51, 174; problems caused by, 14, 29–30, 31, 141, 159; responses to, 235
cultural belonging, 21
culture(s): Anglophone, 114; collectivist, 98, 114, 118, 238–41, 246, 292n18; differences between, 5, 20, 21, 84, 98, 113, 118–26, 156, 168, 169–70, 175, 168, 169–70, 175, 188, 215, 218, 229, 231, 234; East Asian, 114; and happiness, 7, 10, 20–21, 43, 56, 91, 93, 94–95, 202, 214, 236–44, 246–47; heritage, 125; individualistic, 87–88, 98, 114, 238, 246, 292n18; liberal, 48; Muslim, 112–13; patriarchal, 139, 142, 143, 145, 275n26

Daoism, 132, 277n42
Darwin, Charles, 76
Davies, William, 36

Davis, Lydia, 127
democracy, 52, 69, 102
depression, 15, 24, 29, 30, 38, 49, 114, 122, 152, 153, 155–58, 174, 175, 232
Diagnostic and Statistical Manual of Mental Disorders (DSM-5), 156
domestic abuse/violence, 141, 142
Dong Zhongshu, 143
Duncan, Grant, 101
Durkheim, Emile, 67

Eagleton, Terry, 206
East Asians, 113–15, 217, 221–23, 238, 239, 244, 246, 247. *See also* Asians
Easterlin Paradox, 31
economics, 43; happiness and, 31–32; and well-being, 16
education: in East Asia, 222–23; and a good life, 233; and happiness, 50, 195, 201; for immigrants, 123; intellectual, 63; and life satisfaction, 41; and mental health, 156; for minorities, 124; moral, 63, 230; philosophical, 4; physical, 63; provision of, 55, 202; public 14, 16; as right, 195; and socioeconomic status, 17; in the Sustainable Development Goals, 39; theological, 4; value, 10; and well-being, 11, 45, 51, 53, 221–22; for women, 140
El Salvador, 111
Emotional Patterns Questionnaire (EPQ), 271n30
emotional state theory, 186

emotions: aptness/fittingness conditions of, 109–10; associated with well-being, 119; as autonoetic experiences, 127–28; basic, 88–89; basic emotions theory, 76–77; cultural fit of, 123–24; culturally certified, 120; culturally normative, 122, 175; cultural variations of, 111–15, 120–23, 220–21, 246; as goals, 121, 122; hedonic, 20, 250n8; intensity of, 110; language of, 78, 88, 186–87; modeling for children, 84–85; multiple dimensions of, 109–11; philosophy of, 91; positive/negative, 68, **70**, 72, 83, 92, **103**, 107–9, 111, 113, 114–15, 119–20, 120, 121–22, 163, 175, 192, 220–21, 239–41; science of, 91; social-cognitive view of, 86–87, 91; valence and intensity of, 91
empathy, 113, 201. *See also* compassion
empiricism, 229
employment rate, 53
England, 246
epidemiology, 158
equality, 23, 25, 42, 44, 145, 150, 187, 189, 192, 194, 202, 215, 224, 225; economic, 16, 29, 39, 53, 61, 67; gender, 22, 39, 139–41, 143–44, 196, 216, 275n26; political, 53, 67; social, 16
ethics, 4, 5, 85, 109, 129; of happiness, 189
Ethiopia, 41

ethographies, 185
eudaimonia, 11, 36, 43, 55–56, 59, 61–62, 85, 129, 149, 193, 208, 229–33. *See also* flourishing
European Quality of Life Survey, **8–9**
European Social Survey, **8**

fairness, 124, 232
familial devotion, 133
fear, 19, 77–78, 89, 90, 107, 241
feeling rules, 23, 153, 175
feminism: in China, 139–45, 277n41; and Confucianism, 277n44; socialist, 139–40, 143–44; Western, 143–45
filial piety, 133–34
Finland, 67, 69, 83–84, 216, 245. *See also* Nordic countries
Fitoussi, Jean-Paul, 34
flourishing: Aristotle's view of, 61–62, 64, 208–9; in China, 22, 145; global human, 35, 206, 207, 225; and the happiness agenda, 16; of the individual, 87, 130; Rawls's view of, 55; study of, 43; and true happiness, 86, 129, 193; of women, 145. *See also eudaimonia*
Foot, Philippa, 205
forgiveness, 113
Foucault, Michel, 2
frame-switching, 125
France, 86, 246
Francis (pope), 233
Frederickson, Barbara, 107–8
freedom, 40, 42, 52, 57, 99, 154, 194–95

Fricker, Miranda, 151, 152
friendliness, 114, 241
Frijters, Paul, 12

Gallup World Poll (GWP), 176, 228, 235–48
gender equality, 22, 39, 139–41, 143–44, 196, 216, 275n26, 275–76n26
General Social Survey, **8**
generosity, 50, 52, 79, 91, 113, 137
German Social Economic Panel, **9**
Germany, 86, 223, 246
Global Emotions Report, 83, 102, 111
Global Gender Gap Report, 140
goals: agreement on, 192; collective, 225; cultural, 121, 123; culturally valued, 118–19, 122; emotions as, 121, 122; for good lives, 97, 201; happiness as, 2, 3, 57, 62, 64, 67, 73, 197, 199, 205; individual, 3, 114, 219; life satisfaction as, 67; personal, 119, 218; political, 3, 13, 20, 99; priorities of, 118; of public policy, 33, 38, 48, 73, 215; of research, 161, 220, 222, 223; social, 3, 119; universal, 197, 199; for well-being, 120. *See also* Sustainable Development Goals (SDGs)
good life, 18–19, 24, 55, 75, 92, 185, 201–2, 224, 228, 229, 233, 234; in China, 22–23, 132, 138; as normative concept, 44–47; social meanings of, 131; vs. well-being, 59
goodness, moral, 36

goodwill, 114
government, role of, 14–15. *See also* public policy
Gross National Happiness Index (Bhutan), 37, 113
guilt, 241

Halonen, Tarja, 83–84
happiness: analysis and assessment of, 213–25; aspects of, 49–50; authentic, 32–33; average evaluations of, 98–102, 104; as basic emotion, 88–89; behaviors resulting from, 79; capabilities approach to, 34, 39, 55, 195; in China, 22–23, 127–45; cognates of, 11; as cognitive–evaluative state, 46–47, 51; components of, 94–95; as conditional good, 191; as condition of being happy, 82; content of, 85; cultural variations of, 185, 188–89, 201, 223, 235–48; and culture, 20–21; duration of, 90; and economics, 31–32; as emotion, 19; as emotional state, 46, 51, 58, 60, 75, 82, 84, 85, 94, 112; empirical–philosophical view of, 92–93; ethicized conception of, 69; ethics of, 189; eudaimonistic, 33, 35, 36; as evil, 56, 113; existentialist, 33; genetics of, 95; as goal of human life, 2, 3, 57, 62, 64, 67, 73, 197, 199, 205; and goodness, 10; humility about, 3–6; as life satisfaction, 9, 186; and meaning, 56–59; meaning

happiness (*continued*)
of, 16; measurement of, 7, **8–9**, 9–15, 36, 48–49, **70–71**, 80–82, 97, 98–102, **103**–4, 104, 111, 228, 235; as normative concept, 44–48, 56, 64–65, 200; and personal relationships, 123–24; as pleasure, 46; and political neutrality, 64–73; polysemy of, 92–94; predictors and correlates of, 52–53, 79, 94–95; as *prima facie* good, 2, 64, 72; as psychobiological state, 35, 64, 98; and public policy, 200; ranking of, 19–20; self-reports of, 86, 230–31; semantics of, 85–88, 206; of sentient beings, 5; subjectivist perspective, 206–7; as *summum bonum*, 2, 7, 14, 15, 17, 21, 32, 33, 34, 94, 104, 191, 199, 227–28; theories of, 95, 119; thin/thick sense of, 10; true, 2, 4, 7, 32, 33, 36, 46, 56, 57, 62, 64, 65, 71–72, 86, 97, 112–13, 129, 130, 193, 201, 211; as universal psychological state, 19; value neutral, 97; and well-being, 6–7, 9–15, 82–83; worth of, 10.
See also *eudaimonia*; well-being
happiness agenda: and affective injustice, 153; assessment of, 191; and economics, 32; elision of happiness with well-being in, 3, 16, 18, 33–34; and happiness as life satisfaction, 10, 95; and the happiness industry, 36; human-focused aspect of, 5–6; in the liberal state, 13; and the meaning of happiness, 75–76, 97, 101, 130, 205, 206, 211; and the measurement of happiness, 7, 19–20, 21, 33, 69, 80, 216; political, 13; and public policy, 2, 12–13, 15, 29, 33, 41, 193, 198–99, 227, 228–29; responses to, 53; in the United Arab Emirates, 40
Happiness Agenda (UAE), 40
happiness experience (HX), 40
happiness-income paradox, 31
happiness industry, 36
happiness metrics, 25, 185–88
Happiness Movement, 2–3, 249n1.
See also happiness agenda
happiness politics, 15–18
happiness theory, 59, 193
harmony: differing associations of, 243; as indicator of happiness, 7, 21, 68, 69, 72, 80, 102, 104, 223; judgments about, 63; with nature, 113; promotion of, 14, 120; relational, 121; social, 67.
See also balance
Haybron, Dan, 92, 93, 94
health care, 38, 55, 67, 195, 202; mental, 154–59
hedonic balance, 164
hedonic tone, 107–10, 115, 250n8
hedonism, 11, 88, 256n21
Heine, Steve, 5
Helliwell, John, 231
Henrich, Joe, 5
Henry, John, 157
Hinduism, 112, 118
Hispanics, 30

Hitokoto, Hidefumi, 223
Hochschild, Arlie, 153, 175
Hong Kong, 238, 246
hopelessness, 30, 57, 58
human rights: in Bhutan, 37; in China, 128; as condition for flourishing, 35; as goal, 227; happiness and, 11, 199, 228; in the happiness resolution, 198; importance of, 42, 69, 88, 227, 233; lack of respect for, 193; in the Middle East, 192; protection/advancement of, 14, 198, 234; respect for, 196; and subjective well-being, 40; in the Sustainable Development Goals, 195–96; universal, 35; in the Universal Declaration of Human Rights, 194–96; and well-being, 45. *See also* Universal Declaration of Human Rights (UDHR); universal rights
Hume, David, 210
humility, 3–6
Huxley, Aldous, 207

Iceland, 37, 38–39
ideals: differences between cultures, 21, 239, 240; fulfillment of, 117; for a good life, 85, 97, 188; measurement of, 236–39, 240, 242, 290n3; moral, 109; normative, 18–19, 44, 185, 214; political, 128; sacrificing for, 208. *See also* values
identity: implicit/explicit, 135–36; religious, 135–36

ill-being: defining, 186, 189; and emotions, 115, 122; eradication of, 6, 14, 193, 195, 196, 198; and hermeneutical injustice, 23; and the individual pursuit of happiness, 120; masking, 161; measurement of, 152, 185; and the metrics of well-being, 163; and public policy, 188, 193; sources of, 159–60, 188; study of, 16
immigrants and immigration, 124–26, 201
immoralism, 36
income: distribution of, 99; equality of, 216; and personal happiness, 31, 34, 35, 38, 41, 42, 50, 51, 75, 159, 169, 187; provision of, 55; and well-being, 45, 159, 166, 170, 231. *See also* wealth
India, 41, 112, 118, 247
individualistic cultures, 87–88, 98, 114, 238, 246, 292n18
inequality, 187, 225; and African Americans, 150; economic, 29, 39, 61; gender, 140–41, 143–44. *See also* equality
injustice, 142, 187; affective, 23–24, 124, 153–54, 158–59, 171, 187; epistemic, 151, 216; gender, 102; hermeneutical, 23–24, 124, 151–54, 158–62, 171, 187; social, 152; substantive, 124. *See also* justice
interdependence, 223
Interdependent Happiness Scale, 223
ipsatizing, 245

Islam, 112–13, 132, 135, 136
Italy, 86, 102

Jakobsdottir, Katrin, 38
Jamaica, 69, 104
Japan, 102, 219–24, 238, 242, 246
Jin Tianhe, 277n41
John Henryism, 157
Joshanloo, Mohsen, 112, 115
Judaism, 136
justice: for African Americans, 153, 161; in China, 145; climate, 44, 193; environmental, 39; ethnic, 193; gender, 16, 22, 193; as goal, 192–96, 202; and a good life, 230; and happiness, 4, 14, 15, 25, 33, 75, 95, 162, 209; and the happiness agenda, 33, 69; hermeneutical, 152, 154; importance of, 42, 189, 191, 215, 216, 225; inequalities in, 99; intergenerational, 16, 38; and life satisfaction, 95; and public policy, 224; racial, 16, 193; social, 44, 161, 187; as virtue, 15, 132, 205; and well-being/flourishing, 22, 55, 139. *See also* injustice

Kant, Immanuel, 233
Karasawa, Mayumi, 241
kindness, 91, 137
King, Martin Luther Jr., 157, 202, 208
Kitayama, Shinobu, 241
Korea, 223, 246
Kurtz, L. E., 108
Kyrgyzstan, 69, 104

Latin America, 68, 104
Latinos, 178
LeDoux, Joseph, 127
Leninism, 162
Lepper, Heidi, 92
liberalism, 13–14
Libya, 41
life expectancy, 17, 24, 30, 52, 75, 179
life satisfaction: among African Americans, 18, 30, 150, 153; in America, 57, 222; cognitive judgments about, 7, 12, 19, 32, 35, 60, 63–64, 65, 75, 79, 81, 93, 173; of East Asians, 223; and the Gallup World Poll, 235; happiness as, 2, 7, 9, 14–15, 19, 67, 82, 107, 118, 186, 192; and the happiness agenda, 97; and human rights, 192; indicators of, 49–50; as individualistic, 87; measures of, **8–9**, 20, 24, 45–46, 48–49, 57, 60, 66–69, **70**, 72, 81, 93, **103**, 118, 150–51, 165, 166–67, 169–70, 173, 235; national differences in, 244; self-evaluation of, 164, 168–75, 187, 219, 244; and student performance, 222–23; subjective, 21, 41, 51, 52, 69, 72, 95, 102; as theory of happiness, 186; and well-being, 17, 120, 165, 167. *See also* subjective well-being
Lincoln, Abraham, 58
linguistics, 186
Lithuania, 68–69, 104
loneliness, 30, 93, 231

love, 2, 6, 15, 56, 88, 107, 131, 207;
   filial, 132, 134, 138
lovingkindness, 11
Lyubomirsky, Sonja, 92

Maimonides, Moses, 4, 205
Malta, 68
Maoism, 162
Mao Zedong, 139
Marx, Karl, 56
Marxism, 162
McIntyre, Alasdair, 67
meaningfulness, 56–59
mental health, 48, 154–59, 202
Mesquita, Batja, 241
meta-happiness paradox, 41–42
Metzl, Jonathan, 155
Mexico, 41, 246
Midlife in Japan (MIDJA) study, 220
Midlife in the U.S. (IMIDUS) study, 220
migration, 126. *See also* immigrants and immigration
Mill, John Stuart, 83, 110
Millennium Development Goals (MDGs), 195–96, 198–99
Morality: in China, 136–37; theories of, 129–30
multiculturalism, 126, 201
Muslim cultures, 112–13

narcissism, 46, 66, 85, 194
National Performance Framework (Scotland), 39
National Study of American Life, 150

neoliberalism, 132, 133, 134
neurochemistry, 79
neuroscience, 76, 87, 165, 214
New Zealand, 37–38
Nicaragua, 111
Nicomachean Ethics (Aristotle), 62, 149, 229
Nietzsche, Friedrich, 56, 67
Nigeria, 41
Nordic countries, 68, 169, 216.
   See also Finland
Norenzayan, Ara, 5
Norway, 111
Nussbaum, Martha C., 55

optimism, 31, 178, 180, 217–18
Organisation for Economic Co-operation and Development (OECD), 38, 41, 221–22
orientalism, 37

Paraguay, 69, 111
patriarchy, 139, 142, 143, 145, 275n26
peace, 7, 39, 68, **71**, 72, 102, **103**, 104, 114, 194, 240; inner, 112–13; social, 232; universal, 195
perfectionism, 61, 120
personal relationships, 12, 50, 53, 84, 107, 143, 164, 166, 169, 176, 209, 210, 218, 219, 221; in-group, 125; of minorities, 123–24
phenomenology, 79–80; universal, 91–92
Philippines, 69, 104, 111
philosophy, 10, 43, 44–45, 75, 85, 87, 205, 211, 236; Chinese, 130; classical, 208; Confucian, 22;

philosophy (*continued*)
  of emotions, 91, 186; Greek, 11, 130; of happiness, 87; Indic, 6; of language and logic, 186; of mind, 108–9; political, 4, 12–13; well-being in, 16; of well-being, 82; Western, 4
physical health, 44, 47–48, 62, 64, 122
Plato, 4, 5, 36, 45–46, 63, 149, 205, 209
platonic lineage, 4–5
pleasure, 46, 88, 110, 118
pluralistic traditions, 134–39
Poland, 86
political neutrality, 64–73
political theory, 10
politics: benevolent, 132; class, 144; collective action through, 229; corrupt, 52, 232; gender, 144; goal of, 13; happiness, 15–18; and happiness, 33; narratives about, 131
Politics, The (Aristotle), 229, 230, 232
Portugal, 68–69, 104
positivity biases, 175, 178
poverty: acceptance of, 231; in Black neighborhoods, 24, 179; eradication of, 191, 192, 193, 195, 197, 198, 202, 215; prevention of, 14; and suffering, 6, 196
Programme of International Student Assessment (PISA), 222–23
prosociality, 231, 292n18
psychiatry, 10, 85; racism in, 154
psychological states, 54
psychology, 43, 44, 87, 201; brass instrument, 5; cross-cultural, 236; cultural, 5, 9, 10; of emotions, 108, 186; folk, 65, 79, 89, 92; positive, 32, 108; scientific, 79, 92; social, 9, 214; well-being in, 16; Western, 5
psychosocial prosperity, 176
public goods, 16
public policy: capabilities and, 34; emotions and, 229; gender equality and, 39; goals of, 2, 7, 12, 33, 38, 48, 72, 73, 94, 200, 215; happiness and, 2, 3, 15, 18, 21, 25, 32, 47, 63, 69, 97, 227, 228, 229; use of happiness metrics in, 161, 185–88, 215; well-being agenda in, 37

quality of life, 3, **8**, 36, 154, 161, 170, 174; moral, 66

racism, 15, 29, 61, 152, 153, 154, 179, 202
Rappleye, Jeremy, 221
Rawls, John, 55, 233
relationships. *See* personal relationships
religion: Abrahamic, 4, 11; Catholic social gospel, 35; in China, 133–35, 136–39; and life satisfaction, 189; monotheistic, 136; and sustainable development, 233; and thick senses, 10. *See also* Buddhism; Christianity; Confucianism; Islam; Judaism
religious studies, 9, 236
resilience, 30, 150–51, 153
Rofel, Lisa, 133

INDEX 343

Romania, 68–69, 104
Rush, Benjamin, 154
Russia, 86
Ryff, Carol, 220
Ryff Psychological Well-Being
  Scale, 220

Sachs, Jeffrey, 35
Said, Edward, 37
Sarkozy, Nicholas, 33–34
Saudi Arabia, 68, 102, 104, 192
Schachter, Stanley, 76
schizophrenia, 155–56, 158. *See also*
  bipolar disorder
Scotland, 37, 38, 39
self-control, 232
self-esteem, 56, 61, 83, 121, 220
self-respect, 56, 61, 83
semantics, 85–88, 206
Sen, Amartya, 6, 34
sexism, 15, 39, 61, 143, 152, 202
sexual harassment, 141, 142, 151, 152
shame, 121, 176, 241
Singer, Jerome, 76
Slovenia, 68
socialist feminist movement,
  139–40, 143–44, 275–76n26
social justice, 44, 161, 187
social media, 142, 242
social safety net, 31, 45, 51, 68, 69, 84
socioeconomic status, 17, 22
sociology, 10, 201, 236
Socrates, 4, 36, 45–46
Somalia, 41
South Africa, 41, 179
South America, 41
South Korea, 238

Soyinka, Wole, 73
Spain, 102
Srinivasan, Amia, 153
Stevenson, Betsey, 31
Stiglitz, Joseph, 34
Stoicism, 71, 129
stress: absence of, 46, 80, 93, 180;
  and depression, 158; differing
  meanings of, 175; and emotional
  well-being, 176; financial, 166;
  increase in, 29; and the measure
  of happiness, 72, 93; and the
  pandemic, 14, 49; physiological
  measures of, 163; and race, 158,
  177–80; self-reported, 24, 30,
  160, 175, 180
Sturgeon, Nicola, 38
subjective well-being (SWB): affect
  balance, 164; among African
  Americans, 150, 160; causes and
  preconditions of, 53, 66, 112–13;
  Chinese, 128, 145; components
  of, 21, 164; connection with
  objective well-being, 54;
  cross-country differences in,
  231; as cultural project, 21,
  117–18, 120–26; as happiness,
  16–17, 32, 35–36, 42; hedonic
  balance, 164; measures of,
  22–24, 33, 39, 40, 51, 67, 93, 97,
  107, 111–12, 149–50, 160, 163, 164,
  166, 168, 170, 175, 182, 187,
  227–28; predictors of, 114, 118,
  120, 126; psychology of, 92; as
  public good, 16; and public
  policy, 33, 187–88; and SDGs,
  39, 44; studies of, 48, 80, 151, 152,

subjective well-being (SWB) (*continued*)
159–62, 166; theories of, 49, 53, 162; in *World Happiness Report*, 63. *See also* life satisfaction
suffering, 6, 14, 189, 195; of others, 21; psychosocial, 23–24
sustainability, 14–15, 25, 215. *See also* sustainable development
sustainable development, 14, 15, 35, 191–200, 202, 215, 227, 228, 233, 234
Sustainable Development Goals (SDGs), 39, 44, 192, 195–96, 198, 199, 227

Taiwan, 68, 104, 114, 238, 246
theology, 44–45, 75, 205, 211
Thomas Aquinas, 4, 11, 205
Tibet, 93
trust: communal, 69; and happiness, 82, 83, 102; measures of, 60; social, 50, 60, 216
trustworthiness, 132, 170
truth: folk, 198; about good living, 216; about injustice in health care, 159–62; about subjective experiences, 151; universal, 5
Tsai, Jeanne, 84
Turkey, 247

Uchida, Yukiko, 223
unhappiness, 6, 14, 16, 58, 95, 99, 115, 161, 185, 186; study of, 16
United Arab Emirates, 37, 40–41, 102, 192
United Kingdom, 41
United Nations: Fourth Women World Conference, 144–45; "Happiness" resolution, 197–200, 228; and the independent self, 218–19; individualism in, 216–17; Millennium Development Goals (MDGs), 195–96, 198–99; NGO forum, 145; Resolution 65/309, 3; Sustainable Development Goals (SDGs), 39, 44, 192, 195–96, 198, 199, 227; Universal Declaration of Human Rights, 194–96, 14, 192, 198, 227
United States: affective states in, 238, 240, 242–43; Chinese Americans in, 246; compared to Japan, 218–24; European Americans in, 113, 238, 241–42, 246; freedom in, 52, 57; happiness evaluation in, 41, 223; happiness in, 57–58, 72–73, 86, 131; immigrants in, 124–25; life evaluations in, 174; life satisfaction, 244; racism in, 179; subjective well-being in, 170; Twitter posts in, 242
Universal Declaration of Human Rights (UDHR), 14, 192, 194–96, 198, 227
universalism, 5
universal rights, 25, 35, 192–93, 196, 200, 215. *See also* human rights
utilitarianism, 6

value divergence, 181
value-fulfillment theory, 117–18
value judgments, 47
value(s): aesthetic, 251n14; Buddhist, 66; Catholic social gospel, 35; in China, 130, 133–34, 137,

138–39; collectivistic, 241, 246; commitment to good, 71; Confucian, 130, 134, 137, 138; cultural, 118–22, 123; education, 10; of emotions, 69, 85, 113–14, 119–20, 242; ethical, 127, 130, 200; evaluation of, 165, 167, 171, 201, 236–39; expression of, 44; and happiness, 46, 88, 94, 193; of happiness, 9, 64, 81, 86; hedonic, 110; historically derived, 217; individual, 231; individualistic, 246; measurement of, 236–39; moral, 137, 251n14; neutral, 67, 97; noninstrumental, 2; objective, 180; personal, 134; political, 66; prosocial, 231; prudential, 251n14; and public policy, 163; sacred, 138; shared, 53, 117, 139; superficial, 110

Vietnam, 69, 104

virtue, 206, 209–10

wealth, 38, 39, 40, 62, 69, 75, 141, 216, 235. *See also* income

Weber, Max, 67, 133

Weijers, Dan, 112, 115

WEIRD people, 4

well-being: advancement of, 149; aspects of, 49–50; in China, 127–45; complicated picture of, 126; conditions for, 192; cultural variations of, 168, 185, 188–89; distribution of, 232–33; emotional (EWB), 93–94, 119, 128, 175–77; emotions theory of, 120; and the Gallup World Poll, 235; goods associated with, 45; gross national, 38; vs. happiness, 36; happiness and, 3, 6–7, 9–15; hedonic, 119; in India, 112; indicators of, 149; intergenerational, 38; meaning of, 11–12, 16–18; measurement of, 48–49, 223–24; as normative concept, 44–48; objective, 24, 51, 54, 123; philosophical view of, 35; psychological, 123, 220–21; psychosocial, 48; self-reports of, 24, 163–82; studies of, 20, 92, 167–68, 251n14; theories of, 49–56, 83, 119, 162. *See also* ill-being; subjective well-being (SWB)

well-being agenda, 31–41

WELLBYs, 60

Wex, Michael, 169

Whitehead, Alfred North, 4

Wierzbicka, Anna, 86

Winslett, Justin, 138

Wolfers, Justin, 31

World Happiness Movement, 2–3, 249n1. *See also* happiness agenda

World Happiness Report, 8, 30, 36, 40, 52, 53, 60, 63, 68, 81, 82–84, 95, 98, 102, 111, 169, 214, 225, 228, 229, 235, 241–45, 247–48

World Health Organization (WHO), 47

World Values Survey, **8**

Wundt, Wilhelm, 5

Yang, Mayfair Mei-Hui, 275–76n26

Zimbabwe, 41

GPSR Authorized Representative: Easy Access System Europe, Mustamäe tee
50, 10621 Tallinn, Estonia, gpsr.requests@easproject.com